LIVING IN A
TECHNOLOGICAL CULTURE

Technology more than ever has become an established part of our everyday lives. Its sophistication offers us power that can either dazzle or threaten us.

Living in a Technological Culture examines the relations between science, technology and culture, introducing basic concepts in ethics and in the philosophy of science and technology. Some of the issues raised include facts, values, efficiency, instrumental rationality, pure and applied science, culture, politics and moral responsibility. Mary Tiles and Hans Oberdiek reveal not only the embeddedness of technologies in cultures, but also the distinctive ways in which modern technology is embedded in the cultures of Western industrialized countries.

This book, by questioning our existing uses of technology, opens up the wider debate on the shape of things to come. The authors argue that unless we address the questions posed by technology, we will continue to use technology to do stupid things in clever ways.

As an introduction to the philosophy of technology, *Living in a Technological Culture* will be valuable to students, but in assuming no prior background in philosophy, it will engage all mindful users of technology.

Mary Tiles is Professor of Philosophy at the University of Hawaii; she is the author of various books including *Bachelard: Science and Objectivity* (1984); *An Introduction to Historical Epistemology* with Jim Tiles (1993) and *Mathematics and the Image of Reason* (1991), which is published by Routledge. **Hans Oberdiek** is Professor of Philosophy at Swarthmore College in Pennsylvania.

PHILOSOPHICAL ISSUES IN SCIENCE
Edited by W. H. Newton-Smith
Balliol College, Oxford

THE RATIONAL AND THE SOCIAL
James Robert Brown

THE NATURE OF DISEASE
Lawrie Reznek

THE PHILOSOPHICAL DEFENCE OF PSYCHIATRY
Lawrie Reznek

*INFERENCE TO THE BEST EXPLANATION
Peter Lipton

*TIME, SPACE AND PHILOSOPHY
Christopher Ray

MATHEMATICS AND THE IMAGE OF REASON
Mary Tiles

METAPHYSICS OF CONSCIOUSNESS
William Seager

* THE LABORATORY OF THE MIND
James Robert Brown

*COLOUR VISION
Evan Thompson

*Also available in paperback

LIVING IN A TECHNOLOGICAL CULTURE

Human Tools and Human Values

Mary Tiles and Hans Oberdiek

London and New York

First published 1995
by Routledge
11 New Fetter Lane, London EC4P 4EE

Simultaneously published in the USA and Canada
by Routledge
29 West 35th Street, New York, NY 10001

© 1995 Mary Tiles and Hans Oberdiek

Phototypeset in Bembo by Intype, London
Printed and bound in Great Britain by
T. J. Press (Padstow) Ltd, Padstow, Cornwall

British Library Cataloguing in Publication Data
A catalogue record for this book is available from the British Library

Library of Congress Cataloguing in Publication Data
A catalogue record for this book has been requested

ISBN 0–415–07100–3 (hbk)
ISBN 0–415–07101–1 (pbk)

MARY TILES
to my Mother
Mary B. Tollyfield

★

HANS OBERDIEK
to my Son
John Oberdiek

'The acorn seldom falls far from the oak.'

CONTENTS

CONTENTS

PREFACE

The book before you exemplifies its central themes. Because we live nearly half way around the world from each other, the book would not have been written without the aid of modern technology. And while computers, fax machines, and electronic mail made the project possible, they imposed their own discipline. This is to say that the book would have undoubtedly been different (if neither better nor worse) had its authors shared the kind of daily face-to-face discussions joint authors often enjoy and we would have liked. The project grew out of a jointly taught course on *Philosophy and Technology* at Swarthmore College and subsequent discussions in Oxford, Reading and Swarthmore. The ease of air travel brought us together to learn from each other yet has also kept us apart, and so acts as a metaphor for the promise and frustrations of technology. Despite the miles between us, the book is fully collaborative. While each of us had principal responsibility for various chapters, each chapter was read and criticized often many times by the other.

Decisions about the general shape of the book – what to include or exclude – proved especially difficult. The reason is not far to seek. Until recently, technology was science's neglected stepchild. Science was originally done by 'gentlemen'; technology was not. In the academy, naturally enough, science was studied by another class of gentlemen: professors. Philosophers were especially late in coming to technology, long after historians and sociologists. The neat and deep division between science and technology was supported by the assumption that technology is nothing but applied science. (It is odd that no one ever thought that gourmet cooking is nothing but applied chemistry!) Few now believe that this division or the assumptions on which it is based can withstand scrutiny, for science depends on advances in technology as much as technology depends on science. Still, many continue to write and act as if a bright line can be drawn between science and technology. Not only is the line barely discernible, it is neither hard nor fast.

Technology offers rich terrain for philosophical reflection. As the centrality of technology to our age becomes increasingly evident and studies of it acquire increasing intellectual legitimacy, it is as if new continents await philosophical exploration. As with all explorations, the explorers are likely to find themselves and their disciplinary culture transformed by the process. Without changing our core theses, we might have written several, substantially different books. Because our own explorations have been, of necessity, limited, we have mapped only those features closest to our philosophical shores that were most salient from our perspective; we simply gesture toward the vast hinterland, some of which is already being explored by others. So our map – our book – looks like those old maps of the New World which depict a bit of the Atlantic coastline but then trail off in the direction from which the rivers seem to flow. Our hope is that readers will be enticed to make their own journeys.

Many people contributed to the book before you. Each of us individually would like to acknowledge our specific thanks.

Mary Tiles The jointly taught course which formed the basis of this project took place at Swarthmore College in Fall 1988 and I am grateful to the Philosophy Department of Swarthmore College for the visiting professorship that made my participation possible. Since then I have, thanks to Professor Peter Manicas and the students of the Liberal Studies Program, been able to create and teach a similar course at the University of Hawaii at Manoa. Jim Tiles has, as always, been an invaluable source of supportive criticism of draft material.

Hans Oberdiek I would be especially remiss if I did not acknowledge the enormous contribution of Carl Barus, late professor of electrical engineering at Swarthmore College, to my own interest and under-standing of the philosophical implications implicit in technology. Carl's conviction that science, technology and values intertwine coupled with his passion for intellectual honesty and social justice helped not only me, but generations of engineering students at Swarthmore College, to see the importance of humanizing a techno-logical culture. It was Carl's tenacity that helped create a course we twice taught together and served as the forerunner for the course

Mary Tiles and I taught. I have also taken much from Hugh Lacey, whose concern for the way science embodies values manifests itself throughout. Constance Cain Hungerford deserves thanks of a different sort for her unfailing support and helpful comments on drafts of various chapters. Finally, I would like to thank Swarthmore College for funding a sabbatical leave in which to complete the manuscript.

INTRODUCTION
Technological culture and its problems

That humans have been designated *Homo faber* (man the maker, tool user) rather than *Homo sapiens* (man the wise, thinker) indicates the centrality of technology in the life of even those primitive communities which we classify on the basis of their stage of technological development – stone age, bronze age, iron age. But as the Prometheus myth reminds us, fire and the metal-based technology it confers, although essential to the development of human civilizations, was surrounded by ambivalent attitudes: it promises to confer god-like powers of control over nature, but it is not clear that mere mortals are sufficiently god-like to be able to wield this (stolen) power wisely. It is a power which can be used to destroy as well as to create: medicines developed to restore health become poisons when used negligently or maliciously; presses invented to enlighten are used for propaganda; and computers which extend our knowledge exponentially can invade our privacy in ways unthinkable only a short time ago. Even the most benevolent technology carries with it the potential for harm; implicit in every ploughshare there is a sword.

Since World War II the pace of technological development has increased dramatically, trailing in its wake problems of which our grandparents did not even dream. Waste disposal has always presented problems for settled human communities, but none remotely comparable to those presented by nuclear waste disposal, which, if not carried out properly, could contaminate portions of the earth virtually forever. But what are the proper methods of disposal? Here a public consensus is strikingly lacking. Genetic engineering opens up the possibility of manipulating hereditary material in such a way that species, including our own, can be significantly altered. Do we know enough about the development of organisms or about ecological

1

balances to pursue this possibility prudently? Even granting that we have sufficient knowledge, should experiments of this kind be allowed, and on what species? Should experimentation on human genetic material be allowed? Computers have altered so extensively the way information is collected, interpreted and disseminated that it is appropriate to speak of an information revolution. Much of this development was prompted and funded by military interests. That generals have the latest computer-generated information seems desirable; that 'decisions' to launch nuclear missiles may be made by computers rather than people, because people cannot respond quickly enough to (possible) enemy attacks, engenders terror and a feeling of helplessness.

Developments in First World countries generating dilemmas such as these have accentuated the divide between developed and developing nations. Can this gap be narrowed by a transfer of technology from developed to developing nations, and if so should developed nations give aid in this form? Not to do so may retard development to such an extent that the lives of hundreds of millions of people will remain materially and spiritually impoverished. Yet technology which may make perfect sense in a developed nation can be inappropriate when transferred to a developing nation. The use of chemical pesticides can bring benefits, but is also hazardous. Peasant farmers, unused to handling such substances, may cause serious damage to themselves and the environment. The emergence of resistant pests means that increased crop yields are frequently sustainable only by increased dosage or use of new types of pesticide, which have to be purchased using scarce foreign exchange. In transferring its technology a donor nation inevitably transfers its own ways of thinking and doing, its own institutions and values. These interact profoundly but unpredictably with the ways of life of the recipient nation.

The course of technological development in First World countries reflects their dominant values and institutions, their ways of thinking and doing. The results of science and technology are familiar enough, and can mesmerize us. But they are the results and embodiments of human problem solving practices, results which in turn shape the lives of people employing them. (Pesticides are a response to crop destruction. To be used effectively and safely, however, farmers must take all sorts of precautions, study crop development and carefully determine time and rate of applications. To do so with modern pesticides they must be numerate and literate.) As practices, science and technology involve presuppositions, the acquisition of skills, norms of behaviour, and value commitments. Any practice will initially present itself to initiates as 'objective' in that it will exist as an ongoing concern in which they must learn to participate and whose rules must be learnt much in the way that the language and manners of one's society are learnt. Usually a practice is simply accepted as it is; its underlying assumptions and values are absorbed without ever being made explicit, unless or until it faces troubling internal problems, such as those posed by the rapid development of technology. Internal problems are characterized by their seeming intractability; one finds oneself baffled, confused, torn between opposing intuitions.

It is here that philosophical reflection may be able to make a contribution to the discussion of issues which have drawn the thoughtful attention of reflective scientists, engineers and policy makers. This contribution cannot take the form of answering or solving the problems, since that is beyond the scope of any single discipline or any purely reflective process. Philosophical reflection may, however, hope to render a practice intelligible to those involved in it by not only revealing the sources and tracing the development of what seems troubling, but also by seeking to understand how the practice itself, as something humanly devised, is capable of alteration, amendment or reinforcement. In short, one may see how to rethink and thereby begin to restructure a practice so that what troubles, bothers, perplexes and sometimes torments need not arise in so acute a form. And even if restructuring cannot be done all at once now (as surely it never can), at least one understands more clearly why things are as they are and what directions might be explored in making the practice accord better with what our understanding of it requires.

Yet philosophy has a long tradition of ignoring technology; that is, of treating it as something not within the range of its reflective gaze. Is this not puzzling? How could technology and its problems be invisible to philosophical reflection in the industrializing and industrialized Europe and North America of the nineteenth and twentieth centuries? Why has it been so difficult for the relatively new philosophical subdiscipline labelled 'philosophy of technology' to establish itself? To see why this has been so may already be to make a contribution to understanding something about the interlocking of our technological practices with our deeply held cultural assumptions.

In the nineteenth and twentieth centuries industrialization and unprecedented technological innovation were accompanied by the professionalization of science and its assumption of a progressively increased public role. This growth of science and of its influence was paralleled by the emergence of a strong tradition in the philosophy of *science*, whereas the corresponding technological innovations did not generate a philosophy of *technology*, even though technology figures more prominently and often more problematically in the lives of most people than does pure research science. But then most people, including such shapers of public opinion as politicians and journalists, do not draw the clear distinction between science and technology that philosophers and scientists themselves have insisted upon. Scientists and philosophers of science have insisted that science is concerned with acquisition of the most accurate knowledge possible of the natural world, and that scientific research is pursued to this end without concern for, or regard to, any application this knowledge may or may not have. Politicians and industrialists, on the other hand, seem to view science primarily as a means of access to new technologies. Recently many governments have set up science policy units with the aim of trying to determine what scientific and technological research should be funded in order to keep up with, and hopefully steal a march on, industrial and military competitors. New 'advanced' technology is seen as the key to industrial competitiveness and military supremacy and hence to national prosperity and security.

Philosophy of science has mostly concerned itself with the nature of scientific knowledge, the kinds of rational justification that can be afforded for scientific claims, criteria for making choices between competing theories and the mechanisms of scientific change (or progress). With increased public interest in the development of technology it was not unnatural that philosophers of science should think of extending their domain of enquiry to include technology. And since at least some philosophers of science have suggested that there are methods by which scientific progress can be secured, this kind of research has been given encouragement in the form of financial support by those with an interest in determining what are the methods by which technological advances can be made. Could a philosophy of technology yield the kind of theoretical understanding of the processes of technological change which could be used to provide a rational basis for policy decisions aimed at securing technological dominance? To believe so would be to continue, in modern guise, the age old pursuit of the philosopher's stone – a recipe for securing knowledge, wealth and power.

What these ways of looking at science rest on is an implicit view of technology, an unreflective 'philosophy' of technology, according to which technology is simply applied science. And if sophisticated technology is the product of applying scientific knowledge in practical, problem solving contexts, then surely technological advance depends on and will automatically flow from scientific research. Hence many research scientists have supported the case for continued funding for fundamental scientific research by arguing that without this research new technologies will not be forthcoming, even though technological development is not the aim of the research, and the argument has frequently been accepted, with generous government and company funding for fundamental scientific research being based on this premise. But as budgets get tight and fundamental scientific research and development gets more expensive, questions are being asked about the effectiveness of such a strategy. And as research funding is increasingly linked to technological dividends, questions are also being asked about the 'purity' of pure research. Hence we find that in current debates the concepts both of science and of technology are highly contested. We shall return to the concept of science in Chapter 3, but here let us give a preliminary indication of why the equation of technology with applied science must both be questioned and taken seriously.

WHAT IS TECHNOLOGY?

Many histories of technology are histories of the stages of development of tools (such as the plough), of machines (such as the steam engine), of structures (such as bridges) or of instruments (such as the microscope). Here technology is being equated with material *devices* designed and manufactured to make existing human activities easier or to make possible activities which people have dreamt of engaging in, but to which they are not biologically adapted (flying, swimming under water, looking at minute objects). Technological devices are designed to perform some function. They thus embody practical and also, often, theoretical knowledge together with creative problem solving. Simple lever and pulley systems make it possible to move and lift heavy weights (the blocks of stone used in building the pyramids). By working out the theory behind these (found already in the works of Archimedes) it is possible to design maximally efficient systems. The creative practical challenge is then to find suitable materials (strong enough levers and ropes), to get pulleys to run freely, and so on. From this point of view advanced electronic technology is not different in kind from a stone-hammered flint arrowhead; modern technological devices may be more complex and be put to more sophisticated uses, but there is no real basis for regarding the former, but not the latter, as part of a technological culture. Any tool using culture will be 'technological' in the sense of having its own characteristic technology.

Such historical studies suggest that there is no consistent pattern to the relation between technological development and scientific progress (for further discussion see, for example, Volti, 1992, pp. 56–7, Gibbons, 1984, Webster, 1991, Mowery and Rosenberg, 1989). Although some technologies have arisen out of fundamental scientific work, many, particularly those in earlier historical periods, did not. Even in those cases where the path from pure theory to practical outcome was most direct, as in the case of the development of the atomic bomb in the Manhattan Project, much more than pure science was involved (Gowing and Arnold, 1979). In other cases, such as the steam engine, widespread adoption of a new technology preceded and seems to have spurred scientific research in the direction of developing the theory of thermodynamics (Kuhn, 1959, Musson and Robinson, 1969, Ch.XII). So even in this narrow sense of technology, the idea that it is just applied science is hard to sustain. It might, however, be possible to argue that since technological devices embody technical discoveries and increased technical know-how, it might be possible to develop a methodology for the progressive acquisition of this kind of technical knowledge. But such a methodology would not be an adequate base for technology development policy. The mere ability to construct a device on a one-off basis, its invention, does not ensure the feasibility of its future manufacture or its widespread adoption. The Alexandrian Greeks discovered steam power in the sense that they used it in creating moving statues of the gods, self-opening temple doors, etc., but they never developed a steam technology. Various people prior to the twentieth century built mechanical calculators and reasoning machines, but they were never anything more than 'curiosities'.

A first broadening of the term 'technology' would be to include 'techniques'. Any tool or machine has itself to be manufactured and then put to use. Early steam engines, such as Stevenson's Rocket, were individually built by craftsmen. In the absence of established standard techniques, engineers developed their own, modifying and learning from the experience of others. The history of the development of engineering production techniques, including things like welding, improvements in the quality of steel, accurate machining of parts (such as pistons), is an integral part of the history of the development of the steam engine. More efficient and more widely used engines presuppose the development of techniques for building them successfully in large numbers.

The steam engine also provides a striking example of the way in which tracing the development of steam technology, as a culturally significant phenomenon, requires that one look beyond the basic devices to the techniques for using them. The very earliest steam engines were stationary beam engines used for pumping water out of mines. These were enormous machines. The use of steam to power a locomotive required the production of very much smaller, lighter engines. This development again occurred within the mining context, where horse-drawn carts running on metal or wooden rails were already used for transporting ore, coal and slag. For steam engines to gain a use outside the mining context ways of using them for transport had to be developed (railways, steamships); a whole new set of techniques and practices had to arise bringing profound social, economic and industrial changes with them. Steam engines could come to be widely used only once they could be manufactured in sufficiently large numbers and at a price which would make investment in them attractive. This in turn required the development of standardized production techniques. In this respect steam differed significantly from water or wind as a power source. Windmills and waterwheels and their accompanying gearing, belts and drives could usually be locally manufactured by skilled carpenters and blacksmiths who also had the necessary practical, mechanical knowledge. The tolerance on the uniformity and accuracy of parts was large. Steam is a much more demanding power source. The results of a boiler explosion are dramatic and catastrophic, pistons must be able to move freely in the cylinders without allowing significant amounts of steam to escape, replacement parts must be available. Here the technology starts to impose standards of accuracy, quality and standardization in engineering production. Thus the development and use of steam technology both presupposed other economic and industrial developments and in its turn imposed forms of organization and made demands upon industrial and social organization.

Under 'techniques' one thus has to include the whole complex of ways of doing and making in which a technological device has a place. A plough plays a role in an agricultural system. Different kinds of plough may be best suited to the demands of different kinds of system, which in turn depend on soil conditions, terrain, crops grown and size of farms and fields. Equally the introduction of a new kind of plough makes new kinds of agricultural practices possible. Grain farming on the scale practised on the plains of the American mid-west is practicable only with the introduction of large tractors pulling multi-furrow ploughs, yet such machinery would be of no use to a hill farmer in North Wales. Because the modern plough disturbs the earth much more than older ways of planting, soil erosion and soil depletion become greater problems. Again, in a country with no roads, a motor car is useless for transportation. Where it had not been the custom to transport goods using wheeled vehicles, such as carts and carriages, the motor car would not have been developed as a way of facilitating an already existing activity. It might be introduced to such a country, from outside, making possible a form of transport which had not been used before, but only if accompanied by a massive road building programme. Its introduction would then necessarily entail changes in the way of life of the country concerned.

Thus an understanding and appreciation of technological devices, as devices designed to perform a function, requires a knowledge of the background practices and techniques in which it has or had a role. It cannot be derived simply from looking to see how science was applied to solve a practical problem. It is quite clear that technology choices are never made by determining, in a narrowly technical sense of 'best', which device best performs the task in question. The 'best' chosen is relative to all sorts of constraints other than those of performing a certain technical task as well as possible. This is another way of saying that the problems technology is introduced to solve are never purely technical problems. Technologies, to be widely adopted, have to be mass manufactured, marketed, purchased and used successfully. The extra constraints thus derive from the contexts in which the device is to be manufactured, purchased and used. Many of these have to do with material infrastructure and existing practices, which of course vary from one country to another and have both technical and social aspects. This means that technological change, in the sense of change in widely adopted technology, whether military or civilian, cannot be understood by looking simply at technical problem solving and its methods, those practical– cognitive contexts of engineering research and development which are most closely analogous to theoretical science. Instead it requires understanding of the complex economic, political, socio-cultural and infrastructural contexts of technological decision making (see for example Mowery and Rosenberg, 1989, Ch. 11).

However, even when our conception of technology is broadened to include associated techniques, it does not yield an understanding of technology which would entitle us to think of the culture of developed countries in the twentieth century as specifically 'technological', i.e. in a way which would distinguish them from the cultures of medieval Europe or Ancient Egypt. Yet we are frequently said to live in a technological age. What does this mean? What further is embodied in this conception of technology? What does it mean to live in a 'technological culture'?

Here the discussion of steam technology can perhaps give us some initial clues. We have already noted that the production of steam engines begins to impose demands of standardization, accuracy and quality control in construction and in the supply of component materials and parts. This in turn entails a degree of industrial systematization and organization not required by the use of water or wind power. In addition, the use of steam power involves an ongoing cost after the initial installation; unlike water or wind steam had to be generated from coal (or wood) which has to be paid for. There is thus a pressing economic incentive to improve the efficiency of steam engines. It was in this context that a much more exact study of steam engines, their characteristics and the determinants of their efficiency was undertaken and the theoretical aspects of engineering design started to come more into play. The technology became an object of scientific study and theoretical results were applied in the design of new engines. The knowledge required by an engineer is now more than practical know-how; it increasingly comes to involve a theoretical, scientific component. That is to say, a technology which was not originally an instance of applied science becomes one to which science is applied. It is in the nineteenth century that science and technology really start to come together in the way in which Francis Bacon had dreamt of at the end of the sixteenth. It is here perhaps, with the emergence of theoretically directed practices, that we might look for an attitude or approach which could be said to be technological in a sense which does not find application in earlier cultures. As a provisional conjecture we might say that the move *towards* a situation in which technology (including techniques) is applied science is what has created a 'technological culture' and is what perhaps differentiates it from previous cultures.

In other words, technological culture is a product of, and continues to embody, a vision of what constitutes human progress, one in which the equation of technology with applied science plays an important role. (The desire for a science/technology policy founded on a rational methodology would itself be a manifestation of this vision.) As Woolgar (1989, p. 312) remarked, discussions of technology are the reverse side of the coin to debates about human nature. Recognition of this connection between human ideals and technology, which goes via the conception of progress through technology, can help us understand why the definitions of science, technology and their interrelation should be highly sensitive. To contest them is to contest presuppositions deeply embedded in modern cultural ideals. Moreover, modern philosophy both helped to shape and has in turn been shaped by those ideals, hence its inability to 'see' technology as anything other than applied science. Consequently there are no neutral positions, for no definition of such sensitive central terms can be philosophically neutral. For the increasing number of people who, like ourselves, wish to discuss and understand technology, to start from a definition of technology would be premature, since our enquiry is directed towards acquiring a better understanding of its actual significance in our culture. Such an enquiry may, in itself, be interpreted as a challenge to dominant philosophical and cultural ideologies, in that it suggests that they be subjected to critical scrutiny. There is no way to sit on the fence. For even if we do not presuppose a precise definition of technology, we do need to give a preliminary demarcation of the domain with which we will be concerned, and this will already require us to make some commitments. Exactly what these commitments are will become clearer as the investigation progresses.

We will take it that technologies are ways of doing and making which are both affected by and affect ways of thinking. Thus when considering any technology one would minimally expect to consider technological devices (artefacts), techniques for their production and use, the relative roles played in each of these by technical and manual skills, practical knowledge (know-how) and theoretical knowledge. In addition, we would suggest that one cannot grasp the significance of any complex technological device, such as a hydroelectric generator or a nuclear reactor, without understanding its history, complex support system, social meaning and political implications. Just as a satisfactory understanding of the ceiling of the Sistine Chapel cannot be confined to a mineral and chemical analysis of the paint used, even if supplemented by attention to Michelangelo's tools and state of mind, so the great bridges of the world cannot be satisfactorily understood without tracing their connections with the Industrial Revolution, the self-confident, explorative urge prevalent in the nineteenth century, the expanding needs of a youthful, vigorous capitalism, and the moral and political commitment to universalism over parochialism.

Thus, clearly we have rejected the simple equation of technology with applied science, but at the same time we must acknowledge the technological significance of this conception of technology, since it has been part of the context of technological development in the twentieth century in particular. Therefore we shall have to take time (in Chapter 3) to consider in more detail the relations between pure science, applied science and technology. Before doing so, however, we need to probe more deeply into our ambivalent attitudes towards technology.

1

CONFLICTING VISIONS OF TECHNOLOGY

Throughout this century, and certainly since World War II, technological developments have solved or alleviated problems that long
plagued humankind. We rejoice that scientific and technological
advances have either eradicated or brought under control many
childhood diseases and gratefully take advantage of vastly increased
opportunities for speedy travel and long distance communication.
Yet it often seems that technology creates more problems, and more
intractable problems, than it solves. This is true even in medicine,
where dramatic and obviously beneficial advances have been made.
Both at the beginning and at the end of life physicians now have
the power to keep alive indefinitely people who would have merci-
fully perished quickly were nature simply allowed to take its course.
Even programmes of immunization against childhood diseases such
as measles and chicken pox have contributed to overpopulation and
hunger in developing nations. Attempts to increase crop yields to
avoid starvation have required the introduction of costly fertilizers
and pesticides which, in turn, have caused chemical pollution and
medical disorders. Population increases and the introduction of intensive farming, or the famine resulting from an inability to increase
agricultural production, have brought about traumatic changes in
age-old patterns of life. It can seem that the technological 'solution'
to one problem leads just to the creation of many, unanticipated
new problems.

Out of these ambivalent feelings towards technology have grown
two conflicting visions, one optimistic the other pessimistic, one
of technical omnipotence the other of technical impotence, one of
control of the environment and human destiny through technology
the other of technological systems running out of control. The
optimists see technology as fulfilling the biblical injunction to 'fill

the earth and subdue it, and have dominion over the fish of the sea and over the birds of the air and over every living thing' (Genesis 1:28). Although dominion can be construed either as stewardship or as domination, the aim inherited from seventeenth century movements that inaugurated 'modern science' has been that of domination. Thus Bacon (1561–1626), regarded by many as the father of modern science and technology, talks of subduing and dominating nature. Bacon was confident that by deploying our intellectual powers it would be possible to gain knowledge of nature's secrets and so acquire the ability to bend the course of nature to our will. He had faith that humans would co-operate to acquire this knowledge and that they would deploy it to improve the lot of humankind. His vision of a scientifically developed and organized society, presented in *New Atlantis* (Bacon, 1627), reflects his optimistic view of human beings, their moral as well as intellectual perfectibility. On this optimistic view, we are firmly in control of the technologies we produce. Technology provides us with instruments which can be used and further developed by us, or not, depending on our purposes. As such, any technology is value neutral: we impose our values in deciding which technology to use and how. Our success in controlling certain aspects of nature and in harnessing its secret powers (atomic energy) has exceeded Bacon's wildest dreams. Isn't it therefore reasonable to suppose that the methods which have served us well thus far will enable us to continue to overcome obstacles, to solve problems and to expand our control over nature indefinitely?

On the other hand there are those who have become deeply pessimistic as a result of observing the path of so-called technological 'progress'. As they see it, we are strangely impotent in the face of, indeed are enslaved by, a pervasive technology that, ironically, we ourselves have made. Not only is the goal of dominating nature a mere dream, but our ability to control the effects and course of development of the technology we have unleashed is also illusory; mute structures and blind forces are causally far more potent than human will and intelligence. At best, and if we are lucky, we can give technology a little nudge in this or that direction, perhaps slightly retarding its inexorable course. Technological development may have been initiated by humans, but it has become autonomous, has gone beyond the point where, individually or collectively, we can exercise control over it.

Each of these visions overdramatizes. Each is just a caricature of what any one person actually believes. Curiously most of us find ourselves captivated by first one and then the other, depending on the technology, or features of a technology, under consideration. Word processors are likely to be thought a boon by writers and students. They can now control and manipulate a text with greater ease and speed than ever before. Computers generally provide those who use them with enormous power to manipulate data. But this very power can pose a threat to those on whom data is collected, stored and transmitted. Those who have had their credit privileges removed because of a computer error often find it nearly impossible to have their credit rating restored. Computer booking for air travel, computer holding of medical records, academic records, police files all make it possible for a governmental agency to amass a file on an individual without that individual being aware of the information being collected or having the opportunity to scrutinize or correct it. Each of us is thus likely to have occasion to feel the attraction of both visions of technology, and this suggests that much can be said for each. This seems to offer the depressing prospect of interminable, inconclusive debate between optimists and pessimists. After outlining the positions and showing what can be said for and against them, however, we will suggest that the battle lines should not be drawn here. The tendency to see technology issues in one or other of these lights is itself a reflection of deeper, culturally more pervasive assumptions which are shared by optimists and pessimists. By making these presumptions explicit it will be possible to shift the terms of debate away from simply having to adopt pro- or anti-technology positions. We can move instead towards providing a framework for thinking through what is at stake in any given controversial techno-logical decision.

OPTIMISM

Optimists hold that technology and its products are value neutral; technologies are passive tools which can be used for good or evil. If technology is sometimes used improperly and causes harm, the fault lies with its human operators and developers, not with the tech-nology. As the proverb goes, 'It is a poor carpenter who blames his tools.' It has thus been labelled an instrumentalist view of technology (Feenburg, 1991). This optimistic vision is a familiar part of capitalist technological cultures and is dominant within them. It finds expression in the advertising designed to sell us the latest 'state of the art' dishwasher, computer, insecticide or toothpaste. For example, in an advert for Sinclair computers we find:

> information technology has a long and benign history. The computer, the telephone, the telegraph, the printing press, the invention of writing itself – all of them led to increased prosperity and universal improvements in the standard of living. . . . The more information we have, and the more sophisticated the use we make of it, the more exciting and effective our decisions and actions become.
>
> (Sinclair, 1983)

The same optimistic vision was used by President Reagan to sell his Strategic Defense Initiative, or Star Wars, programme – the vision that the problem of providing an impenetrable defence against incoming nuclear missiles can be solved, providing sufficient human resources and money are devoted to it. This was coupled with the message that this would be a benign technology because it was developed purely for defensive purposes. So far from seeing human beings as helpless in the face of inexorable technological progress, optimists tend to see technology as a route to virtually unlimited power over nature as human capabilities are dramatically extended. Optimists, for instance, see the micro-chip as representing a quantum leap in the technology of humankind:

> the microcomputer is rapidly assuming huge burdens of drudgery from the human brain and thereby expanding the mind's capacity in ways that man has only begun to grasp. With the chip, amazing feats of memory and execution become possible in everything from automobile engines to universities and hospitals, from farms to banks and corporate offices, from outer space to baby's nursery.
>
> (Time, 20 February 1978, p. 38)

and:

> By massive physical changes deliberately induced [through technology], we can literally pry new alternatives out of nature. . . . We have the power to create new possibilities, and the will to do so. By creating new possibilities, we give ourselves more choices. With more choices, we have more opportunities. With more opportunities, we can have more freedom, and with more freedom we can be more human.
>
> (Mesthene, 1983, pp. 110–11)

This vision is persuasive because it has a foundation in our experience of technological development. Our society has changed dramatically since the nineteenth century and even since World War II. Electronic technologies based on the transistor and the micro-chip have brought within the reach of the average person both aspects of culture (music, film, information of all kinds) and complex, easy to operate, tools (computers, calculators, microwave ovens) which were once accessible only to the wealthy. New drugs, vaccines and surgical procedures mean that many medical conditions which were once life threatening or fatal can now be treated or prevented from occurring. Agricultural productivity has increased beyond what was conceivable at the beginning of the century, and consequently the level of nutrition of most in developed countries has been markedly improved. And so one could go on.

We recognize that it is the carpenter's lack of skill which leads him or her to make a rickety chair; and that were he or she to attack someone with his or her hammer, we would blame the carpenter, not the hammer. Although modern technologies are far removed from the simple tools of a carpenter, the principle, we can be readily persuaded, is the same. Disasters involving advanced technologies – nuclear power plant accidents, plane crashes, and oil spills – result from faulty design or control, or from faulty operation, not from anything inherent in the technology itself. In cases such as the use of concealable explosive devices to destroy aircraft, where advanced technology is used maliciously, the blame for the resulting loss of life lies with those placing the explosives, not with explosive or electronic technology.

Such reasoning lends plausibility to the picture of technology as simply providing us with tools which can be used to good or bad ends. Technology simply augments human abilities so creating new possibilities. Devoid of intrinsic value and lacking both will and intelligence, it plays an entirely passive role in the human exercise of power and control.

Optimists do recognize that technological development carries a price. It inevitably destroys as it creates. Pure running water in every villager's home undermines the communal life focused on the village well. They also recognize that since technology brings increased power over nature, it also carries the risk that this power may fall into the wrong hands, being used for destructive rather than constructive purposes.

Technology spells only possibility, and is in that respect neutral. Its massive power can lead to massive error so efficiently perpetrated as to be well-nigh irreversible.

(Mesthene, 1983, p. 111)

But to emphasize this negative possibility shows a lack of resolve, and is to go against the spirit of the age, which is 'witnessing a widespread recovery of nerve' (Mesthene, 1983, p. 114). For the first time since the Greeks, Mesthene argues, we are convinced again that there is nothing in the universe that cannot, in principle, be known. 'The commitment to universal intelligibility entails moral responsibility', and this is hard work, but (if we do not lose our nerve) 'we have the means at hand to make the good life, right here and now' (Mesthene, 1983, p. 115).

By referring to the Ancient Greeks Mesthene points us to the source of the vision of human fulfilment which has been crucial in forming and sustaining the optimistic, instrumentalist view of technology. Already in Plato and Aristotle we find clearly expressed the idea that it is reason which marks humans off from animals. For humans fully to realize their human potential is thus for them to rise above their mere animal nature by cultivating and employing their rational capacities allowing these, rather than animal instincts and appetites, to direct their action. This means that only those who have the time (the leisure) to cultivate their rational faculties, freed from concern with the material necessities of biological life, can live truly fulfilled human lives. Practical work, whether of the skilled worker or the agricultural labourer, is thus devalued. It is something humans need to be freed from if they are to become fulfilled. Moreover, it is activity whose function and direction should ideally be the product of knowledge, of understanding the nature of the goals to be achieved and the means to achieve them. The bridle maker (weapons manufacturer) needs to receive design specifications from those who will use it (military personnel) and these in turn are directed by generals (military strategists) who determine the role of cavalry (bombs and artillery). Generals in turn look to politicians for their military objectives. In a well-ordered state (Republic) the means–end hierarchy maps onto a social–political hierarchy, an authority structure, in which direction flows from those who are qualified, in virtue of their theoretical and practical wisdom, to deliberate about ends and the best means of achieving them, to the skilled workers and labourers who must bring them about. (See, for example, Plato's *Republic* 601c and Aristotle's *Nichomechean Ethics* 1094a10–15.)

For the Greeks, the freedom of some to lead fulfilled human lives was contingent upon the labour of others (slaves and females) providing for the material necessities of life (production and reproduction). Slaves are explicitly likened to tools (Aristotle's *Politics* Bk.I iv 1253b23) and one might thus say that slave labour and its management formed a 'technology'. It was even argued that slaves would be necessary unless or until technology was developed to take over the labour performed by slaves. Here the instrumental vision both of labour and of technology could not be more clear.

Marx and Engels made only a minor modification in this vision when they dreamed of overcoming the need for the division of labour, the division between those who deliberate about ends and those who carry them out and by their labour provide for the necessities of life. They dreamed that the development of industrial technology could be used to overcome this division. Technology, provided it belongs to and is managed by the whole community for the communal good, was envisioned as replacing slaves, freeing everyone from the necessity of labour and so making available to all the possibility of a fulfilled human life (Marx and Engels, 1970, p. 61). (This dream was already outlined, in somewhat different technological terms, by Bacon when writing his *New Atlantis*.) In other words, both the programme of modern science and Marxist revolutionary politics were founded on an instrumental view of technology and on a vision of science as that which delivers the rational tools for controlling nature, freeing humans from enslavement to it. It is an instrumental vision founded on a separation of the distinctively human from the natural and hence on the conception that humans can only realize their full potential when freed from the practical demands of the work and labour necessary to ensure their biological well-being.

The fact that this view of technology has transcended the political divide of the Cold War years has lent credibility to the view that technology is value neutral – it seems to be neutral between the very different value frameworks of democratic individualism with free-market capitalism and totalitarianism with state capitalism. On this view, the way to advance technology is to advance science. Technology is applied science. That is, the application, via rational problem solving techniques, of rationally acquired understanding to material situations to achieve freely chosen ends. The assumed independence of both science and material problem situations from social determination gives a double-edged objectivity to technology. It is a product of rationally acquired, universal knowledge of the laws of nature, laws which hold no matter where one is in the universe. This knowledge is applied to material situations and could be similarly applied, with similar results, to such situations wherever they arise. Success or failure is evident: the goal is achieved or it isn't. Technological progress consists in making more possibilities available (being able to do more things) so that more desired ends can be achieved and can be achieved more efficiently.

This scheme is implicit in Western philosophical tradition and is reinforced by its recurrent returns to classical Greek texts, those of Plato and Aristotle in particular. It also underlies the decision making practices of many contemporary national and international institutions. Stamp (1989) illustrates this in the case of development agencies. A vision of development is founded on the belief that lack of development is a result merely of lack of financial resources to get available technology. This is to assume that a machine or process which works in one place will work when transferred to another. Development aid then takes the form of financing for technology transfer. Stamp also illustrates the fallacies of this approach. Most poignantly these are demonstrated in the failures of development policies and their consequent human suffering and social disruption.

It is precisely in the problems of technology transfer that the limitations of viewing technology in purely instrumental terms have become most evident. Technologies, by their very specification, are introduced not into purely material contexts but into social contexts. They are to be used by human beings, to perform tasks previously done in other ways by other means, possibly by other people, or to do wholly new things. Their introduction is bound to have social effects.

Optimists such as Mesthene would not deny that this is the case, but would argue that the problems that have arisen with transfer are the result of human, moral failings resulting in irresponsible use of technology. Mesthene's appeal to moral responsibility is both an injunction to those who use technologies and an indication of what becomes a key concern for those optimistically pursuing new technologies. The concern is that the technology does not fall into the wrong (morally irresponsible or reprehensible) hands. Control over the development of technology demands control over its dissemination and this can be assured only if control is exercised over (other) people. This was clearly seen by those involved in the decision to develop peaceful uses for nuclear power. Weinberg, curator of the Oak Ridge National Laboratory from 1955 to 1973, suggested that a 'technological priesthood' would be necessary to ensure that nuclear power was managed properly and in perpetuity (Weinberg, 1972, p. 34). Observing that the development of nuclear weapons had already created a military priesthood whose function was to guard against the inadvertent use of nuclear weapons and to prevent them or the expertise and materials for building them from falling into the wrong hands, Weinberg realized that the development of peaceful uses for nuclear energy was going to require the creation of a similar group of trusted people as both possessors and guardians of nuclear expertise.

Thus the vision of domination of nature through technology contains within it the seeds of social paranoia:

> Once we have multiplied the power of our body by a machine, then we have lost the self-regulating features of nature. We want that power for our self, but we do not want it to be used on our self. Thus, as we use it we tend to distance ourselves from it. The machine is turned against the Other, whether this be the soil, a bird, a bacterium, or other people. In the process we become grandiose and abstracted from the concrete immediate flow of life.

> (Kovel, 1983, p. 121)

In this way thinking that one can control technology, and so seeing it as conferring power, leads naturally to thinking also that one can, and must, control other people, namely those who do not share one's goals and values, and who might therefore put technology to uses other than those intended or even turn it against oneself.

If this mind-set is accompanied by the tendency to see every problem of control as a technological problem, one to which a technological solution can be found, then it can lead to the development of technologies not designed to 'better the lot of all humankind', but to control and manage one part of humankind in the interests of another part. In *Brave New Workplace* Howard examines the extent to which computer technology has been perceived and used to increase managerial control over a workforce (Howard, 1985). The performance of a telephone operator, or any other person working at a computer terminal, can easily be continuously monitored for speed, efficiency, errors made, etc. Computers and the numerical control of production line machinery allow for the deskilling of many jobs, making it possible both to pay workers less and to give them even less input into the control of the production process. However, it must be remembered that there is no necessary connection between an optimistic attitude towards the technological domination of nature and the adoption of a technological approach to the management and control of people. Computers can be introduced into the workplace so that workers are empowered, acquiring new skills and having more control over their work. They can allow a person to work from home while keeping an eye on small children and make flexible hours more possible. What we have seen is that the development of ever more powerful technologies does entail great risks that this technology may be put to destructive use. Therefore those justifying its development on the grounds of the benefits it will bring have to envision a scenario in which there are some measures of control over access to the expertise and materials necessary to develop and deploy it. There is an incompatibility between the pursuing power through technology and the ideal of a completely free and open society.

PESSIMISM

It is for this reason that pessimistic critics of technology talk about technological systems and technical practices (techniques) rather than about devices. They see these systems as embodying values beyond those which are evident in selection of the ends intended to be achieved by technological means. The instrumental criterion 'efficiency' masks the presence of those values. If efficiency is a measure of the ratio of costs to benefits, how costs and benefits are counted becomes crucial; costs to whom, benefits to whom and of what type? The purely instrumental approach of the optimist, because founded in a bifurcated vision of the world into natural and individual human, tends to overlook the social costs of implementing a technology by not according any reality to the social or the socially constructed. Pessimists, on the other hand, tend to treat technological systems as part of the reality within which people live and work; indeed technological systems constitute this environment by functioning to create and sustain it.

The best and most widely known proponent of a pessimistic view of technology is Ellul. He somberly argues that 'technique' autonomously and irresistibly enslaves everything: art, family life, economics, science and even leisure. Technologies, being ways of doing and making, undeniably shape our moral, social and political lives to a degree unthinkable in earlier periods. The pervasiveness of their impact does tempt us to think of technologies not only as self-governing but also as governing and controlling our lives. Workers in a computerized office must work to the demands of the computer and have tasks shaped and conditioned by the particular communications and reproduction technology surrounding them. In such situations, where the experience is of being dominated by technology, of impotence in the face of an inhuman force, it is easy to feel that technology is beyond our control. It is this kind of manifestation of a technological, managerial mind-set, one which has the maximization of efficiency as its *raison d'être*, rather than a technological system, in and of itself, which would seem to be the real target of Ellul's criticisms, and indeed best fits his definition of 'technique'. As he defines the term, technique consists in 'the totality of methods rationally arrived at and having absolute efficiency (for a given stage of development) in every field of human activity' (Ellul, 1964, p. xxv). For him 'the new technical milieu' is distinguished by six salient characteristics:

(a) It is artificial; (b) It is autonomous with respect to values, ideas, and the state; (c) It is self-determining in a closed circle. Like nature, it is a closed organization which permits it to be self-determinative independently of all human intervention; (d) It grows according to a process which is causal but not directed to ends; (e) It is formed by an accumulation of means which have established primacy over ends; (f) All its parts are mutually implicated to such a degree that it is impossible to separate them or to settle any technical problems in isolation.

(Ellul, 1983, p. 86)

If technology is truly self-governing, then it is clearly out of *our* control and therefore easily thought to be simply 'out of control'. Frankenstein movies express in fiction what has taken place in fact: our inventions have become our masters (Winner, 1977, contains an excellent discussion of this). Ellul's vision, like Mesthene's, captures and brings to the fore ways of thinking about ourselves and our relation to the world which are very deeply rooted in Western culture. For this very reason his pessimistic view of our relation to the technology that moulds our culture seems persuasive. But let us take a closer look at his six salient characteristics.

(a) Undoubtedly technologies and the environments they create are human artefacts and so in that sense they are indisputably artificial. Moreover, as advertisers of everything from popcorn and shampoo to clothing and footwear know and encourage us to continue to believe, 'natural is good, artificial is bad'. In other words, the terms 'natural' and 'artificial' are heavily value-laden terms. Yet 'all natural' shampoo is as much an artefact as a motor car. The ingredients may all be derived from naturally occurring substances, but one could argue that ultimately the materials in a car (steel, rubber, plastic) themselves derive from naturally occurring materials. Once we start to think about it, it is not easy to see how to draw the line between natural and artificial. It may be easy enough to distinguish between imitation pearls and real ones, but how much more difficult to classify domesticated animals (Siamese cats, Jersey cows, Swaledale sheep) or f1-hybrid tomatoes. Advertisers play both on the attitudes which Ellul expresses and on the near impossibility of drawing any firm distinction between natural and artificial. All civilizations surround themselves with artefacts and shape their environment by building houses and cities, engaging in agriculture and so on. In what sense, then, can it be said that the technical milieu is artificial, whereas that of pre-technical cultures was not? This is a question to which we shall return (in Chapter 4). For now it is sufficient to note that to employ 'artificial' as a way of expressing alienation from our dislike of technology, though rhetorically effective in contemporary culture, is a move which needs further justification.

(b) and (c) These two characteristics go together. (c) is in effect an elaboration of what is entailed by (b). To say that a person or a system is autonomous is to say that it has the power of self-determination. (c) makes the stronger claim that the technical milieu is actually wholly self-determining; it forms a closed system, one immune from outside interference. Implicitly Ellul sees our world as compartmentalized into at least three independent segments – nature, technology, human affairs. When he compares the technical milieu to nature he presupposes that nature forms a closed system, one with which humans cannot interfere and whose course cannot be altered by human action. We are thus pictured as caught up in two orders of reality and as powerless in the face of both of them. Instead of mastering nature through technology, humans have created another, equally ungovernable, non-natural world.

Again, this vision has a partial grounding in our experience of the world of technology. Technologies present us with realities which place demands on us independently of what we either individually or even collectively might wish for or think desirable. Use of the automobile and of electricity derived from oil requires the global transportation of millions of gallons of oil. Inevitably there are spillages, destruction of the marine environment and spoiled beaches. In a culture built around the automobile and presupposing its widespread ownership and use, individuals who want to exclude reliance on that technology from their lives will find living almost as much of a challenge as those who try to cultivate naturally dry, but fertile, land and who must constantly irrigate their crops. The hydraulic civilization of ancient Sri Lanka relied on an elaborately organized irrigation technology. This irrigation system required centralized oversight and maintenance for its operation and was thus possible only with the perpetuation of a centralized form of government. We must acknowledge both that no individual can control or direct the development of a way of life extensively shaped by and dependent upon specific technologies and that the existence of such technological systems constrains governmental action. Neither admission, however, establishes that the technical milieu is either autonomous or forms a closed system. It would be difficult to maintain that any technological system is causally closed. Nature is quite capable of unleashing forces which destroy systems made by humans in minutes (think, for example, of the devastating effects of earthquakes, volcanic eruptions, floods, hurricanes, tornadoes). Our technological systems stand in intricate causal relations to natural systems. This we are learning to our cost from the complex debates about global warming, acid rain and the fragile ozone layer. Such issues might indeed provide a test case for Ellul's vision. Is it the case that a growing human concern to reverse adverse effects on the global environment will necessarily be ineffective because the technical milieu is such that it is autonomous, unresponsive to human values and goals? Are technical systems any less responsive to control than human political systems? Neither individual human beings nor their national governments can control the fate of a nation, yet we would be reluctant to conclude that the actions, goals and ideals of individuals and governments have no impact. Is Ellul perhaps moving too swiftly from lack of total control to total lack of control?

(d), (e) and (f) Here again the appeal of Ellul's vision rests on recognizable features of the way in which technologies have developed. Technologies grow like topsy, with neither rhyme nor

24

reason, with little regard for individual human intentions and purposes. 'The Pill', for instance, was originally developed for a variety of purposes, including that of helping married women increase their chances of conceiving by regulating the menstrual cycle. Its role in ushering in a sexual revolution was neither intended nor anticipated. It is not that technological devices are invented without purpose, but that once created they are picked up by other people who see in them uses and avenues of development other than those for which they were originally designed. We use screwdrivers for opening paint cans, washing up liquid for killing white fly, computers for playing video games.

From the point of view of any one person, it then appears that a technological device, once created, assumes a life of its own, its development and deployment governed by principles that no single individual or group of individuals can control. This is what Ellul means when he stresses that the bits and pieces making up any technology ('the accumulated means') establish primacy over ends. But is this development process wholly internal to and dictated by the technology itself, as Ellul appears to suggest, when he says that means establish primacy over ends? Development directed to a multiplicity of different people's ends may lead to results no one of them desired or foresaw. This is especially true when the use of technologies is so pervasive that they form complex, interdependent networks. The various parts of modern technological culture are so interwoven that no technical problem can be solved in total isolation.

Modern technologies, in short, behave like ecosystems. When we intervene here, unexpected consequences pop up there. We are familiar with the difficulties governments have in trying to regulate their economies. A similar story could be told of attempts to make safe nuclear power plants, develop environmentally benign pesticides, design aircraft or space shuttles: no technical problem can be solved in isolation, so the solution to one problem creates others elsewhere. In this respect existing technical interconnections do limit the scope for realizing human ends, but it does not follow from this that the network of technological systems is immune to human intervention and develops only according to its own internal laws. Some problems can be solved in relative independence, for though everything may be ultimately interrelated, it is still possible to distinguish and use specific parts for specific purposes as if they were separable. This may get us into trouble as unnoticed interconnections cause unforeseen

25

problems, but this is a more apt description of the human condition than that requiring us to solve all problems at once before being able to solve any. We have not yet stopped trying to communicate using words even though, in the end, the meaning of any word in a language depends on its interconnections with every other word and every use of language has the potential for altering those interconnections in unforeseeable ways. Not to look up a word in a dictionary to determine its (partial) meaning on the grounds that one knows that ultimately all words are interrelated and none can be defined in isolation would be a recipe for illiteracy, not realistic prudence.

Ellul presents a persuasive case for the autonomy of technology and the pessimistic mood it engenders. In stressing the autonomous nature of technology, however, those who follow Ellul come perilously close to espousing a kind of determinism, if not fatalism: once having released the genie – or atom – from the bottle, once having created the technological monster, the forces unleashed must inexorably play themselves out. We have no more choice in how to respond to them than had Canute in the face of a rising tide. We delude ourselves if we think we can harness the tremendous power of technology, bending it to our will: at best we are only along for the ride. Those who regard technology as beyond control, sometimes yearn for earlier, less technological times, when attunement, rather than domination, best described the way we regard our environment. Ellul, however, would regard such longing as delusive wishful thinking.

Although proponents of Ellul's view provide deep insights into the ways technology penetrates and pervades our lives, the claim that technology is autonomous and therefore out of control cannot be sustained. We have granted that technologies and the environments they create are artificial, that technologies present us with realities no individual or institution can fully control, and that technologies grow and develop in ways which may be wholly unintended and unforeseen by their originators. But after making these concessions we can still dispute the claim that the technical milieu is 'self-determining in a closed circle', independent of all human intervention.

Indeed, the claim (d) that the technical milieu grows according to a process which is causal but not directed to ends would seem to be in direct conflict with Ellul's own definition of the term 'technique' as 'the totality of methods rationally arrived at and having absolute efficiency (for a given stage of development) in every field of human activity'. 'Efficiency' is a term employed in the assessment of the means used to achieve a given end: it requires a weighing of costs against benefits. As Borgmann incisively notes, efficiency 'is a systematically incomplete concept . . . [for] we need antecedently fixed goals on behalf of which values are minimized or maximized', Borgmann, 1984, p. 9). If technological systems are closed and causal, they cannot also have goals and therefore cannot be said to fulfil them either efficiently or inefficiently. To take a non-technical example, as a paperweight, a rock might work efficiently because it does exactly what one wants with a minimum of fuss; used as a doorstop, however, we might judge it inefficient because it is not heavy enough. Similarly television cannot be beaten for bringing us instant news and the advantages of instant potatoes. That we need either may be disputed, but undoubtedly television efficiently brings us both, as intended by large corporate enterprises. If our only concern is with getting the most out of fossil fuels we will define an efficient power plant to be one which converts a high proportion of the heat energy released by burning a fossil fuel into electrical energy – it produces a maximal amount of electricity per ton of fuel. However, if our aim is to produce electricity from fossil fuels in an environmentally safe way, then a plant giving high energy conversion but at the cost of serious atmospheric pollution might be rated less efficient than one whose energy conversion rate was lower but which caused less pollution.

Unless one endows technology with its own goals and the intelligence to work towards them, its ability to achieve autonomy and power through efficiency remains totally mysterious. In other words, the view that technology is autonomous because it is ruled by the standard of achieving maximal efficiency anthropomorphizes technology, usually by demonizing it. Our attitude to computers illustrates the way in which our attitudes easily oscillate here. When using a personal computer with a familiar and not terribly sophisticated program one will regard it as just another machine, no more endowed with a will of its own than a mechanical typewriter. But confronted with a large machine running sophisticated software we regard it as an authority: inhuman only in the perfection of its rationality, the ruthlessness of its logic, it assumes the proportions of a superior being.

In this way technology can come to assume a life of its own, apparently undirected yet operating with a ruthless, rational efficiency, sweeping away impediments in its path. Even the creators of technology seem helpless in the face of its inhuman, non-human, or demonic urges. Here again popular culture provides innumerable examples of technological marvels acting as if possessed with minds of their own, from lovable R2D2 to ominous HAL (a.k.a. IBM?).

PESSIMISTS AND OPTIMISTS

As we have suggested, the experience of those who live in a so-called technological culture can be called on to persuade us of both optimistic and pessimistic views of technology. Most people will oscillate between these attitudes depending on the particular form of technology that they happen to be thinking about and on their relation to it. A home mechanic who repairs and introduces adjustments and improvements to his or her car, or a personal computer enthusiast who understands its software, adapting it to his or her own use, will have decidedly optimistic attitudes towards these technologies, being eager to know about new products coming onto the market, wanting to have, or at least have an opinion on, the latest developments. These same people might, however, be deeply pessimistic about nuclear or medical technology. We are often powerless to resist the trends of development in specific technologies, in part because of the economic and political powers these represent. Technology itself may not be autonomous and out of control, but industries which have accumulated political and economic power through the development, marketing and use of technology are out of the control of individuals and their governments. This does indeed present us with a real problem. Yet in many respects it is an old problem, and perhaps we can derive some comfort from that. It is the problem of the many under the domination of a few.

Both optimism and pessimism, though initially tempting, provide us with distorting visions. Although clearly the optimistic picture is too optimistic and needs to be critically scrutinized, the swing to a wholesale pessimistic rejection of technology is neither feasible for most of us, nor, in the light of the above considerations, would it seem to be justified. Do we have only these two options? We shall suggest that this is not the case; that our tendency to oscillate between these two extremes indicates that neither adequately reflects the character of our relation to technologies and technological systems; and that both are founded in suppositions which are deeply embedded in our way of thinking about ourselves in relation to the rest of the world. What we thus need to explore is the possibility of finding a middle ground, a conceptual base that does not, in advance, commit us to either a global pro- or anti-technology stance. One way in which such apparently exclusive choices can be finessed is to look for the framing assumptions, underlying both, which limit our options. These need to be made explicit if we are to begin to make sense of the technological culture in which we live and of our relation to it rather than oscillating between contradictory feelings of impotence and omnipotence. Our aim should not be to take up a certain stance towards technology, but to see various technologies for what they are, in their varied contexts and without the mystifications of supposing them to be either fully under our control or wholly out of control.

The pessimistic/optimistic, impotence/omnipotence visions of technology are founded on a pair of closely interconnected dichotomies: values versus facts and humans versus nature. These oppositions shape the way one sees the problems posed by technology. Technology itself must be located either in the realm of values or in the realm of facts, either as an extension of human beings or as an extension of nature. Both optimists and pessimists assign technology the same location; it lies within the realm of the factual as an extension of nature. Both think that knowledge of nature is the factual knowledge delivered by the natural sciences. Such knowledge is objective, gained by rational methods employed in the disinterested pursuit of truth. Technology, they believe, is the product of the rational application of that knowledge. Its development is a rational result of advances made in science. The development of technology is then perceived as also a rational, objective process – it acquires the characteristics attributed to the scientific knowledge seen to generate it. The divergence between the two visions rests on whether it is thought that humans gain their autonomy by exercise of reason in the service of a free will so that they can come to dominate nature by directing technological development to serve human ends. Or whether it is thought that science and technology, governed solely by the standards of rationality and objectivity, fail to embody any distinctively human ideals and to this extent form an extension of the domain of reality determined by laws which place it beyond human control. For the latter, to be dominated by the standard of rationality is to lose one's autonomy and to be caught up in an inhuman, deterministic framework. To this extent the opposition is a replaying, in a new context, of the opposition between free will and determinism. If humans are part of nature, they must be bound and determined by its laws and therefore cannot be free. If, on the other hand, they are free because not a part of nature, then how can they act in the natural world and so demonstrate their freedom?

This way of viewing the relation between humans and nature is problematic because it makes the issue of freedom an all or nothing affair. Either humans are a part of nature, or they are not; therefore either they must be wholly determined by natural laws or they must be wholly free. There is no space for a middle ground. Similarly it seems either we must be totally in control of technology or technology must be wholly out of our control.

These distinctions, between fact and value and between humans and nature, are integral to the instrumental conception of technology which is quite explicitly endorsed by optimists. Instruments, belonging to the factual realm, are value neutral; they are the mere means to ends which are set in the light of values held by human beings. Technology as a whole is envisioned as instrumental in enabling humans to free themselves from the necessities of nature; so conceived its role depends on the assumption that what is essential to human fulfilment lies beyond the confines of nature. But pessimists with their emphasis on technology as inhuman and the claim that the dominance of technology is the dominance of means over ends, are also taking an instrumental view of technology. The difference between the visions is a difference of values, a difference grounded in differing visions of what constitutes human fulfilment. Pessimists are pessimistic precisely because they do not accept that technology can be a vehicle for human progress since human fulfilment does not consist merely in the exercise of reason to secure material satisfaction, security and comfort. Instead they tend to emphasize artistic creativity, intellectual culture, development of interpersonal relations, or religion as being the realms in which human freedom finds expression and in which human fulfilment is to be found. The values inherent in these visions of human fulfilment are seen as overridden by the implementation of technical systems as ways of life needed to sustain them are destroyed. In this sense technology cannot be regarded as value neutral since its introduction elevates one set of values at the expense of others, not merely at the level of ideological preference but at the real level of making choices of alternative values unavailable. In this sense values are destroyed and technology, far from creating human possibilities, destroys them.

Technological systems turn human beings into mere natural objects by leaving them no alternative to be anything else.

The enlightenment spirit which fostered the growth of natural science as a route to technological achievement placed its faith in reason as a route to freedom via a knowledge of the laws of nature. Knowledge of laws confers power over and lifts one out of the natural order, frees one from domination by natural forces, enabling the manipulation of these forces to human ends. The optimistic vision of technology rests on this same faith. The pessimistic vision echoes humanist themes critical of and sceptical about the possible achievements of science, critical of the conception of reason as that which makes us human. The image of Faustus selling his soul (his humanity) to gain the knowledge which yields power captures this – to be governed by pure reason is to cease to be human. The difficulty of resolving the conflict between these attitudes towards reason as the highest human power or as essentially inhuman emerges in our ambivalent attitudes to computers. They are valuable to us precisely because they lack certain human characteristics – they do not get angry, impatient, resentful . . . they are perfectly rational. But does that mean that they are superior beings to which we should defer, or are they just tools for our use? Are they artificial intelligences? There are no easy answers to these questions.

2

FACTS, VALUES AND EFFICIENCY

In order to begin to construct a middle way between the pessimistic/
optimistic, impotent/omnipotent vision of technology we need to
question oppositions on which they are founded. Perhaps the most
central and crucial of these is the opposition between facts and
values. To question this opposition we need to look more closely at
the concepts 'fact' and 'value'. Our scrutiny of these will then be
used as a basis for an argument to the effect that technologies are
not value neutral and that certain terms, quite crucial to discussions
of technology, such as 'efficiency' are inseparably factual and evaluative.

JUST THE FACTS

When contrasting facts and values, philosophers have focused almost
exclusively on values. Facts barely rate a mention: they seem trans-
parently clear, rock solid, objectively discoverable, and grounded in
reality. They are what *is*. Values, by comparison, seem hazy, fleeting
and subjective – merely a matter of opinion, commitment or senti-
ment. They concern what some feel *should* be the case or would be
desirable or what some *wish* were true. They do not, however, mirror
the world as it is.

A little reflection reveals that facts aren't as unproblematic as they
seem. We invoke talk of 'facts' primarily in contrast to something
else (Lucas, 1986, p. 24). Sometimes we contrast fact with fiction:
Mark Twain and Samuel Clemens are one and the same, but events
narrated in his novels never happened. Or we contrast fact with
forecast: current interest rates may lead an economist to predict
increased inflation. We sometimes contrast fact with interpretation:
we may know what the Prime Minister said, but what does he

mean? Closely linked with this contrast is another. We may be less interested in interpreting facts than in commenting on them: comment is free, it is said, but fact is sacred. In still other contexts we contrast facts with suppositions, theories, hypotheses and guesses: whales mysteriously beach themselves, and various hypotheses are advanced to explain why. In law, 'the facts of a case' refer to the circumstances and incidents of a case, as distinct from their legal bearing. And, of course, we contrast facts with values. More about this later. As even this brief survey indicates, when we want 'just the facts', we have to be keenly sensitive to context. This is especially true when we examine how 'fact' is used in science and technology.

In their *practice*, scientists and engineers *inter alia* make careful observations, manipulate objects, make instruments, and invent processes. This they do to find out about nature, to invent other devices, and to alter the world. They come to the attention of one another, institutions and the public, however, primarily by producing laboratory reports, learned papers, technical specifications, e-mail bulletins and (less often) books. These contain drawings, tables, graphs, formulae, hypotheses, theories, arguments, proofs and persuasive discussion.

So far there has been no mention of 'facts'. For facts belong to discourse *about* what is found, drawn, studied and invented. Scientists and engineers never say; 'Eureka! I've discovered a *fact*!' Their thrill comes when they figure out causal connections, where something is, or how to design a device elegantly and efficiently.

Appeal to 'facts' is thus remarkably absent from the day to day work of scientists and engineers. Where, then, do we find mention of them? When utterly convinced that they have found something out about nature or how to make something, scientists will *write* and *speak* about these discoveries and inventions as 'facts'. So, for instance, a scientist might say 'It is a fact that a virus causes AIDS' or 'It is true, in fact, that the continents of Africa and South America were once connected'. In place of 'It is a fact that . . .' we could equally well substitute 'It is the case that . . .'. When scientists or engineers say they want 'just the facts' about some matter, they mean that they want to hear only what is *beyond controversy* about the matter. Latour makes the point succinctly:

> a fact is what is collectively stabilized from the midst of controversies when the activity of later [scientific and technical] papers does not consist only of criticism or deformation but also of confirmation. The strength of the original statement

does not lie in itself, but is derived from any of the papers that incorporate it. In principle, any of the papers could reject it.

(Latour , 1987, p. 42)

So facts are *made*, not discovered.[1] Typically, something becomes a matter of fact only gradually, after scientists and engineers generally become fully confident about what they have discovered or invented. In becoming 'fact' what is discovered or invented becomes, for all practical purposes, closed or settled. Note that facts occur at every level of abstraction. It is, for instance, a fact that children inherit some phenotypical characteristics (e.g. eye colour) from their parents, half their genes from each parent, and that an extra chromosome causes Down's syndrome.

Some facts are 'harder' than others. 'Hard' facts are those that no scientist or engineer working in a particular area can realistically imagine being called into question: for example, that the earth revolves around the sun, that the heart pumps blood. Those who *do* deny hard facts are dismissed as quacks, charlatans or unreasoning fanatics. Those claiming that God created the world in 4004 BC, for instance, are simply not taken seriously by mainstream scientists. One sure way of putting oneself beyond the pale, scientifically speaking, is by rejecting 'hard' facts, either directly or by implication.

'Soft' facts are those scientists and engineers base their work on, but acknowledge that much relating to this base remains poorly understood. Smoking causes lung cancer – but how? While confident that better understanding will come eventually, prudent scientists know that further investigation may threaten any fact. It is a 'hard' fact that dinosaurs vanished virtually overnight, geologically speaking; that this occurred because of a cataclysmic event, however, is a comparatively 'soft' fact. The line between 'hard' and 'soft' shifts, of course, as the state of scientific and technical knowledge changes. Here a point needs to be made about what happens when something taken as fact ceases to be taken as such. If dislodged, fact-claims, like knowledge-claims, have to be 'taken back'. Just as we don't say 'I once knew Labour would defeat the Conservatives at the next election, but now I don't', so we don't say 'It was once a fact that Bush told the truth about swapping arms for hostages; now that we know he lied, it no longer is a fact'. Instead, just as we say 'I once thought I knew that . . .' or 'I once mistakenly believed that . . .', so we say 'We mistakenly took it as fact that . . .'. To put the point differently, we never lose faith in facts: the moment we lose faith in that to which they refer, they lose their privileged status as 'facts'. It often happens, of course, that what once was fact no longer is: for example, that the sun never sets on the British Empire.

It must be added, and indeed emphasized, that this account of how 'fact' is used in scientific *discourse* in no way denies that scientists make discoveries about a structured, changing world that exists independently of our knowledge of it. To think otherwise would be to commit the *epistemic fallacy* of equating the analysis, or definition, of what *is* in terms of our knowledge of it.[2] In learning about the world, scientists use formal proofs, models, experiments, reliable apparatus, new discoveries, consistency with established theory (among other things). 'Facts' simply do not play this same kind of role in discovery and justification. They do not, as it were, lie alongside observations, proofs, models, experiments, etc. We don't ask, 'Thanks for the observations, now what about the facts?' Facts simply aren't in *that* toolbox. Instead, an appeal to facts marks a completion ('At last we know the facts') or a basis for the next stage of enquiry ('Before we begin theorizing, let's get straight about the facts'). There is a sense, then, in which science and technology could proceed almost as well without facts. In another sense, however, they could not. For to know when to rest, when to build, what need not be questioned, facts do real work. So while facts may lack the glamour of models and theories, they have their own distinctive work to do.

When we aren't pushing a philosophical doctrine, we use the language of 'fact' in much the same way as scientists and engineers. Importantly, what we take as fact may fall on either side of the descriptive/evaluative divide – or straddle it.

If Jones jumps up in church to announce a fire sale following the service, we take it as fact that he was disruptive, disrespectful and culpable. While we can classify 'disruptive' as a purely descriptive term, 'disrespectful' is not purely descriptive and 'culpable' is primarily normative or evaluative. If we question the veracity of accounts of what Jones did, we are not yet taking the reports as fact. If we eventually accept them, it is not because we find something queer, like a 'fact'. Instead we investigate by making enquiries, interrogating witnesses, and evaluating evidence. We try, in short, to make sure what happened. Once we take it as fact that Jones disrupted the service, we may still question the further factual claim that he was being disrespectful. Was he, perhaps, warning of a fire, not advertising a fire sale? Suppose Jones mistakenly thought that the church was on fire; is that disrespectful? Finally, even if we agree that Jones acted disrespectfully in announcing a fire sale, does it follow that he is culpable? Well, was he sane? Was he being deliberately disrespectful because he thought, perhaps rightly, that the service itself was thoroughly corrupt? (Was Jesus disrespectful and culpable in chasing money-changers from the Temple?) Answers to such questions may not be easy or fully satisfying. Once members of a community become fully convinced of the answers, however, these become 'facts'. The community may be mistaken, of course, but so can a community of scientists and engineers. Each may overlook something, misinterpret it, or give it false emphasis.

Ordinary facts, like scientific facts (which may be ordinary to scientists), can also be hard or soft. Many ordinary facts are about as hard as hard can be; for example, that people cannot breathe under water. Because we ordinarily have neither need nor interest in accuracy or precision, we often overextend our factual claims. We take as fact that fire burns when this does not hold of things which burst into flame at extremely low temperatures. Many ordinary facts, of course, are exceedingly soft, easily overturned on further investigation.

In saying that facts belong to the *language* of science, we are implicitly denying them any special *ontological* status. Facts are not, as it were, part of the 'furniture' or 'fabric' of the world; our appeal to them expresses our confidence about what is so. That facts belong to the language of science does not mean that they are unimportant: practising scientists need to know what is reliable, what can serve as uncontested as they pursue their research.

There is nothing, then, to stop scientific or ordinary facts from being descriptive, normative, evaluative or partaking of all. It is fact, for instance, that automobiles have contributed to the growth of suburban living, that an automobile culture tends to weaken parental authority, and that many people drive irresponsibly. Anyone contesting these factual claims will not look for contrary facts. Instead one will challenge the veracity of government reports, raise sociological questions, or probe reasoning for shaky premises, false inferences, implicit but undefended value judgements, and the like. One will, in short, engage in further investigation and argument, both of which require evaluation. Midgley makes this point nicely and reiterates our general point:

> [W]e can . . . only understand our values if we first grasp the

given facts about our wants. Moral philosophers in the first half of this century, however, made great efforts to discredit all reasoning that assumed this connection. Half the trouble in this controversy resulted from a mistaken notion of *facts* – from assuming that they were simple neutral things, easily defined – matters seen and described infallibly, without reference to standards, which arose separately as a kind of practical convenience or even luxury. Actually, . . . in talking of *description*, we are never neutral even in what we 'see' – we must always select, interpret, and classify. This is just as true of scientific observers as of ordinary ones. By *facts* we usually just mean 'data', that is, everything we count not as part of the particular problem before us, but as what is safe enough to be taken for granted in solving it, and needed to do so. But *facts* are never confined to the raw data of sense, and seldom to 'physical facts' (the kind that can be stated in terms of physics). It is a *fact* that this is a food or poison, that it is dangerous, dirty, unique, or legal, that it is an ancient totem pole or the flag of my country. Yet standards quite alien to physics must be grasped before we can 'see' these facts. They are thus never logically isolated from some kind of 'evaluating'.

(Midgley, 1978, p. 178)

We said at the outset that we employ talk of facts as contrastive, and that the contrast is not always or even usually with values. When, for instance, a scientist or engineer says that something is a 'factual matter', he or she means that it is a matter open to scientific enquiry, instead of (for example) meditation, philosophical reflection, or appeal to authority. It does not mean that evaluations and value judgements are excluded if, as we will see in subsequent chapters, they are implicated in scientific enquiry.

VALUES AND EVALUATION

As with many commonly used terms, the meaning of the term 'value' is impossible to pin down precisely. It originally meant 'that amount of some commodity, or medium of exchange (e.g. money) considered to be the equivalent of something else'; or 'the material or monetary worth of a thing'. In this original sense, there is little difference between the value of something and its price. Hobbes (1588–1679) denied that there was *any* distinction:

37

The Value, or Worth of a man, is as of all other things, his Price; that is to say, so much as would be given for the use of his Power: and therefore is not absolute; but a thing dependant on the need and judgement of another.

(Hobbes, *Leviathan*, Part I, Ch. 10)

We still say that some paintings are overvalued (i.e. overpriced) while others are undervalued (i.e. underpriced), or that certain stocks are 'good value' (i.e. the cost of buying them is low in comparison to the likely return). We now, however, also distinguish between prices and value: Oscar Wilde, for instance, said that the cynic is someone who 'knows the price of everything and the value of nothing'.

It is no accident that 'value' entered language as commerce came to depend increasingly on monetary systems that were becoming a dominant force in European economic life. In a barter economy goods are exchanged on a basis of available surplus and need, so there is no fixed quantity of any single commodity that would be suitable payment for helping harvest a neighbour's crops or supplying him or her with milk. With the introduction of money as the principal medium of exchange, a particular commodity or service comes to be exchangeable for a sum of money – the price or value. Price is something involved in transactions between individuals – the seller has his or her asking price and the buyer the price he or she is prepared to pay and, in the end, does pay. An individual, of course, may well pay either more or less than the 'going rate' – that is, the market value. The individual may get a bargain, pay a fair price or feel that he or she paid too much and was cheated; the individual may have paid less than the item was worth, what it was worth or more than it was worth. Here we see how the separation between price and value comes in and how value can come to seem to be an intrinsic characteristic of something. A work of art can have a (market) value that may bear no relation to the price paid for it (it may have been a lucky find in an antique shop, and it is possible that neither the seller nor the buyer had any idea of its value). But it is also true that the amount a buyer is willing to pay for something, both in monetary terms and in terms of the sacrifices that finding the money might require, is a reflection of the value he or she places on it, or on its possession. The buyer might be prepared to pay over the market value just because it is important to him or her. Someone might pay substantially more than the established market price for an old recording because his or her beloved grandfather was a member of the orchestra; another might ask substantially less than the established market price for a rare stamp because of a sudden need for quick cash. Such examples illustrate the distinction between individual (or subjective or extrinsic) values and socially established market values (objective or intrinsic).

Use of the term 'value' has by now been extended into all kinds of contexts that do not involve monetary exchange. But the two-sided nature of the term present in its origins plagues its extended uses too. Sometimes values appear subjective (extrinsic) being just a reflection of the goals of individuals or groups of individuals, sometimes objective (intrinsic characteristics of things) possessed independently of people and their desires.

Just as facts are not simply 'there', so values are not simply expressions of subjective feeling. But what are they? Some think that they are transcendent objects, like distant stars which inspire commitment and loyalty. Although misguided, this picture picks out two significant features: values do present themselves as outside us and demanding our allegiance. Those who value efficiency, for example, think of it as valuable independently of their subjective wishes and thus feel that schemes ought to be judged in terms of efficiency. These features, however, do not entail that values exist in some separate, non-human realm.

As ordinarily used now, 'value' can refer to many things:

1 A fundamental good that a person pursues consistently over an extended period of his or her life; one of the person's ultimate reasons for action.
2 A quality (or a practice) that gives worth, goodness, meaning, or a fulfilling character to the life a person is leading, or aspiring to lead.
3 A quality (or a practice) that is partially constitutive of a person's identity, as a self-evaluating, a self-interpreting, a self-making being.
4 A fundamental criterion for a person to choose what is good (or better) among possible courses of action.
5 A fundamental standard to which one holds the behaviour of self and others.
6 An 'object of value', an appropriate relationship with which is partially constitutive both of a worthwhile life and of one's personal identity. Objects of value can include works of art, scientific theories, technological devices, sacred objects, cultures, traditions,

institutions, other people, and nature itself. Appropriate relations with objects of value, depending on the particular object, include the following: production, reproduction, respect, nurturance, maintenance, preservation, worship, love, public recognition, and personal possession (Lacey and Schwartz, 1995).

How can values be other than expressions of feeling and impose themselves on us as something 'objective?' The answer lies in how values arise. To see this, we need to understand an everyday human activity, that of *evaluating*. People have desires, usually many and various. They are never lucky enough to satisfy all, and not all at once. Even someone who, racked with pain, succeeds in killing him- or herself seldom does so wholly without regret. Now just because all wants cannot be satisfied, it does not follow that those that cannot be satisfied disappear, nor that they should. Wants, desires and interests differ in this way from beliefs. If someone believes two inconsistent things, then that person is unreasonable if he or she does not abandon at least one of them. This is not true of desires: we often want to eat our cake, and have it, too. At worst, it is *childish* to desire the objects of two clashing desires. It need not be irrational, however, and often is not unreasonable or even childish. Whether a set of desires is unreasonable turns on the desires in question and social possibilities.

But what have desires, wants and interests to do with evaluating? One's desires characteristically clash with each other, and do so on two different levels. Someone who wants to eat his or her cake and have it too, experiences a *first-order* conflict. To resolve such conflicts one weighs the objects of one desire against one another. Usually, though not always, the result can be expressed in quantitative terms: I want this more than that, but less than something else. If things go well, the result will often be a change in desires. The person may decide that cake is not healthy, and so give up desiring it.

There are, additionally, clashes of a different kind. For besides wanting to eat one's cake and have it, most people want to be a certain kind of person. This may entail altering one's first-order desires and acquiring new desires more consistent with the kind of person one wants to be. This may involve freeing oneself from certain first-order desires altogether or simply keeping certain desires 'in their place'. Often, however, first-order desires need to be *transformed* in the light of our 'higher' or *second-order* desires, wants and aspirations. Unless one brings this about, one will not be the kind of person one wants to be.

Values result from these two kinds of evaluating. Under the pressure of our need to be a certain kind of person, our first-order desires evolve. This evolution takes place against a social backdrop that gives meaning to our evaluations. A person may then come to value, say, family life more than a career (or conversely) and foster one instead of the other. The value of family life, then, will present itself as much more than an expression of feeling, and so it is. It also will present itself as a demand on one's allegiance, and so it is. People need not feel oppressed by the demands values place on them because, through the activity of evaluating, they help bring them into being.

Yet this is only part of the story, the *subjective* side of the story. For so far we have only talked about individuals developing their own values through valuing. But individuals do not live isolated lives. Just as water is the natural medium of fish, so the natural medium of humans is *culture*. Nerlich aptly characterizes culture as 'an engineering programme for producing persons' (Nerlich, 1989, p. 185).[3] By 'person', Nerlich means something other than a biologically produced human being. Human beings become persons in this sense when they become free, deliberating agents. These, he explains, are social qualities whose shape and content vary from culture to culture. If we think of different cultures as carrying out different engineering programmes, we can better understand how values arise. All societies, of course, have the same 'raw material' to work with: namely, biologically determined human beings. But just as engineers do different things with the same building materials, so do cultures. One implication is that distinctive cultures present distinctive values to their members. One, for instance, may place a high value on machismo behaviour in men; another, a high value on material progress. This highlights another implication: a person with a certain cluster of native and acquired abilities may be favoured in one culture, but disfavoured in another. Cultures are in this way like games: chess favours people with one set of skills, football those with another.

A specific culture conditions, not fully determines, the kind of first-order desires a person has and the kind of person he or she wants to become. A man may regard his wish to be more nurturing as a vice, a defect of character, in one culture but not in another. At first glance, the values and choices a culture presents to any given

41

member seem both inevitable and immutable. They are as 'hard' as any 'fact'. A woman in the United States or United Kingdom today who wishes to combine a career, family and leisure confronts daunting obstacles. Subjectively, a person wants one thing, but, objectively, one's culture may demand something else. These problems can and do overwhelm and crush many. But they also set the stage for profound cultural change, and it is important to see how.

A culture may be an engineering programme to produce persons, but it differs significantly from more conventional engineering programmes. In particular, those subject to the programme can reflect on the values it fosters and, either individually or in concert, try to modify it. We can, as it were, deliberately throw a spanner in the works. Now in doing so, we will be trying to change the programme so that it accords better with the results of our own valuations, our own sense of what we hope to become. This will not be easy. Probably many will be satisfied with the way the programme is working out. This is not surprising, as everyone is – in a loose sense – a 'product' of the programme. But events may conspire to foster change. Wars and plagues not only destroy, but create possibilities of significant change. By altering political or social consciousness, too, perceptions change of what is 'just' or 'natural'. And rapid developments in technology are especially effective in making elements of an existing cultural programme obsolete.

We can return to the plight of women for an example. Because of profound economic, political, social and technological changes the traditional role 'assigned' to women is under attack. Yet the values fostered by that role remain: woman as primary parent, nurturer and homemaker. These values clash with emerging roles and their attendant values. For many women, however, the new roles do not *replace* the old, but are simply *added* to them. So, many women work one shift for pay and a second shift for no pay, at home (see Hochschild, 1989). This 'double day' places enormous stress on marriage and the family. Significantly, the second shift brings more than additional work: it carries with it additional values demanding allegiance.

No one knows how it will end. But we can use the example to illustrate how values get formed, challenged and doubly transformed. The first transformation occurs within a particular woman as she tries to integrate her various desires, wants and needs to become the person she wishes to be. Typically, one first tries to do it all: to have one's cake, and eat it too. When this fails, as it usually does, a woman must re-evaluate both her first- *and* second-order desires.

This usually leads to compromises, both with herself and with those around her: husband, children, co-workers and superiors. Here, incidentally, we see the clash of values *between* and *among* people, not simply *within* one person. Certain traditional ways of dividing up household responsibilities, for instance, may come under scrutiny. Success is not guaranteed. A woman and her husband may agree to split household chores evenly, yet old patterns may reassert themselves quickly. How much does she value domestic tranquillity? Unless she can draw on the experience of other similarly situated women, enlisting their political and moral support, the cultural programme will hardly hiccup as it either absorbs or marginalizes her. With concerted action, however, the programme may change, perhaps dramatically. Others not immediately involved may help alter the programme. Corporate managers, for instance, cannot be pleased to know that, on average, their women executives receive less sleep and fall ill more often than their male counterparts. So the programme may be radically – and unpredictably – transformed.

Individuals are distinct, though not separate, from the engineering programme that is culture. All struggle to see their values reflected in culture or to embody their values in culture. This includes the considerable technological aspects of any culture. To see this, consider an analogy with professional basketball. Rules designed for players under six feet tall (e.g. the width of the free-throw lanes, the length of time a player may stand under the basket, even the height of the basket) threatened to destroy a game now dominated by players nearly seven feet tall. A clash of values resulted in a challenge to what it even means to be a good player: is it sufficient simply to score more points than anyone else? Presumably tall players think so! But the game is not played just for the (tall) players; it is also played for the public, and they did not like the game as it was fast becoming. What was valued became re-evaluated. The resulting changes encode new values into the game. There is, of course, enormous continuity with the old, including its values. But the game has changed and now favours players with different skills. Even here technology plays a role. That the game now favours 'leapers' is only possible because baskets have been designed and built that do not snap off when struck. The 'spring' basket thus embodies a (sub)culture's programme of what counts as a good player, of what constitutes value. In altering the game through its rules, practices and technological innovations all sides, both traditionalists and revolutionaries, must rely on the resources of the tradition from which it comes. Because of this give

43

and take, challenge and response, values become objective, if only for a time and provisionally, until another major challenge.

Cultures, of course, are not games: they are entered without consent, deadly serious, all encompassing, and not easily manipulated by deliberate, enforceable rule changes. Still, on the principal points we wish to make, the analogy applies. The double transformation of desires into values, then, consists in this. As individuals struggle to become who they wish to be, they create values as they strive to forge their desires into an integrated whole. Only when these values link with salient elements in one's culture, perhaps transforming it, do they become objective by commanding the allegiance of most. If this occurs, the engineering programme – culture – has itself been transformed.

THE INTERPLAY OF FACTS AND VALUES

We can distinguish between facts (what is widely agreed to be the case) and values (what is good or has worth) without committing ourselves to the further thesis that they belong on either side of some unbridgeable ontological divide. It would seem to be a fact, for instance, that health is a primary good, that being subject to physical and psychological abuse is bad, that living in a thriving community is good, that lacking any appropriate relationship with objects of value is bad, and so on.

Our judgements often reflect the easy mix of fact and value. Consider, for instance, a headline in *The Washington Post* (Saturday, 16 July 1994, p. 16) 'Rwanda Sets Sad, New Record for African Tragedies'. 'Record' refers to quantifiable numbers; 'sad' and 'tragedies', however, are evaluative descriptions. Accompanying stories describe/evaluate the mass exodus of Hutus from Rwanda to Zaire: the head delegate of the International Committee of the Red Cross 'described the situation as "unmanageable . . . not hopeless, but overwhelming" ' (p. 1) and a reporter concludes (on p. 16) that 'Perhaps the biggest obstacle to agencies confronting the new crisis is a general sense of exhaustion among a donor community grown wary of Africa's seemingly perpetual state of hopelessness'. Stories abounding with numbers interweave seamlessly with evaluative descriptions of chaos, violence, horror, hopelessness, despair and pathos. As used in this context, these words are both genuinely descriptive *and* evaluative. And, isn't it a fact that the slaughter and displacement of Rwandans is a terrible tragedy?

We generally accept this intermingling until we find ourselves *disagreeing* with the evaluative descriptions. Critics of a government's foreign or domestic policy may describe it as in 'disarray' or as a 'shambles'; supporters will dismiss such judgements, urging voters to 'look at the facts' or 'read the record'. But which facts? Which records? For records, too, involve descriptive evaluations: which statistics bear the most significance, and for what purposes? It is doubtful whether we can ever simply report 'the facts' free of any descriptive evaluation. For supposing we could, what would we have? Nothing more than list upon list of 'raw data'. Once we impose *any* kind of order on the data or make *any* selection among the data, we are engaged in evaluation, in determining what we deem significant.

Thus, for example, Polyani, when seeking to characterize science in such a way as to distinguish it from technology, notes:

> Not all empirical knowledge forms part of science: the contents of a telephone directory for example do not. The *scientific value* of a piece of knowledge is determined by three factors: (*a*) its reliability, (*b*) its systematic significance, and (*c*) the intrinsic interest of its subject matter.... A discovery is interesting to science only if it has a bearing on the existing system of science.
>
> (Polyani, 1955, p. 37, emphasis added)

In other words, science itself is a product of the evaluation of empirical information. But Polyani's attempt to distinguish science from technology also illustrates how someone can acknowledge this point, even using the phrase 'scientific value', while at the same time maintaining that values have no place in science, that it is value free, or value neutral. He says:

> By contrast [with a technological invention], the validity of a scientific observation cannot be affected by a change in values. If diamonds became as cheap as salt is today and salt as precious as diamonds are now, this would not invalidate any part of the physics and chemistry of diamonds or of salt.
>
> (Polyani, 1955, p. 37)

This is true, but it is true because here 'value' is being used in a strictly economic sense, so that literally speaking the point being made is that the scientific value of a piece of knowledge is (relatively) independent of the economic value of the things (diamonds, salt, etc.) with which it is concerned, whereas the value of a technological invention is not.[4] But if Polyani had expressed himself this way his contrast would have lacked the rhetorical force necessary to make it seem sharp enough to justify his view of pure science as something which transcends fluctuating values, as something which operates on a 'higher' more universal plane than technological disciplines. His rhetoric plays on the reader's willingness to make the metaphorical transfer of 'value' from the strictly economic context to the much wider range of contexts in which we make evaluations and hence bring our 'values' into play.

It is in this wider sense, in which 'values' are manifest in the making of evaluations and of choices based on those valuations, that it is possible to say that values become embodied in technologies.[5] Just as artists naturally express their artistic values in their art, so do the makers of technologies. If, for instance, price is more important than safety in the minds of manufacturers, their products will undoubtedly embody that trade-off. Where manufacturers have a captive market of a necessary product, to take another example, their indifference to their customers' interests often shows up in unwieldy designs. Genuinely free markets among true equals help bring about an integration of conflicting values. For here interests of sellers and buyers interact dynamically, often spurring innovations in design that embody values satisfying both. But genuinely free markets among true equals are far rarer than we think: costs (of entry, design, advertising), market recognition, power imbalances exclude many from even entering most markets.

As we saw previously, once embodied in a technology the values of its creators tend to persist. But this point needs to be modified, as we also argued. For users of technology can themselves regard the embodied artefact as 'raw material' and do what they can to turn it to their own purposes. Sometimes this will be relatively easy; sometimes, relatively difficult. In any case, and contrary to the worries of the more extreme pessimists, there is no need for any *general* attitude of helplessness or hopelessness.

To admit that technologies are never uniquely 'valenced', that the values they embody are dependent on the wider socio-cultural context, might be taken as support for the instrumentalist view that the technologies themselves (intrinsically) are value neutral, even though they can only ever exist in a context and as soon as they are inserted into a context they inevitably take on values. Again we can draw on the analogy with language. The word 'rot' in isolation may simply be a sequence of marks on paper; it takes on a meaning (semantic value) only in the context of other words from a specific language and in the context of a specific use. 'Der rose es rot', 'The roof timbers in this house have dry rot', 'He was talking a load of rot' all signal different semantic values for 'rot'. Now even though there are many divergent views of language, most would agree that words have their being as components of a larger unit – a language – and that their identity is, at least in part, constituted by the role they play in that language, i.e. in relation to other words. Thus isolated marks on paper are not yet words. In this sense words have no · intrinsic properties, properties wholly independent of their function in language. Words differ in this respect from rocks, which have chemical and physical properties in virtue of the material they are composed of, independently of the context in which they are found and independently of the way in which they are classified. In treating something as a natural object we treat it as a given, as something which has an identity independent of any of the uses we may put it to or any values we may impose on it.

The more radical forms of instrumentalism attempt to treat tools as natural objects (hunks of junk), and yet it should be clear that the very concept of a tool already removes an object so identified from the purely natural category. To identify a piece of flint as an artefact, as possibly an arrowhead, is already to regard it as having been made with an end in view and a characteristic use, i.e. as embodying the values of a particular stone-age culture, even though these cannot be directly read off an isolated, but obviously worked, piece of flint. We can properly identify it as a tool only when we can fill in enough of its cultural context to be able to make a reasonable guess at how it was normally used and for what kinds of purposes.

A less radical form of instrumentalism might concede these points but at the same time also insist that we are free at any time to alter the use of a tool, to put it into new or non-standard uses, or not to use it at all, if we object to the end for which it was fashioned. Guns can be used for defence as well as attack and if we object to any killing or maiming of human beings, on whatever pretext, we need not buy a gun. But not buying one does not prevent others from using them on us or on other people. This is the reason so many people give for buying a gun; the existence of guns creates the perceived need to have one's own, just for self-defence.

Just as one person cannot effect a reform of language, purging it of all sexism, so one person cannot control the use of a technology.

Rather individual ends and values tend to be influenced by the forms of technology surrounding them. This is the entanglement whose existence is denied by technological optimists and whose existence is acknowledged but resisted by technological pessimists. To accept it would mean accepting that humans are moulded and constrained by the material environments they create for themselves, that they are not fully free in relation to them and hence do not, and could never, fully control or dominate them. Both share a vision of what is ideally human as autonomous of human material embodiment; their ideals, their ability to recognize or confer values is what sets them apart from the rest of nature. But they differ over their conceptions of the extent to which this is currently realized and over ways of ensuring its future realization. For pessimists the ideal can be realized only by withdrawing from technological culture and the dominance of instrumental rationality. But what exactly do the pessimist and others find so objectionable about instrumental rationality? Reasoning about the best means to achieve the ends we wish to pursue seems an integral part of any human life, not something limited to the context of technology or a technological culture. The beginnings of an answer can be given by taking a detour through the concept of efficiency.

EFFICIENCY

Polyani gives an interesting characterization of technology:

> Technology devises the means for the achievement of certain ends and such a process is rational only if it is economic ... any invention can be rendered worthless ... by a radical change in the values of the means used up and the ends produced by it.

. . .

> A technological advance is (*a*) a commercial enterprise or (*b*) part of a commercial enterprise. (*a*) The inventor developing a new technical process or device, whether by his own means or by borrowed capital, undertakes an essentially independent task which he must perform to the satisfaction of the market. By keeping his activities aimed at the greatest profit their results remain simultaneously coordinated to the similar activities of all other productive units within the same market.
>
> (Polyani, 1955, pp. 37–42)

48

Here he is expressing a view of technology which has dominated, and continues to dominate, the climate of technological development in capitalist economies. In this conception of technology we find that fusion of instrumental rationality with economic rationality and of economic rationality with efficiency to which Ellul so strongly objects. Although he rejects the total package, Ellul does not try to take the package apart; he does not question this fusing of concepts and seems to take it as inevitable. And while these things may be difficult to pull apart in the context of industrial capitalism, we nonetheless think that it can and should be done.

The concept of 'efficiency' plays a crucial role in binding instrumental and economic rationality together with technological development. The terms 'efficiency' and 'efficient' were not used in anything like their modern senses before the mid-nineteenth century. Earlier uses of these words can be traced back to the Aristotelian notion of an efficient cause – the event or action immediately responsible for producing a given effect. Striking a match in the presence of a gas leak, might, for example, be the efficient cause of an explosion. Such an action might have greater or lesser 'efficiency' or 'efficacy' depending on the magnitude of the effect produced. 'Efficiency' does not start to become a term of quantitative comparison by which to rate systems, processes or machines until the mid-nineteenth century. This shift of use seems to have come about in the wake of the development and widespread use of steam engines and the adoption of steam engines as a favourite source of metaphors and analogies.

Steam engines were originally developed in England to power the large pumps necessary to prevent flooding in deep mines. So they were initially invented and developed in the commercial context of mining and were not a direct product of theoretical advances in science. The earliest engines were very large stationary beam engines. The crucial concern for mine owners was to get pumps that were technically capable of pumping the volume of water required at the rate required to keep their mine workable, and to get ones which would do this without being so expensive to operate that they would threaten the economic viability of the mine. It was therefore necessary for engineers to develop ways of rating their engines with respect to these two factors:

> The mechanical effect of the steam engine may be considered
> either in respect to the mechanical power exerted by a given

49

machine, in a given time, or in respect to the expenditure of fuel, by which a given mechanical effect is produced. These are separate considerations, but both of them are important, and in particular cases, one or other of them may demand preference, according to the circumstances.

For instance, if a mine is to be drained of water, and if, by becoming deeper and more extensive, its engine is scarcely equal to the task, the principal object will be to augment the power of the engine by every possible means, without regard to the consumption of fuel. This is a very common case in coal mines, where fuel can be had free of expense. On the other hand, an engine for a lead mine, or a copper mine, may be fully equal to the task of draining the water, and yet the expense to fuel may be so great, as to take away the profit of the mine. In this case, the main consideration will be to obtain the greatest mechanical power, with the least consumption of fuel.

(Farey, 1827, Vol. I, p. 169)

In this context the notions of mechanical power and mechanical effect are precisely defined and can be measured so that machines can be rated and compared one with another. Farey describes an experiment, conducted in the presence of witnesses, to compare a high pressure steam engine, made by Woolf, with a Watt low pressure engine. These engines were designed to power mill stones for grinding wheat. The engines were used to drive the same size and kind of stones and the amounts of wheat ground, fuel consumed and time taken were compared. The Woolf engine ground twice as much wheat per bushel of good coal as the Watt engine and in two-thirds of the time. Convinced by this demonstration London millers bought engines from Woolf, although as Farey also notes:

Mr Woolf's engines, being the most complicated, require more care and attention to keep them in equally good order, with those of Mr Watt, and their performance is impaired in a greater degree, if they are allowed to get out of order.

(Farey, 1827, Vol. I, p. 75)

Again Farey explains that machines may be rated for mechanical effectiveness (efficiency) either in respect of the maximum power that they can exert or in respect of the amount of power they are capable of deriving from a given 'exertion of the moving force by which they are actuated', noting that 'it does not follow that a machine which is acting so as to exert its utmost power, will also afford that power at the least expense'. (Note how an economic concept has entered the mechanical discussion.)

> To obtain the maximum of effect from a given expenditure of motive force a machine must be adapted to receive all the power of that motive force, without permitting any of its activity to escape, or be expended in waste, so as to fail of exerting its full effect, to impel the machine. This depends chiefly upon the manner in which the machine is constructed.
>
> (Farey, 1827, Vol. I, p. 66)

In other words, the more mechanically efficient machine is that in which least energy is lost (in the form of heat dissipated) in overcoming internal resistances. A little paraphrasing will show the way in which the concept of efficiency was subsequently analogically transferred from the purely technological context, where it is precisely defined and measurable, to the industrial context:

> To obtain the maximum productivity from a given labour force a production line must be organized so as to utilize all the labour power of that labour force, without permitting any of its activity to escape, or be wasted, so as to fail to exert its full effect to produce. This depends chiefly upon the manner in which the production line is organized.

Just as nineteenth century mine owners and millers were concerned with getting the maximum amount of (mechanical) work out of steam engines for the minimum amount of fuel, so industrialists generally exhibit an overriding concern to get the maximum productivity from the minimum labour force. In the case of steam engines there is a fairly direct connection between the interest in mechanical efficiency ratings and economics although even here there is strictly a distinction to be drawn between fuel efficiency, which depends additionally on the combustion process, and mechanical efficiency, which depends on the working parts of the engine and on its use of steam pressure. But for a fixed combustion process the mechanically more efficient engine will get more mechanical work out of a bushel of coal, and so will, on the face of it, cost less to run. Thus instrumental reasoning, economic reasoning and mechanical reasoning tend to run together into the evaluation of machines for mechanical efficiency. Although even here, Farey's caution about Woolf engines serves as a reminder that the economics of the deployment of steam engines is not so simple as the 'economics' of energy or fuel use in the machine. Engines need maintenance and hence persons to maintain them and more maintenance by more skilled people will be an additional cost. And his point about the economic differences between coal and lead mines which make fuel efficiency much less of a concern in the former context than in the latter, shows that whether the more fuel-efficient engine is the economically rational choice, that based on maximizing profits, depends on the context in which the choice is being made.

In current political discourse increased productivity is frequently equated with increased efficiency, and increased efficiency with increased profitability. Increasing efficiency seems sometimes to be regarded as an end in itself, and as something for which there are absolute measures. But outside the strictly mechanical context the measures are no longer precise. As the notion of efficiency is metaphorically extended it comes to have many different senses. Even the moral injunction 'Do not waste anything' could not succeed in uniting all these senses to promote efficiency as an end in itself. To be efficient in one respect – to use one's time to achieve the maximum number of tasks – often requires being inefficient in others – not making all possible use of every part of a fish one is preparing by discarding the head and bones. In what sense is that to be considered a waste? From the point of view of a hungry person who might have time and ability to make use of them in fish soup, it is waste – discarding something potentially useful. From the point of view of people who would never dream of eating fish heads or of making fish soup it is not a waste. In an energy conversion process, energy loss can be calculated. But even to regard energy lost from a mechanical system as energy wasted is already to introduce an element of evaluation; it presupposes that one is looking at the mechanical system as a machine designed to perform a task, and is thus to begin to put the mechanical system into the context of instrumental reasoning. In more complex processes it is not even always clear what to count as a significant loss (waste). When a typist spends five minutes every hour getting up, stretching and looking out of the window is this to be counted as time wasted (inefficient use of labour)? Or is it to be counted important to the typist's physical well-being and hence part of what is an efficient way to use labour (people like machines need maintenance)?

Profitability clearly depends on the balance between the financial costs of *all* inputs (labour, materials, energy, services) and the incomes received from outputs (whether services or products). Unlike the mechanical context, the financial output from a production process can exceed the financial input (there are always energy losses when operating machines). Productivity depends not only on the efficient use of labour, but also on the technology used, its efficiency and how efficiently it is deployed. These are all slightly different senses of efficiency and each would have to be assessed in different ways, but all draw on the idea of drawing up an energy equation to see how much energy is lost in a mechanical process. The transfer to the wider context of instrumental and economic evaluation generally is made by analysing other processes with a view to drawing up a balance sheet of inputs (means) and outputs (ends) and thinking of inputs as costs and outputs as benefits. The introduction of new technology to automate a production line, so decreasing the labour force and increasing the rate of production, while it would be an increase in productivity of the workforce (amount produced in a given time per person employed), may or may not result in an efficiently organized production line (one operating at maximum productive capacity, given the machines purchased and the labour force employed); may or may not represent an efficient use of capital (a good return on the capital investment required to purchase the machinery); may or may not make efficient use of raw materials, and so on. So there is no single notion of efficiency with which to equate increased productivity. Indeed, whether increasing the productivity of each person employed by means of a heavy invest-ment in automated technology constitutes an efficient use of a labour force depends on the scale at which things are considered. At the level of an individual company or plant it may be efficient, but if in the process many skilled people are laid off without prospect of future employment elsewhere, then at a regional or national level this constitutes a very inefficient use of the available labour force.

Why do Ellul and others so object to the notion of efficiency and link it integrally to their pessimism about technology? We suggest that this is because it is a concept which has its origins in technology and is at its most measurable as a way of evaluating the suitability of machines for specific purposes. To assess a production process or an organization in terms of efficiency is, however, to treat an assembly of people as if it were an assembly of mechanical parts. It is expressive of an attitude of treating people, particularly those constituting a workforce, as if they were just objects, as if they along with the machines they operate were just part of the means being deployed to achieving someone else's ends. Thus the tendency to evaluate all production, service systems and organizations in these terms becomes symbolic of the dehumanizing effect of technology about which pessimists complain. It runs counter to what Kant regarded as an absolute moral imperative – human beings are always to be treated as ends in themselves, never as means.

HOW TECHNOLOGIES EMBODY VALUES

We have discussed how values arise in the life of individuals situated in a particular culture, and how an economic context can set the framework for evaluating machines. What bearing does this have on the question of how – or even whether – technologies embody values? A particular person, class or culture may hold certain values, but can we make sense of the notion – which we've used throughout this chapter – of such values becoming embedded in a particular technology?

Certainly narrow, instrumentalist definitions of technology lend plausibility to the neutrality thesis. Particular tools, machines or processes considered in isolation from their social, scientific and economic context seem little more than value-neutral products, to be used as one wishes. If one tries hard enough one can always consider any object or process in isolation, thus seeing it as no more than a physical object or chemical process. Williams does just this when he states that 'Nuclear weapons are neither moral nor immoral – they are just piles of chemicals, metals and junk' (Williams, 1984, p. 100). True, nuclear weapons are composed of chemicals, metals and junk, even if highly sophisticated junk. That they are 'just' this and nothing more needs further argument. Proponents of the neutrality thesis often make this reductivist move, a move familiar enough in philosophical circles: a person is 'just' a collection of flesh and bone, the mental is 'just' complex states of the central nervous system, art is 'just' paint on canvas and so on. Reductivism gains no plausibility merely because it may be found almost anywhere.

This reductivist move ignores the factors that make the difference between a pile of junk and a technological device. A windmill with its sail is nothing more than a quaint adornment to the landscape until situated in a culture dependent on wind power and the organization of other bits of machinery necessary for using it to grind corn or pump water. Yesterday's technological wonders (flying shuttle, gas poker, early electric heater) frequently turn up in junk shops to be recognized only as some sort of machinery or tool by most customers. Reductionism ignores the intentions, values and social understanding of those who design, develop, market and control technology; it also overlooks the understanding of users, consumers, beneficiaries, victims, and those deeply affected by technology whether they are aware of this or not. Finally, this reductivist temptation has as a corollary that only the *users* of technology are responsible for harm, since all technologies are inherently without value.

The reductivist move seems plausible only if we abstract a technology from any possible use. For taken wholly abstractly, we can indeed describe it in suitably neutral terms; for example, as junk. (Taken wholly abstractly, of course, we can do the same for *anything*: a horse race, for instance, can be described wholly in terms of bodily mechanics. We can always empty a term of its meaning if we try hard enough.) The neutrality thesis results from an artificial separation of technology from its *use* (see Davis, 1981, pp. 46–67). Once a use is envisioned a technology loses its neutrality: it will embody a variety of social and evaluative meanings, including symbolic, moral and aesthetic meaning(s).

Technologies can destroy certain values and make others virtually impossible to fulfil. The obverse is also true: technology can create certain (dis)values and make others virtually certain to be realized. We can, of course, regard palm-sized pistols as nothing more than hunks of junk and innocent uses can be imagined for them – destroying a lock for which one has forgotten the combination, for instance. But handguns were not invented for any such purpose: they do not have the place they do in our society for any reason other than to kill and threaten to kill. Speaking of guns generally, Corlann Gee Bush argues that they are 'valenced' or 'charged' with a 'collective significance':

> A particular technological system, even an individual tool, has
> a tendency to interact in similar situations in identifiable and
> predictable ways. . . . Valence tends to seek out or fit in with
> certain social norms and to ignore or disturb others. . . . Guns,
> for example, are valenced to violence; the presence of a gun
> in a given situation raises the level of violence by its presence
> alone.

> (Bush, 1983, pp. 154–5)

The handgun expresses and reinforces the values of a society as much as do apple pie and motherhood. And so too with other technologies, far more sophisticated than handguns. Think of the automobile and the technologies it spawned in engineering, petroleum, steel, plastics and electronics. The automobile – literally, 'self-moving' – spoke, and continues to speak, to our sense of individual freedom, rootlessness and our desire to go where we want when we want for whatever reason – and alone, if we wish. Television, as Bush points out, is 'valenced' to isolation: 'despite the fact that any number of people may be present in the same room at the same time, there will not be much conversation because the presence of the TV itself pulls against interaction and pushes toward isolation' (Bush, 1983, p. 155).

Contrary to a central tenet of instrumentalism, all technologies embody values. Yet how is this possible? A non-technological example provides a useful beginning. Before peace talks begin between (or among) warring parties, there is often a protracted dispute about the shape of the table around which the parties will sit. At first glance, this seems absurd, and too often it is. But it need not be. For the shape of a bargaining table, and who sits where, suggests the relative power of the participants: a round table, for example, signifies greater equality than a rectangular one. Think, too, of the elaborately decorated, raised thrones of kings. Or classroom shapes. An amusing example concerns commercial dining. Restaurants wishing to create an intimate atmosphere slightly lower the height of tables, thus inclining the heads of the diners towards one another; fast-food restaurants both raise the height of tables and use seating that both thrusts the diner forward and makes it difficult to sit back and relax, thus ensuring a fast turnover.

In any of these instances, of course, one can resist the implicit signification, but only with effort, awkwardness and, at least sometimes, personal cost: it is difficult not to adopt an inferior attitude, for example, if the person to whom you are speaking is sitting on a raised chair or speaking to you from a raised podium. (Similar observations could be made about dress; after all, 'Clothes maketh the man', as 'power dressing' attests.)

Technologies are generally charged with signification. The microwave oven, whose principal 'virtue' is the speed with which it cooks frozen convenience foods, embodies the values of people in a hurry, of people who find little value in family dinners, because they have no family, or have no time for a family, or prefer to spend what little time they have for their family in other ways. Even those who have time on their hands think they need a microwave because they, too, feel the need to be in a hurry, because only people in a hurry (we think) are productive members of society. People with time but little money, therefore, often spend their resources on expensive, not very nourishing, frozen foods when they might be spending more time but less money on making wholesome dinners. In a society that devalues the latter, this is not surprising. So we see that the microwave oven imposes its values on everyone.

To think of nuclear weapons as mere 'hunks of junk', therefore, is to consider them in total isolation from their context of signification: how and why they were developed, their use, their environmental impact, and their broader cultural context.[6] Nuclear weapons could not have been developed, for instance, without transforming the norms of behaviour among physicists, chemists and engineers, who before the Manhattan Project used to pride themselves on their openness in discussing their discoveries with their counterparts throughout the world.[7]

So all technologies embody values. But whose? This question needs to be asked, because advocates of the neutrality thesis claim that technology has little or nothing to do with power and control. Consider the rise of the factory system in Britain during the Industrial Revolution. Defenders of the neutrality thesis argue that it came about because of its great efficiency and productivity. But as one biographer of several industrialists of that period attests:

> In the case of many of our most potent self-acting tools and machines, manufacturers could not be induced to adopt them until compelled to do so by strikes. This was the case of the self-acting mule, the wool-combing machine, the planing machine, the slotting machine, Nasmyth's steam arm and many others.
>
> (Dickinson, 1974, p. 81)

In short, technological innovations helped owners to overcome an intractable labour force. Nor does this simply reflect the backward hypothesis of a twentieth century historian. Writing 150 years ago, Andrew Ure said of the factory system:

> This invention confirms the great doctrine already propounded, that when capital enlists science in her service, the refractory hand of labour will always be taught docility.
>
> (Quoted in Dickinson, 1974, p. 81)

So we should not be surprised to learn that a principal reason Henry Ford introduced the assembly line into the production of the motor car during this century was to provide otherwise lazy workers with discipline. This mattered to Ford and other industrialists not only because a highly disciplined workforce allowed them to produce consumer goods more cheaply, but because they morally disapproved of the values of their workers, who seemed more interested in such irrelevancies as families, fishing and friendship than in turning out inexpensively made internal combustion engines and textiles. This illustrates processes discussed in the previous section. Ford wanted an 'efficient' workforce, one which did not 'waste' time pursuing ends other than increasing production. But the vagueness present in the notion of efficiency enables those who advocate it as a general standard to use it as a vehicle for imposing a particular set of moral values. As so used it is not a straightforward quantitative economic or mechanical concept. Ford's values appealed to a rising middle class that saw itself as heir to America's destiny, not to the cherished values of factory workers. To some extent, of course, workers themselves came to accept the values and disvalues of the assembly line, though the degree of their acceptance should not be exaggerated: throughout the 1920s and 1930s owners of factories had to use police and even the army to enforce their power – and therefore their values.

A technology usually reflects the plans, purposes and ambitions of some individual, some institution, or some class. Not surprisingly, it will embody the values implicit in those purposes. While values can be genuinely other directed, we would be amazed if we did not find that those who provide the impetus for technological change hope to advance their own ends. Of course, plans, purposes and ambitions can and do change as technologies develop, so intentions seldom become realized in just the form envisioned by the original inventor, developer or financial backer. As technologies have become increasingly complex, involving many people and institutions with diverse aims, the final product or process often takes on an unexpected shape that may be unwelcome to some of those involved. The aesthetic sensibilities of a line engineer, for instance, may cause a product to work differently than intended. Still, those with commercial, financial or political power can exert enormous pressure, so that those who might not otherwise care one way or another about some technology find themselves trying to produce something conforming to the will of their paymaster: how else could one explain the vast amount of medical and scientific talent expended on inventing and developing cosmetic products?

Technologies are not necessarily sinister just because they embody values: it all depends on the values. The opportunities of misunderstanding, and so abusing, technologies can be diminished if we are on the look-out for ways in which deep-seated value commitments permeate our technologies. Seldom, of course, will only one value or one mind-set inform a technology. To alter the shape of a particular technology, therefore, it will never be enough – or even possible – to remove surgically one value and replace it with another. That is a mistaken picture: values, even those associated with efficiency, are not 'in' technologies as a virus is 'in' a cell. If we need a metaphor, values are embedded in technology as a man's character shapes his conduct.

Goethe once described architecture as 'petrified music', and we can see more concretely how technologies embody values by considering great structures. Where Renaissance churches express the cool rationality of a humanistic age, Roman Catholic churches of the Counter-Reformation respond to this and the rise of Protestantism with architectural motifs which appeal directly to passion and mystery. Every period embodied its own collective significance, valenced to advance purposes and values of those concerned to shape the culture of the period. Churches might be dismissed as unique because they express self-conscious religious purposes. We can make the same point, however, by discovering engineering values as embodied in towers and bridges.

In his engaging book on the new art of structural engineering, David P. Billington reveals how the memorable towers and bridges of the industrial age demonstrate that function follows form. That is, 'the designer is free to set form rather than be bound by some automatic application of scientific laws'.[8] Thus, while Brunel, Eiffel, Roebling, Maillart, Freyssinet *et al.* sought to understand mathematics, physics and their materials, they relied on this understanding less and less as their experience grew: 'they were disciplined but not controlled by nature's laws' (Billington, 1983, p. 267).

What provided the greatest discipline were two concerns: *efficiency* and *economy*. Efficiency led them to find minimum materials because they result in less weight, less cost and less visual mass. This is not, however, a simple, value-free calculation. For sometimes less material entails greater labour costs and extreme thinness can never be achieved everywhere in a large structure. Further, efficiency must be balanced against public safety: what degree of risk should be tolerated? Economy – understood as 'the desire for construction simplicity, ease of maintenance, and a final integrated form' (Billington, 1983, p. 267) – also involves evaluation. For simplicity, ease and integration of form all require judgements of value. Efficiency and economy, each themselves complex, provide a demanding context in which gifted engineers seek to avert ugliness and embody *elegance*. This not only means a visual expression of efficiency and economy, but the expression of contrast and harmony with its surroundings. The resulting structures embody the aesthetic and social values of those who designed them, as modified by interaction with the aesthetic and social values of the broader public.

Architecture may be 'petrified music', but values embodied in technologies are never petrified. We need to correct any impression that technologies are 'valenced' in only one way or always keep the value charge initially given them. A case in point is the French-made *abortifacient* RU-486. Abortion opponents have fought strenuously – with some success – to keep RU-486 from being imported into the United States because it kills. Yet even conceding this, matters are not so simple. For RU-486 also shows promise as a lifesaving and life-prolonging *medicine* in treating breast cancer, glaucoma, diabetes, and several other diseases.[9] The same technology can clearly embody more than one set of values. It is therefore the multi-valenced nature of technologies – not their lack of valence or 'value neutrality' – which supplies the grain of truth for those who argue that technologies are good or bad, depending on how they are used.

Technologically embedded values show their fluidity in another way. If conditions change, a particular technology can come to embody *different* values though the technology itself does not change. Lighthouses, for example, were once elegantly designed within the constraints set by efficiency and economy to help seafarers avoid shoals and other dangers. Some still do. Increasingly, however, navigation relies on more sophisticated and reliable technologies, such as NAVSTAR. Lighthouses now embody different values, at least near inhabited areas. For they now serve to recall a romantic (and romanticized) past and provide a picturesque backdrop for a day at the beach or overlooking a harbour. Were it suggested that favourite lighthouses be destroyed because they no longer fulfilled their original purpose, the suggestion would (rightly) be met with vigorous protests! One set of values is being displaced by another.

As we have seen, technologies may be relatively 'open' or 'closed' with respect to the values they embody. The electric chair, for instance, is extremely closed in at least two dimensions: it is designed with the sole purpose of execution, and it is difficult to imagine it being used for anything else. Microscopes, too, are relatively closed. A microscope can, of course, be used as a doorstop, stage prop, or item of barter, but then its *peculiar* properties are not being used. Other technologies are more open, some exceedingly so. Steam technology, for example, can be used in a variety of devices to express a variety of values, individual and social. Just as words seldom shake off the implications of their etymology, however, technologies seldom completely transcend the purposes for which they were designed or the values they express.

3

SCIENCE, SCIENTIFIC METHOD AND THE AUTHORITY OF EXPERTS

The instrumental vision of (an ideal) technology is of devices which are the product of applied science and which are, to this extent, fully controllable because thoroughly understood. They will be able to deliver the best solutions to practical problems because they are based on the best available knowledge both of the problem situations and of the means available to address them. Technological development in the nineteenth century and, more specifically, in the twentieth century since World War II has been directed by this ideal, and has increasingly moved in the direction of a (partial) realization of it. Vannevar Bush, who played a significant role in shaping US science research policy after World War II, including setting up the National Science Foundation, wrote:

> Basic research leads to new knowledge. It provides scientific capital. It creates the fund from which the practical applications of knowledge must be drawn. New products and new processes do not appear full grown. They are founded on new principles and new conceptions, which in turn are painstakingly developed by research in the purest realms of science . . . publicly and privately supported colleges and universities and the endowed research institutes must furnish both the new scientific knowledge and the trained research workers . . . . It is chiefly in these institutions that scientists may work in an atmosphere which is relatively free from the adverse pressure of convention, prejudice, and commercial necessity.
>
> (Bush, 1946, pp. 52–3)

Here we find basic research equated with pure science, an equation still frequently made. This equation again presumes that it is possible to separate facts from values, means from ends. As pure science, basic research will be regarded as concerning itself only with the factual, seeking to discern what is the case, not with moral or political issues that might arise if one were to start asking about the uses which might be made of the fruits of that research. Although, as Bush also indicates, it has, since World War II, been quite clear in the minds of politicians that governments should fund basic research just because it is thought to represent the long term route to future technological innovation.

To understand the technological character of the culture which these policies have produced we need to look closely both at what science and its application have been thought to be, and at whether recent history suggests that they really conform to this image. To what extent can basic research be equated with pure science? What are the relations between pure science, applied science and technology? Is any general characterization of these relations possible? This chapter will question the notion of pure science. The next will deal in more detail with relations between science and technology.

THE PURITY OF PURE SCIENCE

Pure science would be the disinterested pursuit of knowledge, active enquiry aiming solely at uncovering the truth, without regard to questions of potential utility. In pure science knowledge would be treated as an end in itself, not a means to some further end. In this respect Isaiah Berlin (Berlin, 1981) is correct when he links modern science with a tradition of Western thought traceable to Plato, for whom Truth, Beauty and Goodness are ends which are unified in the form of the Good, that towards which all our enquiries should be directed if we wish to live as fulfilled human beings. Berlin describes the modern scientific tradition as the tradition of those who believe (i) that it is possible to make steady progress in the entire sphere of human knowledge, (ii) that methods and goals are, or should be, ultimately identical throughout this sphere, and (iii) that we have reached a stage where the achievements of the natural sciences are such that it is possible to derive their structure from a single set of clear principles which, if correctly applied, make possible indefinite further progress in unravelling the mysteries of Nature. He goes on to characterize the tradition stemming from Plato as resting on the following assumptions:

(a) Every genuine question has exactly one true answer, all others being false.

(b) The method which leads to correct solutions to all genuine problems is rational in character and is, in essence, if not on detailed application, identical in all fields.

(c) The solutions, whether or not they are discovered, are true universally, eternally and immutably: true for all times, places and human beings.

His reading of the import of these assumptions fills out his character-ization of the presumptions underlying the attitudes characteristic of modern science:

> The implication of this position is that the world is a single system which can be described and explained by the use of rational methods; with the practical corollary that if man's life is to be organized at all, and not left to chaos and the play of uncontrolled chance, then it can be organized only in the light of such principles and laws.

> (Berlin, 1981, p. 81)

Here the accuracy of Berlin's reading of Plato need not detain us. What is interesting is his perception of the antiquity of the concep-tion of knowledge underlying the project of modern science (in its pure form) and his portrayal of modern science. Here he seems accurately to be reflecting the image of science dominant in Western countries forty years ago, and still dominant at many important levels of society, but now also seriously challenged by, amongst others, feminists, sociologists of knowledge, and those in developing coun-tries whose needs seem in no way to be addressed by modern science and whose indigenous cultures seem to be threatened by it.

Let us briefly consider the assumptions on which Berlin suggests the modern scientific tradition rests. The idea (a) that every genuine question has exactly one true answer – i.e. that there is an answer to each such question and that there is no more than one such answer – is justified if all knowledge can be assimilated to factual–descriptive knowledge and genuine questions are restricted to those which in the end amount to asking, in a wholly unambiguous way, 'Is X the case?' In addition it must be assumed that the answer to such questions is determined by the way the world is, independently of any factors relating to the interest, concerns or cultural location of the questioner. This is why (c) can also be assumed, for if answers to questions exist, whether or not they have been, or ever will be, discovered, because these answers are not in any way conditioned by the status of the enquirer, then they are true for all times, places and peoples. The further assumption (b) that there is a rational method that will lead to these answers makes additional requirements on what must be assumed about the world and about human beings. The world must itself be presumed to have an order which is congruous with structures available to the human mind, a congruity which makes the order of the world intelligible to rational human beings. In the Christian tradition this was assured by the assumption that the world was created by a rational, creator-God, who also created humans in His own image, i.e. as, albeit imperfect, rational beings, capable of understanding aspects of His creation. (Einstein's faith in the rationally intelligible order of the universe was similarly evident in the famous remark 'God does not play dice' which expressed his refusal to accept that quantum mechanics, with its non-deterministic laws, could represent the ultimate truth about the physical universe.)

These assumptions about knowledge, the world and human beings are natural in a tradition which valued contemplative knowledge (pure science) and where the value placed on this form of knowledge was itself expressive of a conception of human dignity defined in terms of spiritual and intellectual perfection, and positively opposed to the concerns of material life, the life of the body. In a culture, that is, where there is no sharp separation made between the pursuit of knowledge and the religious life. So for example we find in *Protreptikos*, an early work by Aristotle, which survives only in fragments:

> (B42) To seek from all knowledge a result other than itself and to demand that it must be useful is the act of one completely ignorant of the distance that from the start separates good things from necessary things; for they differ completely . . . .
>
> (B43) One would see the absolute truth of what we are saying if someone as it were carried us in thought to the Isles of the Blest. For there would be need of nothing and no profit from anything; and there remain only thought and contemplation, which even now we describe as the free life.
>
> (B50) . . . to the philosopher alone among craftsmen belong laws that are stable and actions that are right and noble, for he alone lives by looking at nature and the divine. Like a good

helmsman he moors his life to that which is eternal and unchanging, drops his anchor there, and lives as his own master.

(B108) Mankind possesses nothing divine or blessed that is of any account except what there is in us of mind and understanding: this alone of our possessions seems to be immortal, this alone divine.

(B110) For mind is the god in us . . . and mortal life contains a portion of some god. We ought, therefore, either to philosophize or to say farewell to life and depart hence, since all other things seem to be nonsense and folly.

Here we see that in linking so closely conceptions of human dignity and perfection, the quest for this kind of knowledge is also a moral quest, the knowledge is knowledge of the Good as well as the True, of how to be a virtuous human being as well as a learned one. So even though the knowledge sought is itself conceived as absolute, undistorted by human values and limited human perspectives, it is valued by humans precisely because it is incorporated into a model of what constitutes human perfection. This means that the privilege attached to this kind of contemplative knowledge, and even the assumption that such knowledge is possible, had a specific cultural location. This persisted in various modified forms throughout Christendom in the medieval period, where it was associated with a tendency to denigrate the so-called 'mechanical arts' because of their worldly associations. George Ovitt offers the following summary of his study of attitudes towards manual labour in Europe in the Middle Ages:

> with regard to the status of manual labour during the Middle Ages, the evidence suggests the coexistence of two traditions. On the one hand, . . . some writers (notably Augustine and Cassian) argued for the centrality of manual labour to the realization of human spiritual aspirations; on the other hand, virtually every medieval commentator subordinated the *opus manuum* to the *opus Dei*, described manual labour in idealized, often ritualistic rather than productive terms, and – especially beginning in the twelfth century – subscribed to the idea that while work was theoretically blessed, the mechanical arts were tainted by their concern with worldly ends.
>
> (Ovitt, 1987, p. 102)

Hugh of Saint Victor, writing in the twelfth century, says of the mechanical arts:

> These sciences are called mechanical, that is, adulterate, because their concern is with the artificer's product, which borrows its form from nature. Similarly, the other seven are called liberal either because they require minds that are liberal, that is, liberated and practiced (for these sciences pursue subtle inquiries into the causes of things), or because in antiquity only free and noble men were accustomed to study them, while the populace and the sons of men not free sought operative skill in things mechanical.
>
> (Hugh of Saint Victor, 1961, p. 75)

It was against this tradition that Francis Bacon reacted. Bacon was a significant early seventeenth century agent of what has come to be called the 'scientific revolution'. His 'Great Instauration', his 'Masculine Birth of Time', was a call to action, a rejection of the virtues of the contemplative life. He sought to shift the primary focus of scientific attention away from contemplatively perceived truth to the goal of mastery over nature.[1] To this end he urged that the pursuit of truth should no longer be disinterested; its interest should ultimately be in increasing human abilities to dominate and control nature. Knowledge was to be sought and valued to the extent that it confers this ability. As Newton-Smith, a defender of the idea of the value neutrality of science, says, 'without an interest in prediction and control modern science would not exist' (Newton-Smith, 1984, p. 59). But it should then also be acknowledged that this interest is an expression of a particular conception of human beings, of their relation to nature and of their perfectibility, and that this interest, together with its associated values, shapes the conception of what will constitute scientific knowledge, both as regards the form of knowledge sought and the methods thought appropriate to attaining it.

The scientific, intellectual interest in prediction and control presupposes a view of human beings on which such an interest is worthy of their dignity, an expression and fulfilment of a distinctively human potential, which raises humans above animals and the rest of nature. Bacon was well aware that the weight of the intellectual tradition produced by a Christian reading of Plato and Aristotle was opposed to this conception of humans, in that it privileged a form of knowledge oriented not to this material world but ultimately to

God and the eternity of the after-life.[2] It required a disengagement from the technological and the practical as unworthy of concern:

> It may be that there are some on whose ear my frequent and honourable mention of practical activities makes a harsh and unpleasant sound because they are wholly given over in love and reverence to contemplation. Let them bethink themselves that they are the enemies of their own desires. For in nature practical results are not only the means to improve well-being but the guarantee of truth. The rule of religion, that a man show his faith by his work, holds good in natural philosophy too. Science also must be known by works. It is by the witness of works rather than by logic or even observation, that truth is revealed and established. Whence it follows that the improvement of man's mind and the improvement of his lot are one and the same thing.
>
> (Bacon, 1964, p. 93)

Within the Aristotelian framework the goal of scientific knowledge was knowledge of the natures or essences of things, and this would be expressed in terms of their qualities, dispositions and powers. Those disciplines, such as astronomy, which dealt in observing and noting regularities with a view to being able to make predictions, were not unknown to Aristotle, but for him they were not true sciences for they could not yield understanding of why those observed regularities should be present (*Physics* 193b9–24).

Bacon, valuing the ability to intervene in nature, sought to redirect science in such a way as to privilege knowledge of laws of action and of the contexts in which they are applicable (Bacon, 1620, II.ii and II.iv). Others in the seventeenth century, seeking continuity with the tradition of associating genuine knowledge of the natural world with God's knowledge of His creation, privileged knowledge of laws of action for a slightly different reason. They argued that to understand the world as God does would be to understand it from the point of view of one who created it (not one who merely contemplates it). The clock and its relation to the clock maker had become increasingly popular as a metaphor for the universe and its relation to God.[3] The kind of knowledge of the natural world that could lead to a greater understanding of God would be the kind of knowledge that makes it possible to design and construct clocks. This would be very much the kind of knowledge that Bacon was suggesting. It might not have practical application as its primary goal, but its possession would only be convincingly demonstrated by successful design and construction of complex devices. In both cases there is a shift in the value attached to knowledge of regularities and laws which yields prediction and control, and in both cases the ability to control events constitutes a mark of success, although only in the explicitly action-oriented Baconian programme is possession of this ability equated with possession of knowledge of the natures of things.[4]

The significant difference between the Baconian vision of achieving human perfection through knowledge of the natural world and traditional, more spiritual conceptions, was that knowledge was not sought under the guise of timeless truths about the world as it unchangingly is, and hence timeless truths by which to live, but under the guise of universal laws, which although timelessly true, would be used as the basis for human intervention to change the world, to realize fundamentally new possibilities. It is part of a progressivist vision and as such is fundamentally at odds with attitudes of cultures based on the permanence of tradition.

Knowledge of how to divert the course of nature cannot be obtained merely by observing the natural course of events, by watching nature take its course, for the aim is not merely to imitate nature but to gain control over it, to achieve things never naturally achieved. Thus the primary learning will be from attempts to manipulate, from artefacts and from artificially contrived situations. Observations of artefacts were available to Aristotelians, but were discounted by them as not being productive of the sort of knowledge required by natural philosophers. Bacon turns the tables, placing much less value on naturally occurring events and much more on experimentally contrived situations.

Here there is a very strong sense in which an interest in mastery over nature, and hence in knowledge geared towards construction and creation, shapes the content of science, determining the form interesting knowledge should take. It involved redrawing the conception of the natural, thought of as that which does not require explanation. It can no longer be that which is a direct expression of the nature or essence of a thing. It is now that which occurs according to a basic law of action, in the absence of interference. The whole conception of what needs and what does not need explanation, of what is fundamental and what derivative, is changed.[5]

But the findings of pure science are claimed to be value neutral – true for all people's times and places irrespective of their divergent values. Technology, as application of such knowledge to the solution of practical problems, is frequently assumed to inherit the value neutrality of the knowledge on which it is based. It is important to acknowledge that while in one sense this might be true, the sense in which it is true does not serve to justify the claim that science, as a body of knowledge, is value neutral. It would do so only if it were correct to move from the assumption that the world is a single system to the conclusion that there is only one form which knowledge of it can take and hence only one route to this knowledge.

It is quite correct to say that if the second law of thermodynamics is true, it must be true for anyone, anywhere in the universe. No matter what one's culture or values one will not be able to boil a kettle by putting it on an iceberg. But scientific knowledge has never been held to be merely knowledge of a collection of isolated truths. To qualify for the honorific 'science' a discipline has to contain theories, bodies of knowledge in which disparate data are organized by the application of general, fundamental principles and where questions can be answered or problems solved by reference to these principles. To say that knowledge can only take one form would be to insist that all theories have to be organized in the same way, and have the same sort of principles. But if it is acknowledged that changes in the goal of enquiry occurred during the period to which the birth of modern science is customarily traced, and that such changes were an integral part of changing conceptions of how human beings should seek to perfect their lives, the assumption that there is just one form of knowledge which represents the goal of all rational enquiry cannot be justified. In other words, the modernity of modern science cuts it off from strict continuity with classical knowledge traditions and thereby renders the possibility of pure, non-utilitarian, value-free science problematic.

Further evidence of the diversity of forms which scientific knowledge can and does take can be found by looking at twentieth century sciences. Evolutionary biology takes a very different form from quantum physics; the former is expressed with very little use of mathematics, whereas mathematics is absolutely crucial to the latter. Molecular biology, which focuses on using physics and chemistry to try to understand how simple organisms function and reproduce, is quite different from ecology, which is trying to understand ecosystems and the relations of interdependence between species and environment. Both differ significantly from astrophysics with its focus on distant regions of the universe. What theories, as organized bodies of knowledge, offer are ways of understanding, or looking at, aspects of the world. The value placed on a theory therefore does not rest simply on whether the laws it contains or the predictions it makes are true or false, reliable or unreliable, but on whether its particular approach to the world, the kind of problems it addresses and the way in which it does so, is valued which, in turn, depends on how its approach fits with wider cultural values.

In this respect it makes sense to talk of epistemological values, values placed on various forms of knowledge or items of knowledge in the light of wider conceptions about the goal, or goals, of enquiry. Epistemological values thus appear when knowledge is viewed in its social context as a product of particular form of enquiry, a product which is evaluated by reference to the social role of that form of enquiry. The epistemological value accorded to a law, or to groups of laws, may change over time even though they are not rejected and continue to be used. Epistemological values depend on how cognitive goals are characterized.

For example, as Eduard Glas has pointed out, late in the eighteenth century, in the wake of the French Revolution, we can see not just an overturning of epistemological values, but the emergence of two competing schools of mathematicians, espousing distinct epistemological values: those of Laplace and Lagrange on the one hand, and of Monge on the other. All three mathematicians were assigned by the French revolutionary government to the task of converting mathematics into a perfectly transparent and universally learnable language. Mathematics was to be purged of all remnants of metaphysical thinking (regarded as aristocratic) and so be made more accessible to the people. Lagrange and Laplace were analysts who took the opportunity to further their efforts to purge analysis of reliance on geometrical notions and to turn the subject into a rigorous formal calculus, a computational language which would assist with the project of converting fallible human reasoning into an application of infallible mechanical procedures. Monge, on the other hand, was interested in geometry and regarded analysis as merely a shorthand notational system for referring to geometrical transformations. The universal language that Monge invented was descriptive geometry, an extension of plane geometry to spatial situations based on the use of projections. Monge's descriptive geometry provided both practical tools and a means of communicating practical, technical knowledge and this feature assured it a dominant position within the École Polytechnique, itself founded in response to the military and political imperatives of the early years of the French Republic. The programmes of Laplace and Lagrange, on the other hand, carried the prestige of formal, highly intellectual mathematics, and under Bonaparte this displaced Monge's 'egalitarian' programme at the École Polytechnique. The point about these two programmes is that they had different research goals. What was at stake in the competition between them was the future direction of mathematics in France. As Glas sums it up:

> the two groups pointed to different kinds of technical credentials and ideological motives to recommend their own practice as a body of mathematical doctrine and accomplishment that should pre-eminently be trusted to render the most valuable service to the elevation of society and the glory of the nation. Lagrange and Laplace valued Monge as a very able geometer indeed, but these analysts considered geometry as such of minor value for the development of what they perceived as the eminently credible doctrine. Conversely, Monge was far from denying the merits of Laplace and Lagrange for the perfection of analysis, but in his perception their accomplishments were formal exercises rather than contributions to veritable mathematical progress.
>
> (Glas, 1993, p. 246)

The opposition between practical, technically oriented research and more abstract, self-consciously impractical research has repeatedly been, and continues to be, a site of social conflict because it intersects with traditional patterns of social dominance based on the divisions between mental and manual labour and between those who have to work for others for their living and those who do not. These patterns of dominance are not peculiar to European cultures, but can also be found, for example, in India and China. This devaluation of things mechanical manifests itself in all manner of ways and at various levels of the social hierarchy. It can, for example, be seen in the attitudes of doctors to the introduction of mechanical instruments for measuring blood pressure (sphygmomanometers). Where the proponents of scientific, physiologically grounded medicine advocated use of such devices, those who were opposed often argued for retaining the diagnostic art of taking a patient's pulse as integral to their professional status. 'The nerves and tactile corpuscles of the tips of your fingers will have much to do with your skill and success. . . . If your fingers, instead of having their sensibility protected and their tips educated, are rendered callous and clumsy by manual labor or rough usage, their delicate nerves will be unfit for their duties.'[6] Thus different forms of medical knowledge and their social embedding are here brought into a conflict which is not just about use of a type of instrument but also about the value of any knowledge to be gained by using it, something which is in turn judged by reference to a wider conception of the goals of medicine and the form of knowledge required to satisfy them.

Even though the social stigma attached to manual labour was of course present in seventeenth century Europe, nonetheless we do not, on the whole, find amongst the advocates of the new 'natural philosophy' attempts to make the sharp division, which can be found solidified in twentieth century academic institutions, between pure and applied science. Even Laplace and Lagrange would have found it politically unwise to align themselves explicitly with (aristocratic) classical tradition. The separation of pure from applied science, accompanied by stress on the continuity between modern pure science and classical traditions of Western thought, was a product of nineteenth century struggles, especially in England and Germany, for the professionalization of science and for the inclusion of science departments within established universities, which still centred their curricula on the classics. The seventeenth century developments constituting the scientific revolution were, for the most part, instigated and propagated by people working outside the context of universities, people with royal or other wealthy patrons, or private means. Francis Bacon, Viscount St Albans, was a lawyer by profession and was at one time Lord Chancellor to King James I. Gresham College, a non-university philosophical society whose meetings were attended by educated middle-class Londoners such as Samuel Pepys and William Petty, was encouraged by Charles II and under his patronage became the Royal Society. It adopted Bacon as its ideological figurehead, stressing the importance of experimental method. Membership of the Royal Society was by no means restricted to those devoting large parts of their lives or livelihoods to scientific research and by this means its meetings also served as a forum for publicizing the work of those who were so engaged. The rise of modern science was thus associated with the rise of educated classes which were not formed in the traditional, clerical mould but of men of affairs with practical, worldly concerns.

But in the absence of the kind of sweeping educational reforms carried out in France in the wake of the French Revolution, the experimental sciences elsewhere struggled to achieve social status. Their practical utility was difficult to demonstrate convincingly before the nineteenth century, and the very attempt to push for status on utilitarian grounds tended to undermine their credentials as intellectual disciplines suitable for inclusion in universities alongside the classics. The conflict between utility and intellectual status was a product of the ways in which social hierarchies are maintained. In this climate the argument for inclusion within universities had to be based on portraying (pure) science as continuous with classical conceptions of knowledge and foreswearing any practical intent. Yet at the same time, significant funding for scientific education and research, whether from government or business, would not be forthcoming until the utilitarian arguments could be convincingly won. It is this social context, with the split between universities and technical institutes, pure from applied science, that helped to foster the instrumental vision of science and technology and of the particular way in which the relations between them came to be conceived and realized via the setting up of institutions for education and research.

The difference between university and non-university research is nicely illustrated in an account, by Paolo Palladino, of crop breeding research at the University of Cambridge and Reading extension college earlier this century. Describing the situation at Cambridge he says:

> Agricultural education and research did not gain a foothold in the University of Cambridge until the early years of this century, and then only by way of a prolonged struggle with an academic community that viewed the provision of instruction in technical subjects as an improper activity. The prevailing view was that the university should foster the spirit of knowledge for its own sake. If such knowledge could then be applied to resolve practical problems, so much the better; such unintended developments might provide a rationale for greater support of scientific research in the university.
>
> (Palladino, 1993, pp. 307–8)

It was therefore not surprising that when it did get going the agricultural course in Cambridge put heavy emphasis on the scientific foundations of agricultural productivity, paying little attention to farming practices. Agricultural education came to mean education and research in what scientists thought to be of most value to agriculture. The 'pure' research was not directed at the education of more technically skilled farmers.

> In sum, Cambridge scientists viewed agriculture as an activity which, just as engineering and medicine, should come to depend on expert 'scientific' knowledge for its improvement. That is, the improvement of agriculture was for them not so much a matter of educating farmers to adopt more advanced methods of production but a matter of scientific enquiry to be handled by specially trained 'agricultural scientists' who would eventually turn the products of their scientific labors over to the passive farmer for application on the farm.
>
> (Palladino, 1993, p. 310)

By contrast, the University College at Reading, an Oxford University extension college, was founded in 1892 to meet the needs of the local farming community. Significant financial and political support for this venture came from local business families (the Palmer family, of Huntley and Palmers biscuits, and the Sutton family, owners of Suttons Seeds) and from Lord Wantage, a landowner and stockbreeder. These benefactors, who wanted to encourage scientifically informed farming, sought to model Reading College on the American land-grant universities, where the local farming community were given an input into educational and research policy. But they were resisted by the academic community, who refused to allow non-academics to have any voice in educational matters. Even so, Reading was genuinely in the business of educating farmers and many courses were specifically geared to the needs of farmers, who could enrol on a part-time basis and often did not work towards any degree. Its students were required to have farm experience before enrolling and were expected to continue to spend time in the fields. At Cambridge, on the other hand, one could obtain a degree in agriculture without having any experience of farming.

This difference in emphasis led to differences of view about the right direction for plant breeding research. Percival, at Reading, whilst agreeing that agriculture should be treated scientifically, argued for a form of crop breeding research in which farmers themselves would be instrumental in achieving a scientifically improved agriculture. Once they were taught to assess their needs more precisely and how to assess the extent to which the varieties available to them were meeting their needs, they would be able to improve on traditional practices of selection to develop new varieties most suited to their specific needs. At Cambridge, on the other hand, Biffen, the professor of agricultural botany, argued that plant breeding should become an exercise in applied Mendelian genetics and that traditional methods could never be significantly improved. In his view all economic activities, such as agriculture, were technical activities that could be made more efficient only by the intervention of professional scientists (Palladino, 1993, p. 319). He used a Mendelian theory of inheritance, devised at Cambridge by Bateson, to explain the phenomena observed in his experiments on resistance to rust disease in wheat. On the basis of this explanation he successfully produced a hybrid wheat that was both high yielding and rust resistant, by crossing a high yielding rust-susceptible wheat with a rust-resistant but low yielding variety. This work had both a 'pure' research significance – it was interpreted as demonstrating that Mendelian genetics was applicable to non-morphological characteristics – and a significance for the utility of basic theoretical research – it was also interpreted as demonstrating the ability of theoretically informed research to transform plant breeding, to change it from a craft to a science, and more widely as further confirming the ability of scientific research to solve practical, economically significant problems.

Although in the developed world this dispute about directions for plant breeding has been won by the scientific experts and the seed companies, with the introduction of hybrids and now with the promise of genetic engineering, the same issues are very much alive in developing countries.[7] Here the benefits of new, scientifically developed varieties (the so-called Green Revolution) have given rise to concerns about how to conserve genetic diversity and how to develop sustainable farming methods in regions of economic deprivation and less than ideal growing conditions. This is an issue to which we shall return, but what it again serves to illustrate is that the form of knowledge sought and the kind of research programme pursued depend crucially on the location of the person, or people, asking the questions. This determines not only the kind of questions they ask, but what they expect from an answer and the value they place on specific discoveries, observations or theoretical conjectures.

To acknowledge the presence of epistemological values is to allow that there are connections between the reason why a particular kind of knowledge is valued and the form it is required to take. This in turn means admitting that very different forms of knowledge may pass for basic science, where basic science is understood to be science which aims solely at the construction and testing of theories. As we have seen, even when the only interest internal to science is interest in truth and in empirical adequacy as a necessary condition of truth, the form that truth may be required to take is not uniquely determined by the world. Empirical adequacy can mean either predictive observational success, constituted by agreement with a predefined fixed class of possible observations of natural occurrences (saving the phenomena), as in ancient astronomy; the development of a comprehensive systematic taxonomy, as in natural history; or experimental success, the prediction and successful production of novel, artificial phenomena. This latter may also have wider or narrower interpretations. If empirical success means success purely relative to laboratory experiments, this standard may become something wholly internal to a research tradition where prediction and control is narrowed to the ability to predict what will happen in carefully controlled conditions, together with the ability to produce those conditions. Here even experimental science may have no more concern for practical application than Aristotle's contemplative knowledge. Further, empirical success of this sort does not, of itself, warrant claims about practical applicability.

If active involvement with the physical world is endorsed and incorporated into the goal of science, so that interest in successful engagement with the world becomes an interest internal to science (a scientific interest), there is still a question about the basis from which the engagement is made and on which it is valued. For Bacon the basic relation is that between superior and inferior. Through their engagement with the world human beings will demonstrate their superiority, show that they are set apart from the rest of nature, capable by virtue of their intellect of transcending it. The standpoint at which they aim is still a standpoint outside the world, a standpoint distanced from the object of their scientific study and of their manipulation. It is this which continues to feed the conception of the objectivity of scientific knowledge as consisting in disengagement, as being disinterested, not materially conditioned, and hence value free. The intellect places humans beyond nature and there is a presumption that only intellectual knowledge, knowledge from a disengaged, non-human perspective, can confer real power over nature. We are thus heirs to a paradoxical conceit of knowledge characterized as neutral, disinterested, value free, not materially conditioned, but nonetheless sought and valued just in so far as it confers material power. The quest for such knowledge is far from disinterested.

Any proposal which seeks to base science on a relation between human beings and nature in which the two are put on a more equal footing will have the effect of treating humans more fully as a part of nature. This necessarily requires abandoning the presumed availability of a non-materially conditioned viewpoint. This does not, however, entail abandoning standards of objectivity. The importance of successful completion of practical projects and of reliably repeatable methods of achieving results can still be recognized even when it is realized that projects, and hence success or failure in them, are set and judged against a background of conditions which determine and limit their significance:

> there is a tendency to forget that all science is bound up with human culture in general, and that scientific findings, even those which at the moment appear the most advanced and esoteric and difficult to grasp, are meaningless outside their cultural context.
>
> (Schrödinger, 1952, p. 109)

The fact that research programmes take their orientation from their wider cultural embedding does not mean that there cannot be research pursued without concern for practical applications, that there is no objectivity in scientific research, or that the results of research are biased. What it means is that there can be no science which is 'pure' in the classical sense – pursuit of a unique truth about the world, a truth which should be equally valued and recognized by all rational beings. When considering modern science as an institution, as opposed to specific programmes of scientific research, it is clear that disclaimers of any concern for its practical utility are highly problematic, first because an orientation towards practically useful theoretical knowledge is precisely what served to differentiate modern from classical science, and second, because twentieth century scientific institutions owe their financial and political support, the support without which research on any significant scale would not be possible, to claims of utility.

SCIENTIFIC METHOD AND INSTRUMENTAL RATIONALITY

Sometimes it seems to be thought that scientific knowledge is reliable because science deals in hard facts, not idle speculations, superstitious beliefs or folklore. Yet, if the argument of Chapter 2 is correct, this puts the cart before the horse. There it was argued that we accord beliefs the status of facts when they are deemed reliable. So if there is an association between science and facts it must be that scientific methods are regarded as being the most reliable we have available for determining the answers to questions we may have about the world (whether human or natural). The products of scientific activity are accorded the status of facts because of the trust placed in methods of scientific investigation. To say that there is no scientific evidence that any of the food additives currently permitted within the EU have any harmful effects is a way of dismissing as groundless and irrational the fears of those who think that such additives do have harmful effects. Whereas to say that it is scientifically established that smoking causes lung cancer is a way of saying that this is something a smoker ought to worry about. Further, as was noted in the previous section, science is not just a collection of facts, of isolated bits of information, but involves theories which organize and help us to understand the data gleaned from observation and from experimental research. It is therefore necessary, when talking of scientific method, to look both at scientific methods of data collection and at the ways in which bodies of data are used as the basis for theory formation and testing.

The notion of being in possession of a rational method for the acquisition of knowledge of the natural world was a crucial part of the seventeenth century ideology heralding the inauguration of 'modern' science. It is a shadowy reflection of the vision, that Bacon, Descartes and Leibniz shared, of a universal rational method which would be so reliable that discoveries made by employing it would be guaranteed to be genuine just because they were produced by following the right procedures. This would be like having a method for solving all problems in the way that we can do long divisions or solve simultaneous equations: in these latter cases we do have methods of which we are confident that, if they are correctly followed, they will yield correct solutions. Matters are not so straightforward in science and it has long been recognized that the quest for such a universal method has no more hope of being successful than the alchemists' quest for the philosopher's stone which would turn base metals into gold. Nonetheless, the authority of science continues to rest on claims concerning the superiority of scientific methods, even if they do not, and cannot, provide absolute guarantees as to the truth of claims made as a result of employing them. Many people will admit that because research requires funding, what research directions are actually pursued will be influenced by the values and concerns of the wider society within which it is conducted, but would insist that, nonetheless, scientific research methods ensure the value neutrality of research results.[8] What then are the methods of science assumed to be and why are they thought to confer superior reliability on the claims made by scientists?

Bacon's vision was of a science which was to be the product of reasoning from experience. As he saw it the novelty of this vision lay in systematically combining theorizing with practical experimentation and detailed observation:

> Those who have handled science have either been men of experiment or men of dogmas. The men of experiment are like the ant, they only collect and use: the reasoners resemble spiders, who make cobwebs out of their own substance. But the bee takes the middle course: it gathers its material from the flowers of the garden and of the field, but transforms and digests it by a power of its own. Not unlike this is the true business of philosophy;[9] for it neither relies solely nor chiefly on the powers of the mind, nor does it take the matter which it gathers from natural history and mechanical experiments and lay it up in memory whole, as it finds it, but lays it up in the understanding altered and digested. Therefore from a closer and purer league between these two faculties, the experimental and rational (such as has never yet been made), much may be hoped.
>
> (Bacon, 1620, I, xcv)

But how exactly are the experimental and rational faculties to be made to work in concert? Bacon stressed the need for detailed and systematic observations made in pursuit of answers to specific questions put to nature. Reason poses questions in the light of existing knowledge and of research goals. Scientifically useful observations are not randomly accumulated but are methodically acquired and organized according to strategies devised for answering specific kinds of questions. For example, anyone with experience of constructing even a simple bridge, shed or bookcase will have noticed that materials deform when subjected to loads. The seventeenth century vision of people like Bacon was that a whole range of practical activities, such as construction of bridges and houses, could be vastly improved by being done scientifically. That is, approach the problem of construction by analysing the practical situation to determine what kinds of demands are made on materials by specific methods of construction and what kinds of knowledge about the characteristic behaviours of different types of materials, in different kinds of conditions, might make it possible to make improvements and develop new methods of construction. Then set about gaining the necessary theoretical (scientific) knowledge. This kind of approach had already demonstrated some of its power in military contexts. Galileo's work on falling bodies was undertaken in part because it was realized that improved knowledge of the behaviour of projectiles was necessary if the power of the relatively newly introduced gunpowder were to be fully exploited. What Bacon and others did not really appreciate was the length of the route they had mapped out. There was no possibility, in the seventeenth or even eighteenth century context, of developing very many practical techniques by starting from a basic theoretical understanding of the properties of the materials involved, for the route to that, still incomplete, understanding has proved to be very long indeed. It was only in the late nineteenth century and more particularly in the twentieth century that theoretical science has been able to play a really significant role in transforming practical activities.

Suppose that one wanted to know how different materials behave under the various kinds of stresses and strains to be found in the context of bridge building. The scientific approach would be to design experiments that would yield useful information. But what information exactly is it that is required? The whole problem situation requires analysis before any experimentation can begin. Following Bacon's advice one might start by looking at how different materials behave under the same conditions, and at how the same material behaves under different conditions. But what kind of conditions are most relevant and what determines sameness and difference both for conditions and materials? Here Descartes adds further advice – the problem should be analysed into its simplest components. So we might first try to list the basic kinds of stresses and strains that construction materials are subject to and come up with the list – compression, extension and torque (squashing, stretching and twisting). We might then try to devise experiments to examine how a material behaves when subjected to each of these kinds of forces on its own (since in actual structures they frequently occur together in varying combinations). For example, one might focus, as Hooke did, on what happens when a material is subjected to a load tending to stretch it. To do this we would have to devise and perform experiments to measure the amount a material stretches when subject to varying loads, i.e. where everything else is held constant and only the load is varied, recording, for each sample, the amount stretched under each load and what happens when that load is removed, gradually increasing the load until the test sample breaks or starts to flow. In the process one might notice that shape seems to make a difference to the amount of stretch – more on a relatively thin than on a relatively thick cross section. This itself would require further systematic investigation and would require that previous results be checked to be sure that samples tested were all of the same size and shape. Similarly any other variable whose relevance is recognized only part way along in the enquiry can require re-evaluation and possibly more refined repetition of previous work.

Robert Boyle, 'father' of modern chemistry and exponent of the Baconian experimental approach to natural philosophy (science), realized that this frequent need to evaluate past results makes it vitally important that these results not just be recorded as lists of numbers, or sequences of observations, but that the experimental procedures that were employed to produce the results should also be documented. This should be done in such a way that others could possibly repeat the experiments and check the results for themselves, and so that the reliability of the results could later be assessed by reference to the experimental conditions, the factors for which they did or did not provide a control and the way in which measurements were made. This serves to link confidence in experimental data to the possibility of critical scrutiny by others working in the same field.

Both Boyle and Descartes gave advice which has been crucial to the procedures which have become definitive in the conduct of scientific enquiries. To make any advance in developing a theoretical understanding of the complex situations with which the world confronts us, these situations have to be analysed and simplified so that problems are reduced to those which we already know how to solve, or at least have methods which could be applied to attempt a solution. There must then also be ways of 'calculating' the effect of combining the various simple components if it is to be possible, even approximately, to model the complexities of actual situations. It is for this reason that theoretical models tend to be mathematical. The kind of analysis attempted thus depends crucially on currently available mathematical methods and experimental technology. (Descartes advocated trying to reduce all problems to making measurements which would yield sets of simultaneous, quadratic or linear equations since he knew how to solve these.) Moreover, the reliability of currently accepted experimental data depends on it being standard scientific practice to evaluate that data critically in the light of the procedures used to arrive at it; to check not only for reproducibility but also for the way it has been interpreted, for the appropriateness of the methods, whether they are the best available, whether any significant variables were overlooked, etc.

By recording extension under different loads for given samples of materials, such as metal springs, which do stretch significantly when loaded, Hooke was led to propose the law that for a given sample the amount stretched is directly proportional to the load applied, i.e. the graph obtained by plotting load against extension will be a straight line. But for what ranges does his law hold? Very small extensions were too small for Hooke to measure and test samples eventually either break or reach a state of plastic flow as the load is increased. How does tensile strength relate to elasticity? Is it possible to find samples, e.g. of steel, which would make it possible to test Hooke's law beyond the usual range? To answer such questions requires a much more detailed and more theoretical understanding of the structure of materials and of how this structure affects their engineering properties. Much of this knowledge was not available until after World War II, and it is knowledge which could not have been acquired without making and testing theoretical speculations about the nature of materials, their atomic, molecular and crystalline structures. That is, it requires analytic physical and chemical understanding of materials themselves. Such theories cannot be confirmed by direct experimental observation, but must be mediated by chains of inferences leading to the design of instruments and experiments for detecting the conjectured components, structures and their behaviours. The sense in which modern science is experimental, and is not merely speculative, lies in this requirement to seek to test theoretical speculations, or conjectures, by working out ways of detecting the presence or absence of entities and effects that are claimed to be present in specified situations. Once the existence of black holes was predicted by astrophysical theories, the next step was to think about where they might be found and how their existence might be detected. It was for this reason that Popper, perhaps one of the most influential philosophers of science of this century, proposed that only those theories or conjectures which are empirically testable deserve to be called scientific, and insisted that the scientific attitude is to seek to construct empirical tests for any proposed theory, not to seek to defend a theory, in the face of whatever evidence may come along. In other words, scientific rationality is critical rationality, a way of thinking that recognizes the provisional character of its present theories, recognizes that they are likely to be revised in the future and is continually seeking out the necessary revisions.

But Popper emphasized only falsification and suggested that whenever a theory is in conflict with evidence, the scientific attitude is to reject the theory. This picture is, however, oversimplified, in part because it takes a rather simplistic view of the nature of scientific theories, assuming that all scientific theorizing takes the form of proposing universal laws of nature. Whilst such laws form an important part of most theorizing, this is hardly the be all and end all of theoretical activity in science. To illustrate we may return once more to Hooke's law (a proposed universal law of nature). It is true that no sequence of observations, however exhaustive, could establish the complete accuracy of this law; our observations will always be incomplete. Moreover, as we have already noted, the observations available to Hooke were certainly very incomplete, being limited by the instrumental technology available to him. Indeed, with more advanced techniques it has been possible to test the law in these ranges and it has been found not to be strictly true – the straight line graph starts to bend. But how was this achieved? Earlier this century (1920) A. A. Griffiths, in the context of thinking about how to build better aeroplanes, became interested in trying to produce really strong materials and tried to do this by starting from theoretical models based on the strengths of chemical bonds. His first attempts were notable failures and when he calculated the theoretically predicted strengths for various materials, including steel, he found them to be much greater than is empirically known to be the case. The calculated tensile strength for steel was 5 million pounds per square inch, whereas commercial steels typically have values around 60,000 pounds per square inch and very strong steel wires reach strengths of 400,000 pounds per square inch. Instead of rejecting the theoretical basis of these predictions out of hand, as Popper would have a scientist do, Griffiths started to ask why there was this discrepancy. On the basis of studies of visible cracks and the way in which they propagate, often leading to catastrophic failures in large structures, he proposed to explain the relative weakness of the usually sound materials by postulating the existence of micro-cracks, dislocations in the alignments of their molecules. The test was to try to detect such cracks, using electron scanning microscopes, and to try to produce 'crack-free' materials and see whether they had tensile strengths approximating those theoretically predicted. The results of both of these kinds of test tended to confirm Griffiths' theory; dislocation edges were detected and by experimenting with glass fibres he was able to produce samples whose strength approximated the theoretically predicted value for glass.

Here Griffiths provides important confirmation of his theoretical work by proving that a theoretical projected possibility really *was* a possibility and that this kind of confirmation, while not demonstrating the truth of all aspects of the theory, provides a genuine rationale for continued work on it, even in the face of apparent conflicts with other results. This work also illustrates the distinctive way in which the development of explanatory theories guides empirical work – it is not just a matter of making systematic observations, creating the right experimental conditions and methods, but also of conducting experiments in which the aim is to try to create new situations and realize new possibilities. Griffiths' work marked the beginning of the science of strong materials, which has been one of the success stories of scientific research since World War II:[10]

> At the present time the new materials . . . and the new methods of making them offer possibilities for new technologies almost without limit. We can say this because we understand the limits to strength, stiffness and toughness of materials of widely different kinds and how these limits arise in terms of interatomic forces and the microstructure of the solid. From this we can go on both to predict and to make new materials with hitherto unknown combinations of properties and at the same time we can devise new methods of manufacturing both the materials and the articles made from them. To take simple examples, both a boat and a bicycle may be made from light alloy, plastic or ceramic and so can an aeroplane wing or a kettle. Now, and increasingly in the future, the designer will choose his materials so that consideration of final properties and method of making an article are not separate processes but are one and the same. The distinction between materials science and engineering with materials will have disappeared.
>   (Kelly, 1986, p. 117)

Amongst the startling new effects now possible are springs made of cement, glassy metals, plastics as strong as steel, crystals that are liquid, and fibrous tough ceramics.

The methods used to bring about this development are listed as being (i) the identification of crystal boundaries, defects, and the way that the properties of these depend on interatomic and intermolecular forces, i.e. the theoretical work of Griffiths and others; (ii) the development of tools for observing these defects, such as electron and ion microscopes, together with very sophisticated means of determining chemical composition on a minute scale; (iii) the development of new techniques for processing materials, involving rapid quenching and the attainment of very high pressures; (iv) an understanding of how to combine materials from the different classes into composite materials and the development of techniques for doing so. This sort of programme depends on much more than the making and testing of bold theoretical conjectures (Popper's view of scientific activity). It requires the development of instruments and technological processes in the light of theory as well as with a view to testing theories.

The length of the route from the discovery of Hooke's law to a theoretically based technology of new materials, and the length of similar routes (e.g. to biotechnology), had the consequence that the idea of taking a scientific approach bifurcated, taking one form in practical contexts and another in the context of research science. To take a scientific approach to practical problem solving did not, and still does not, entail using lots of theoretical science. Rather it involves using scientific methods to solve practical problems using whatever knowledge is available or can be fairly readily acquired.

Thus in the eighteenth and nineteenth centuries one finds the idea of a universal rational method linked to a scientific and progressive approach both to agriculture and to industrial practices. Adam Smith cites the example of the improvement of pin manufacture resulting from analysing the production process, reducing it to simple components and having each of these performed by separate operatives. In the nineteenth century engineers began adopting a scientific approach to the extent that they started to develop standardized test procedures for creating tables giving the engineering characteristics of standardly used materials. They distinguished between various kinds of steel, demanding standardization and quality control in the production process. Without this standardization there could be no assurance that the tables would give values accurately representing the characteristics of steel actually used in construction. Experimentally derived knowledge could only be of future practical use if uniformity amongst materials could be assured through standardization of production practices and the implementation of quality controls. As brick and steel replaced wood and stone, artificial materials replaced natural ones. It became more possible to ensure uniformity in materials and hence more possible to construct by designing, modelling and calculating in advance and then building to design. Hence it became more possible to treat practical problems intellectually, treating them as design problems to be solved by technical experts, rather than as practical problems to be resolved in an *ad hoc* fashion as the construction proceeds. When materials are naturally supplied and must be found locally this approach is not possible. Boat builders who must rely on the individual characteristics of the tree they find to use for the stem of each boat cannot build to a fixed design, but must adapt to accommodate the characteristics of the materials with which they have no choice but to work, using their accumulated practical skills to make the best out of what they have to work with. With artificial materials daring design innovations, such as metal-hulled ships, suspension bridges and the Crystal Palace, became possible. Success is not always assured, however, as great engineering disasters – e.g. the collapse of the Tacoma Narrows bridge and the Hindenberg airship – remind us.

The use of 'scientific' methods for problem solving, both in science for answering theoretically posed questions, and outside science for answering practically posed questions, is one of the reasons why, in the public mind, 'science' has come to cover engineering and technology as well as theoretical science. The differing approaches to plant breeding research at Cambridge and at Reading at the beginning of the twentieth century, however, illustrate the difference between taking a scientifically theoretical approach and taking one which aims to use scientific methods to improve existing practices. The theory-based approach is more radically innovative because it seeks to improve on nature by producing new varieties, ones which would not be likely to emerge from a continuation of existing practices based on farmer selection, no matter how much these were improved by being done more scientifically. Moreover, the theory-based approach which led to the introduction of hybrids renders the farmer's discriminatory skills, the ones used in selecting the seed to be saved for the following year's sowing, redundant. In the nineteenth century experienced American farmers would have strong opinions about the superiority of roughly indented over smooth corn, or of tapered ears over cylindrical ears. They had learned how to 'read' corn, and how to translate these physical characteristics into meaningful indicators of yield, quality, insect resistance, or simple aesthetic value (Fitzgerald, 1993, p. 329).

After the introduction of hybrid corn in the mid-1930s, however, farmers became convinced that 'their commonsense experience had no applicability in the newly mysterious area of seed selection' (Fitzgerald, 1993, p. 340). This was because, whereas previously farmers had been able to select corn on the basis of visual characteristics of the seed, this was not possible with the new hybrids, different strains of which might be visually indistinguishable from one another. Moreover, visual characteristics of the seed were no longer a reliable indicator of growing characteristics and since hybrids could not be grown successfully for more than one year, farmers now had to purchase fresh seed each year. So farmers could no longer try to select corn in order, over the years, to create a strain suited to their own particular farm conditions.

But even the introduction of scientific methods with a view to producing a scientifically improved practice has the effect of devaluing practical craft skills. It aims to make practice more reliable by basing it more on systematic recording and measuring, thus converting practical judgements as far as possible into intellectual ones, based on tables of data and mathematical analyses of them. Such procedures should be more reliable because they are more 'objective'; in principle they could be repeated and checked by anyone. Practical skills are notoriously difficult to transmit and different people have different aptitudes for acquiring them. They cannot be reduced to lists of rules. Two people may follow the same recipe for making an elaborate sponge cake, using the same equipment, but produce quite different results, just as two witnesses of the same accident may give very different accounts of what happened. But there are objective tests for the possession of practical skills – successful execution of whatever task the exercise of the skill forms a part. The attempt to rely solely on data analysis for making practical decisions is not assured of success unless one can be wholly confident that the analysis of the decision situation is complete and that all relevant factors are reflected in the data to hand, something on which one could never have absolute assurance. In the end this too must be a matter of judgement, something which cannot be reduced to rules and procedures. The judgement in this case will need to be that of experts, those who, in the light of some theoretical understanding of the situation, could justify a claim that the situation has been correctly analysed. And although experts often agree in their judgements, they also frequently disagree.

Either way, then, the introduction of scientific methods into practical contexts changes the way people do things, tending to transfer authority from those engaged in carrying out the practical projects to scientific experts, or requiring those who carry out the practical projects to acquire some scientific expertise for themselves. Thus science became ideologically associated, via the notion of a universal (scientifically) rational method, to notions of progress and instrumental rationality and was set in opposition to tradition and the use of traditional methods relying on practical knowledge and craft skills. Progress meant change and innovation, the refusal to be bound by tradition. Advocates of modern progressivism thus regarded the 'scientific' approach as rational, evidently superior to tradition. In the post-colonial world this leaves us with the problem of needing to know whether the opposition between tradition on the one hand, and science and technology on the other, is inevitable, or whether this opposition is a product of the ideological context within which science and technology developed in the West. Even if the latter should be the case, there remains a question about what to make of this. To what extent do the values of the context within which sciences and technologies develop permeate those sciences and technologies thus creating problems for smooth transfer into cultures which do not share those values?

4

FROM APPLIED SCIENCE TO TECHNO-SCIENCE

As we have seen, there are close connections between the instrumental view of technology and (i) insistence on the distinction between pure and applied science, (ii) the equation of basic research with pure science, and (iii) the equation of technology with applied science. In Chapter 3 we indicated some of the difficulties of maintaining (i), given the distinctive characteristics of modern science, those distinguishing it from classical learning. Once application, prediction and control become interests internal to science, it is no longer easy to draw a sharp line between pure and applied science. In this chapter we will further explore relations between pure science, basic research, applied science and technology, with a view to challenging (ii) and (iii). We will argue that in an increasing number of fields it no longer makes sense to try to distinguish between pure and applied science or between science and technology. It makes more sense to talk, as Bruno Latour does, of techno-science.

PURE SCIENCE AND BASIC RESEARCH

Academic philosophy of science has paid a great deal of attention to pure, theoretical science, but has given very little attention to applied science and has assumed that it can be unproblematically subsumed under the general umbrella of instrumental reasoning – the endeavour to solve practical problems by selecting and developing the best means available, drawing on theoretical knowledge to do so. This is to view pure science itself as a kind of instrument – a heap of information, rather than a heap of material junk – information there to be used or not, in whatever way anyone chooses. The information carries no values with it and its mere presence does not entail that it should or should not be used; those choices are up to potential users. Of course, just as guns are material fashioned with specific uses in mind, theories are information fashioned with a view to answering specific kinds of questions. In so far as these are purely intellectual questions, without practical concern and not directly geared to or arising out of practical contexts, theoretical scientific knowledge is more like raw cognitive material from which intellectual instruments may be fashioned, than like an already constituted instrumental resource.

For example, Watson and Crick's research leading to the discovery of the double helix structure of DNA and to the chemical 'alphabet' of the genetic code has as good a claim as any to have been pure research. Watson and Crick pursued their goal as an intellectual (and professional) challenge, not with any direct view to application. It was not even the research they were officially supposed to be doing, i.e. for which they were sponsored. Their discoveries did not, in themselves, provide a resource usable by plant breeders or anyone else concerned with the production of biological organisms. Much ongoing basic research is required to develop understandings of specific mechanisms, those likely to be most relevant to envisioned practical applications. Such work is closely co-ordinated with the development of laboratory techniques, such as gene splicing and DNA sequencing, and of the laboratory technology that makes these techniques possible. Governments and corporations sponsor basic research because they see it as directed at specific kinds of practical application, such as plant breeding, the production of pharmaceutical products and genetic screening.

Research is basic in that it does not directly produce actual, marketable products. It does, however, contribute directly to the underlying base of information and practical techniques that theory suggests will be necessary for the execution of a whole range of projects that, in the light of Watson and Crick's work, now seem to be realizable theoretical possibilities. The imagining of possibilities, the dreaming up of possible projects, the selection of projects to be adopted as long term goals – none of these is determined or directed by the discovery of the double helix structure of DNA. The crafting of a more detailed knowledge base, what it includes and excludes, the techniques to which it is linked, is the fashioning of a set of scientific tools for specific purposes. To this extent it cannot be equated with pure, theoretical science. For although it has increased knowledge as one of its objectives, directives determining the kind of knowledge sought and valued are set with practical projects in mind. The factors giving priority to some practical projects instead of others must be sought in the wider socio-economic environment within which the research is taking place. Here we need to be careful to distinguish between science as an institution with its various research traditions and specific pieces of research carried out by specific researchers. Individual scientists have often carried out research without concern for its applications being motivated purely by the intellectual challenge it presents. That challenge is itself presented within the context of a wider research tradition, however, whose existence may have a great deal to do with potential applications.

While there may be no such thing as a typical example in this context, there are many others that could be used to make the same point. Think for example of the route from discoveries in atomic physics, in the context of World War II, to Slizard seeing the theoretical possibility of an atomic bomb, and then via the Manhattan Project to the actual production and explosion of such a device. The Manhattan Project required both further basic research and the development of production techniques with a highly specific aim in mind. We would argue that, in general, much of what is funded and undertaken as basic research is not undertaken simply for the pursuit of knowledge for its own sake but with a view to creating the detailed knowledge base necessary to mediate between fundamental scientific theorizing and the kind of practical projects it suggests might be possible.

HOW DOES BASIC RESEARCH SCIENCE GET APPLIED?

One reason academic philosophy of science has not given much attention to applied science is that the process of application has been thought to be unproblematic by comparison with the problem of characterizing the methods by which scientific knowledge claims may be rationally justified. (Another reason may be the generally low esteem accorded to practical knowledge and technical concerns within academic institutions, where more purely intellectual pursuits are privileged.) This judgement is itself encouraged by the tendency to characterize both contexts using simple logical schemata. The justification for resorting to logical schemata lies in part with the equation of the rational with the logical. If this equation is accepted, it can be plausibly suggested that there is a single common form to all theoretical knowledge. Thus, for example, according to Popper, 'Scientific theories are universal statements' (Popper, 1959, p. 59). But evidence comes in the form of singular statements of the results of particular observations. This means that no accumulation of evidence can ever conclusively establish the truth of a scientific theory (Hume's problem of induction), since from Fa & Ga, Fb & Gb . . . one can never validly derive $\forall x(Fx \rightarrow Gx)$. So the epistemological problem, that on which philosophers have focused much of their attention, is how to use empirical evidence to arrive at theories, or how to choose between theories. Popper's proposal was that science proceeds not by trying to verify its claims, but by trying to falsify them, since from Fc & $\neg Gc$ one can validly infer $\neg \forall x(Fx \rightarrow Gx)$. Thus he proposed that theories are scientific when they are empirically falsifiable, i.e. such that they can be refuted by empirical evidence. This requires that they be capable of making predictions about what will or will not happen in specific, empirically realized or realizable conditions. To apply a theory, then, is to use it to make predictions in specified circumstances. There is thus seen to be a single logical schema underlying both theory testing and theory application. In both cases this is represented as a straightforward logical deduction

$$\forall x(Fx \rightarrow Gx), \ Fc \vdash Gc.$$

Because theory application, like prediction, is logically modelled as a valid deductive inference (i.e. one that is always rationally justified) it has been viewed as a straightforward process, one involving no deep problems.

There have been many more sophisticated versions of this 'standard philosophical view of science'; Richard Grandy (Grandy, 1992, pp. 216–17) offers a typical list of the key components:

1 Theories are to be represented as axiomatized systems (sets of sentences) expressed in the language of first-order logic.
2 There is a fundamental distinction between observational and theoretical vocabulary.
3 There are bridge rules or correspondence rules connecting observation with theoretical vocabulary.
4 The axioms or theoretical postulates define internal relations among the purely theoretical terms.

Although philosophers dispute details of this general characterization, the relation between theory and evidence, theory and application is still frequently portrayed as a loosely logical relation: application is basically the same thing as prediction, which is the same thing that is required for theory testing. The underlying schema is then

$$C, T \vdash E,$$

where C is a statement of specific conditions, T is the theory and E is a statement of what will, according to T, happen when conditions C are realized.

However, as people have come to focus on what is distinctive of modern research science – namely, its experimental and increasingly technological character – the logical characterization of the epistemological problems posed by science has come to seem too oversimplified to provide a useful framework within which to pursue questions about the authority status of science. Some of the reasons for thinking such a characterization to be oversimplified were indicated in Chapter 3 when discussing Popper's characterization of science and scientific method. Additionally, this logical framework provides no basis for distinguishing observational sciences (such as ancient astronomy) from experimental sciences, such as modern physics and chemistry. It therefore contributes to the image of pure scientific theorizing as an activity continuous with classical pursuits of knowledge and makes it difficult to reveal the differences, those on which the technological successes notched up to modern science rest.

Although not all sciences are equally experimental, there are some things notable about those that are, and these will be sufficient to show the inadequacies of thinking about the relation between theory and evidence in basically logical terms. Claude Bernard argued in the mid-nineteenth century that medicine could and should become experimental. He was well aware of the difference between observational and experimental science:

> In the observational sciences, man observes and reasons experimentally, but he does not experiment; and in this sense one could say that an observational science is a passive science. In the experimental science, man observes, but much more than that he works on matter, to analyze its properties and to provoke for his benefit the appearance of phenomena, which doubtless always occur in accordance with the laws of nature, but in conditions which nature has realized only infrequently, if at all. With the help of these active experimental sciences,

man becomes an inventor of phenomena, a veritable overseer of creation; and one cannot, with regard to this, assign limits to the power he will be able to acquire over nature, by the future progress of the experimental sciences.

(Bernard, 1984, p. 48, our translation)

The goal of an observational science is to discover the laws of natural phenomena with a view to be able to predict them; but it gives no knowledge of how either to modify them or master them at will. The model for these sciences is astronomy; we can predict astronomical phenomena, but we never know how to change them. The goal of an experimental science, such as physics or chemistry, is to discover the laws of natural phenomena, not only for the purposes of prediction, but in order to regulate them at will and make ourselves masters over them (Bernard, 1984, p. 278).

Writing in 1934, Bachelard used Descartes' discussion of his knowledge of a piece of wax (*Meditations* II) as a vehicle for contrasting observational science with modern, experimental science. Descartes takes a piece of beeswax. It has a characteristic colour, texture and even a smell. He warms it and it melts, loses its smell and changes shape, colour and texture. Descartes uses his observations to conclude that if the nature of wax is to be known it will not be in terms of its impermanently possessed, sense-perceived properties. His object is one presented by nature. It is a substance that can be classified based on characteristics observable without the aid of instruments. But to be constituted as an object for scientific investigation by modern techniques, Bachelard argues, the wax would first be purified, then carefully prepared so that it would depend on the kind of enquiry being pursued and the kind of instrumentation being used to further enquiry:

The physicist would take ... a wax which was as pure as possible, chemically well-defined, the product of a long series of methodical manipulations. The wax chosen is thus in a way a precise moment of the method of objectification. It retains none of the odour of the flowers from which it was gathered, but it constitutes proof of the care with which it was purified. In other words, it is brought into being by an artifactual experiment. Without the artifactual experiment, such a wax – in a pure form which is not its natural form – would not have come into existence.

After having put a very small fragment of this wax in a

95

crucible, the physicist makes it solidify with a methodical slowness. Fusion and solidification are controlled by means of a tiny electric furnace whose temperature can be regulated with all desirable precision by varying the intensity of the current. The physicist consequently makes himself master of the time whose effective action depends on thermic variation. In this way he obtains a droplet of wax which is very regular not only in form but also in its surface structure. The book of the microcosm is now engraved, it remains to be read.

(Bachelard, 1978, p. 173, our translation)

This structure might be read, for example, by an electron scanning microscope, or by using the techniques of X-ray crystallography. The point is that before this stage of 'reading' the object has been carefully prepared and a great deal is already known about it by virtue of the carefully controlled manner of production. It is also the case that without this type of production, there would be no regular structure to read. A fragment from Descartes' piece of wax would be too 'disorderly' to be readable; it is a highly individual piece of wax with elements of its microstructure peculiar to it, depending on the travels of the bees from whose hive it came, etc. Bachelard's piece of wax has had all these idiosyncratic impurities removed. It is a highly standardized and regularized piece of wax. Any other piece prepared in the same way would be expected to yield the same microstructure. It can thus be read as having implications for our knowledge of all of them. This illustrates the way in which laboratory practice contributes to the solution of the problem of induction. Great care is taken to prepare objects and to control conditions seeking, in this way, to obtain stable, uniform results. If a student or another experimenter fails to get results that sufficient scientists with established reputations have repeatedly obtained, it will usually be assumed that they failed to do the experiment correctly, or that there was some fault in the apparatus, i.e. that either the right conditions weren't produced, or that there was some error in measurement, not that the results do not hold in general.

It is for this reason that Ian Hacking says experimenting is not just observing, it is intervening – phenomena are created in laboratories under carefully contrived and controlled conditions. Control of the initial and boundary conditions (maintenance of relatively closed systems) is crucial to the emergence of regularities (i.e. the success of inductions).

Experiment is the creation of phenomena; phenomena must have discernible regularities – so an experiment that is not repeatable has failed to create a phenomenon.

(Hacking, 1983, p. 224)

The creation of phenomena is part and parcel of the process of experimental analysis, where naturally complex conditions and substances are simplified and purified by using methodical controls to isolate their components. The laws governing these isolable components are not created, but they are manifest only under very special, non-natural conditions. Focus on experimental work and the production of phenomena thus makes the transition from experiment to regularities, from particular results to general laws, less mysterious. It is a transition made by making certain kinds of controlled and controllable situations, situations that have been made to behave in a regular manner. Yet this practical mediation of the logician's problem renders more problematic the practical implementation of the logician's solution to theory application. For if the experimental phenomena reveal themselves only under highly artificial, technically contrived conditions, how do they ever find successful application in the world? Bruno Latour poses the question this way: 'How does science get out of the laboratory?' (Latour, 1987).

When we start to think of experimental science in the terms sketched above it becomes clear that laboratory technology, including measuring and recording devices, plays a crucial role in experimentation and that experimentation itself is a complex activity. As Hacking notes (Hacking, 1983, p. 230), it is necessary, at the very least, to distinguish between:

(1) designing an experiment that might work;
(2) learning how to make the experiment work, designing equipment, getting interferences (noise) under control;
(3) getting to know when it is working (when the equipment is functioning properly).

Running experimental equipment involves mechanical skills. The design of workable experiments involves skills not unlike those of the design engineer. So even basic research science depends on practical activities and technical skills. These are absolutely crucial to the reliability of the empirical data base. In terms of the nature of these activities there is no sharp cut-off between pure and applied science or between science and engineering. Consider, for example, the following description of Faraday's attempts to produce improved lenses for optical telescopes to be used by the astronomer Herschel:

> The technical difficulties were as follows. For optical purposes, glass must be homogeneous in composition and structure, otherwise different portions of the lens will possess different indices of refraction. Flint glass is optically the most desirable, but it presents real problems in terms of homogeneity. It contains lead oxide, so heavy that it sinks to the bottom of the mixture. Thus when Herschel received an early batch of specimens from Faraday in 1825, he wrote in response:
>
> > The difference of S[pecific] G[ravity] between the top and bottom in one case exceeds anything I could have supposed possible. It is evident that no accidental defect in mixing could have produced it.
>
> There were other problems as well. The pots tended to crack and fuse under the heat, and ultimately the furnace itself began to go to pieces. The glass contained bubbles and striae, which could not be removed by stirring the molten glass because this shattered the pots. Faraday wrote to Herschel that 'we shall have to feel our way a good deal', and in fact the entire procedure was an excruciatingly tedious process of moving from problem to problem in an area that was without precedent. It was . . . 'an exercise in precision cooking'.
>
> (Berman, 1978, p. 164)

Because of the need to get interference, or 'noise', under control, and because of the need for the greatest possible precision, scientific experiments can only take place in specially prepared situations and at sites set aside for the purpose that will be free from intrusions. What modern engineering design and experimental design have in common is emphasis on prediction and control. The experimenter wants to check specific predictions by controlling everything else, all the boundary and initial conditions. The engineer designing something to perform a desired function wants to be assured that it will perform this function when produced according to the design specifications. But this control can only be secured if the boundaries of the system are defined and held fixed. In this respect engineering also becomes theoretical as design comes to be separated from construction. In the sixteenth century Italian military engineering designers sought and proposed the ideal form for a fortress – a scientific solution to the problems posed by the need to defend against the forms of artillery and siege equipment in use at the time. Subsequent generations of military engineers have pursued similar goals, culminating most recently in the Strategic Defense Initiative with its 'Star Wars' vision of a perfect defence shield against incoming nuclear missiles. The ideal form of a fortress was sought and proposed. But this ideal form was predicated upon fixed conditions regarding the terrain of the site:

> The notion of an ideal form [of fortress] led to a belief in the superiority of a fortress laid out on flat ground, without regard for fortuitous geographic features such as hills and ravines, the protective qualities of which had for centuries dictated the location of castles.
>
> (Ferguson, 1992, p. 69)

The attempt to build only ideal fortresses would lead to ignoring natural, potentially defensive features. So before beginning to build, the terrain had to be modified to suit the fortress specifications: flattening the ground and removing all cover within cannon range of the proposed walls. Indeed, the following has been called the fundamental tenet of engineering:

> Whatever an engineer may be called upon to design, he or she knows that in order for the plans to be effective the system being planned must be predictable and controllable. The designer first defines the boundaries of the system (often involving highly arbitrary judgements), just as the fortress designer set his boundaries at the limits of cannon range. Then the permissible inputs to the system and the permissible outputs from the system are carefully determined. Nothing may cross the boundaries unobserved or unaccounted for. There is no place in an ideal engineering system for unpredictable actions, either by machines or by people. Thus the assumptions and essential procedures of the fortress designer – the fortress mentality – fit naturally the needs of modern engineering design.
>
> (Ferguson, 1992, p. 70)

This similarity between engineering and experimental design provides some clues to how science itself gets applied. In his study of Pasteur's work on bacteria and the development of techniques of immunization, Latour answered his own question by suggesting that *science does not, in fact, get outside the laboratory*. Instead, the laboratory is extended to take over sections of the world where the scientifically produced techniques are to be applied. This would be exactly parallel to the building of an ideal fortress. Technological success in the application of research science can be assured only by changing and controlling the environment in which it is to function to replicate laboratory conditions as closely as possible if successful implementation is to be assured. Relatively closed systems are not just found, they have to be artificially produced and maintained. This needs theoretical scientific and/or theoretical technological knowledge, plus experimental and/or technical know-how as well as knowledge of the possibilities for control of the social setting of the system. Experimental laboratories are typically small and typically experiments only require controlling the boundary conditions for short periods (here the need for social control can seem trivial). A technological project, on the other hand, may often be large scale and long term. If there are problems realizing and maintaining the 'ideal' boundary conditions there will be problems with predicting outcomes. On these scales social control becomes more difficult and much less trivial.

Here we begin to see that applying theoretically worked-out solutions to practical problems – the application of scientific knowledge and of methods adopted from the theoretical sciences – is far from straightforward. In particular the effect of thinking of technology as applied science and thinking of science in terms of a logically structured theoretical discipline overlooks something crucial. Namely, that the application of science understood as implementing a top-down designed technology, if it is to have a chance of functioning successfully, requires creating suitable environments within which to place that technology. This is what the instrumental vision of technology invites us to overlook – the conditions, the infrastructural background, essential to the functioning of sophisticated instruments. Devices create new possibilities only if they can function properly. When their functioning is dependent on altering the environment in which they are to function in permanent ways, their implementation ceases to be a matter simply of making new things possible. It is also a matter of having to commit resources to maintenance of that environment, a process that may well be destructive of all sorts of other possibilities. Aspects of the world and of human lives have to be controlled and this control in itself inevitably means, from the point of view of those whose lives are controlled, a restriction on their previous possibilities. Value issues arise here as elsewhere. Let us take two rather different kinds of cases to illustrate these points.

Not all control of the human environment is negatively valued, even by the more extreme pessimists about techno-science. One obstacle to acknowledging how much environments must be altered for a technology to find a home is that we take so much of the environment we live in for granted. We tend to forget the extent to which our environment is a made environment which has to be maintained by a complex organization of people and technology. We also tend to forget just how much this control of our environment contributes to the possibility of regarding nature as a mostly benign rather than as a constantly threatening force. In early nineteenth century Europe rapidly rising urban populations were constantly threatened by epidemics of infectious diseases, cholera and typhoid in particular. When it was discovered that many infectious diseases are caused by bacteria and in particular by water-borne bacteria, public health measures were taken to provide supplies of safe drinking water and to install sewage and drainage systems to prevent contamination of groundwater sources and to minimize risks of the spread of disease by contact with untreated sewage. The installation and maintenance of this infrastructure represents a form of centrally organized control of our environment (and to that extent our lives) that we take for granted. Only when it breaks down do we realize its importance.

Some technology required to ensure a good water supply had been available since Roman times.[1] The administrative structures required to install and maintain it were mostly unavailable in Europe in the period between the fall of Rome and the French Revolution. The wide-scale provision of adequate supplies of fresh drinking water to a large population presupposes a stable administration, sufficiently concerned for the welfare of the general populace to have the political will to commit resources to public works projects and having the ability to install and maintain the necessary pipes, pumps, filters and treatment facilities. This is a kind of control over, and introduction of an element of uniformity into, the lived environment that people welcome, especially those not otherwise in a position to secure such provisions for themselves. (Of course, there are further questions that arise about who gets how much water, for what purposes and at what cost, about the siting of reservoirs, the depletion of aquifers, restricted access to watersheds, controls of pollutants in runoff from farmland and so on. These breed controversy because of the conflicting interests of various subgroups of the population of any given region.)

One significant difference between the Roman and the modern European context is that the Romans lacked knowledge of the existence of bacteria and of their role in the transmission of certain diseases. Rome's public water supply was therefore neither protected against bacterial contamination nor suspected as a source of disease when epidemics occurred. To this extent it may have been as much a liability as a resource. It has been argued (Cartwright and Biddiss, 1972, Ch. 1) that bacterial contamination of the water supply contributed significantly to the downfall of the Roman Empire, by subjecting the people of Rome to a succession of epidemics. This illustrates the vulnerability of populations dependent on centralized supplies. Social as well as technical control is required to ensure their security to prevent malicious as well as accidental contamination.

Other public health measures have been more controversial. The pasteurization of milk (named after Pasteur) was introduced to prevent the spread of tuberculosis and brucellosis via the consumption of milk from infected cows. Yet the introduction of regulations making it illegal to sell unpasteurized milk was seen by some as an infringement of their right to buy and consume what they regarded as a superior product. And the discovery that fluoride helped to prevent tooth decay led not only to the manufacture and sale of fluoride toothpaste, but also to the idea of introducing fluoride into the water supply so all children would get the benefit of protection against tooth decay. Again this control over our lived environment was welcomed by some people but resisted by others on the grounds that fluoride is a chemical whose other effects on the human body had not been fully evaluated and that people should not have to consume water containing it if they did not wish to. In the United States, some also suspected a Communist-inspired plot to poison US citizens! The problems posed by this kind of issue are clearly no longer purely scientific or technological, but also social and political, as we shall see in more detail in the next chapter.

A rather different kind of example of the complexity of the move from research laboratory to widespread use is provided by the Davy lamp, or miner's safety lamp. At the time (1816) of its introduction the Davy lamp was heralded as a success for science. Humphry Davy had used scientific methods, applying available scientific knowledge, to solve a practical problem. The problem was how to make a lamp that would burn in the methane-rich atmospheres frequently encountered in coal mines without causing an explosion. Davy had analysed the problem, come up with a theoretical solution and tested it in his laboratory. His solution involved shielding the lamp flame by surrounding it with fine wire gauze, so dispersing the heat from the flame and reducing the temperature of contact between the methane-rich atmosphere and the lamp. As a miner's safety lamp, however, it was hardly a success: the numbers of mining accidents caused by explosions and the numbers of miners killed in such accidents rose dramatically in the years immediately following the introduction of the lamp.[2] As actually used in the mines, the lamp caused explosions because the air was not still. Sudden draughts could cause the flame to blow onto the gauze heating it more directly and raising it to a temperature sufficient to ignite the methane and insufficient ventilation in the mine could result in high air temperatures which would not allow the gauze to cool sufficiently to prevent ignition. Davy lacked the knowledge of mining necessary to perceive the difference between his problem, which he had solved, and the problem of producing a lamp which had the required property when used down a mine, which he had not solved, although he did warn that his lamp had limitations. His lamp would have been a solution *if* the mining environment had simultaneously been controlled to approximate the laboratory environment, i.e. if more adequate ventilation systems had been installed to control the flow of air through mine workings. This would have been an expensive solution to the problem of the buildup of methane that the miner owners did not wish to implement. So the problem put before Davy was the mine owners' problem of how to get a light that would function in the methane-rich atmosphere of 'crept' workings, which they knew to be inadequately ventilated.[3]

This example illustrates the way in which knowledge sufficient for success in the laboratory does not on its own confer other wider powers of prediction and control. Nor can the methods used for achieving laboratory success automatically be assumed to be those that will yield success in wider spheres. The theoretical and explanatory endeavour of the natural sciences, physics and chemistry in particular, has been analytic and foundational – the quest for fundamental laws, for basic constituents of matter, the basic building blocks by reference to which the characteristics of all more complex objects and phenomena are to be explained. The empirical investigative methods that form part of this endeavour have been correspondingly analytic, concentrating on the isolation of causal factors, on the creation of controlled experimental conditions in which the effects of variation in a single variable can be studied. But the application of knowledge gained in this way depends on skills and knowledge of different kinds. Analysis has to be accompanied by synthesis. Either work in controlled environments has to be extended to work in much more variable conditions or ways must be devised to limit the variability of the conditions in which the products of research are to be deployed. Knowledge of the variable conditions of application is as important as knowledge of fundamental theory; practical skill is as important as theoretical understanding. One could thus say that Davy's laboratory success did not transfer into great success in use because the introduction of his lamp was not accompanied by the kind of reforms in the mining industry that would have rendered mine conditions similar to laboratory conditions. Alternatively, one could lay the blame at Davy's feet, suggesting that he had an inadequate understanding of the conditions under which his lamp was to be used and therefore that he failed to take the variability of those conditions into account in designing his lamp. He did not, in other words, make the laboratory conditions in which he tested his lamp sufficiently similar to mine conditions. For application of laboratory research to be successful either the laboratory must be extended out into the world or the world must be brought into the laboratory.

Neither strategy could be said to be more or less scientific than the other; they distribute the costs and benefits differently. The second strategy demands more of the research and development phase, increasing its costs and the time it takes. It requires a scientific understanding not only of the device or technique being developed, but also of the contexts in which they are to be deployed together with the ability to model their relevant features, by using wind tunnels, scale models or computer simulations, for example. Sometimes such knowledge may simply be unavailable. Doubtless Davy could have extended his research trying to make a more elaborate lamp that would be safe even in sudden draughts. In that event it would probably have been a more complex device, and hence more expensive to produce; and if it were too bulky it might become too complicated and cumbersome for miners, working in confined conditions, to use. In other words, other factors of the use context would start to come into play.

The first strategy also has its costs. The provision and maintenance of controlled environments on any large scale, such as a coal mine, requires considerable capital outlay and the organization to monitor and maintain equipment. Extending the walls of the laboratory out into sectors of the world requires transforming those sectors and thus often requires social engineering, as well as civil, structural engineering. To be able to make his anthrax inoculations effective, for instance, Pasteur had to transform certain aspects of French farming practices. Records had to be kept of cows. The indoor environment in which they were inoculated had to be clean, and so on.

Assuming that technology just consists of value-neutral devices, tools or instruments encourages the idea that technological devices can be successfully used in any context. As we have seen, however, the reality is otherwise: in many cases there are specific material and social preconditions for the successful implementation of a given technology. Failure to realize this, or to be able to see exactly what they are (especially the social conditions), is one of the reasons why there have been problems with technology transfer. Consider just one example, given by Patricia Stamp (Stamp, 1989, p. 59).

A new hydraulic palm-oil press was installed in a Nigerian village community on a piece of land designated by the village head. Initially 70 per cent of the people used it, but after a year the figure dropped to 24 per cent. Why? Since the manual extraction of oil from palm fruits consumed time and energy, it would be natural to assume that a mechanical press that saved both would be welcomed. One problem, however, was the assumption Western countries make that the operation of heavy machinery is a male role. Machines are thus designed for use by men and aid agencies assume that they should be given to the men in a community, both in their role as heads of households and as users of them. The extraction of palm oil, however, was traditionally a task for women. They continued to assume that this was their task. Since the press had been given to the men, however, they set up the daily schedule for its use and retained all the products from it. Because the press had been designed for men, women found the press difficult to use; and the need for a schedule made it difficult for them to fit in this activity with their other required tasks, such as meal preparation. Furthermore, since the products of the press belonged to the men, women did not benefit from the increase in the amount of oil extracted per unit of fruit pressed. Consequently, women could not set this benefit off against the other inconveniences entailed by use of the press, especially as they also lost an important byproduct of the pressing pit, the fibre that was used as a source of heat. To have been a success *either* the traditional way of life (including distributions of tasks between male and female) would have to have been significantly changed, *or* the technology would have to have been redesigned for use by women and to fit in with the particular social patterns in the community. Neither was done, and so the technology failed in practice.

Ignoring such conditions in technology policy decision making has the effect of reducing socio-political issues to technical ones. It hides the question 'Do we want to fulfil the social conditions needed for this technology?' It consequently turns decision making into a matter of answering technical questions about effects and the adjustments that can be made to ameliorate, or at least keep within bounds, the undesirable effects.

TECHNO-SCIENCE AND THE COMMODIFICATION OF KNOWLEDGE

There are two respects in which modern science, as it developed from the seventeenth through to the eighteenth and nineteenth centuries, became an essentially public, co-operative activity. First, even such early writers as Descartes and Bacon realized that their recommended procedures for acquiring knowledge of the natural world could not possibly be the work of any one person. Unlike a metaphysically based system of natural philosophy, it could not hope to be achieved as the work of a single author working in isolation. The collection of data, performing of experiments, framing and testing of theories would be the work of several generations of scholars working in co-operation with one another. Already in *New Atlantis* Bacon describes such teamwork, with internal divisions of labour. There he outlines the activities of the members of Salomon's House, those who in *New Atlantis* play a role analogous to the Guardians (philosopher-kings) in Plato's *Republic*. As research has become more complex and the facilities required more expensive and elaborate, the need for teamwork and co-operation has increased. It is now almost impossible for an isolated individual to carry out research in the natural sciences, providing his or her own finance and facilities; this was possible for figures such as Isaac Newton and Robert Boyle.

The very imperatives that have required teamwork on specific research projects – complexity and expense – have also started to introduce pressures tending to limit the possibilities for co-operation between such teams and thereby to limit the other respect in which science has been essentially public. This second, important sense in which publicity has played a constitutive role in modern science has been in the publication of experimental results and proposed theories. This was essential not only for the formation of the widest possible community of scientists but also for the exposure of theoretical and experimental claims to the critical scrutiny of peers and research competitors. An individual or a team might be expected to be strong advocates for their own claims and, in their enthusiasm, to have quite possibly overlooked, or failed to take sufficient account of, data that would present difficulties for their theoretical claims, or methodological inadequacies that would make it unwise to rely too heavily on their results. Others, possibly backing conflicting claims, may be expected to spot such weaknesses, to try repeating experiments, and so on. Thus publication of results has been essential for recognition; the work of an individual cannot become scientific knowledge unless those in the relevant scientific discipline come to accept it as such. Further, claims about the objectivity of scientific knowledge rest on the belief that the scientific community, as a whole, subjects claims to thorough critical scrutiny before giving any such provisional acceptance. Awareness that publication attracts scrutiny makes people more cautious, seeking to establish their results and justify their claims as well as possible in order to forestall possible criticism. Although there is no stigma attached to have presented a stimulating and well-worked-out hypothesis that turns out to be untenable, or interesting, carefully obtained new data that turns out to be flawed or misinterpreted for reasons that could not have been anticipated, there is a professional price to pay for being judged to have made the kind of mistakes that experienced workers in that field should not make, i.e. to have been doing bad science.

In many areas of research this public scrutiny through publication still prevails, but in those areas where research has been funded by business corporations or by government for the purposes of military research limits have been placed on the publication of results and methods. These are areas in which basic research is funded with specific kinds of application in mind, i.e. areas where research has explicitly ceased to be disinterested and knowledge has become a commodity to be hoarded or sold. These are the fields, increasing in number, which most deserve Latour's appellation 'techno-science' – fields where it not longer makes sense to talk of a separation between pure and applied science or between science and technology. Computer science, information science and biotechnology

– those much touted harbingers of the better future age of high technology – would be examples. But the trend towards treating knowledge as a commodity goes back to the introduction of the system of patents, copyrights, and varietal registration for seeds. For example, Pickstone argues that:

> By the end of the nineteenth century, at least in Germany, one finds the characteristic conjunctions of university research, pharmaceutical company laboratories, hospitals as proving grounds, plus philanthropic and government laboratories, especially for standardization.
>
> These linked institutions operated in markets or quasi-markets. They were oriented primarily to the production of commodities which people (or governments) purchased. Characteristically, they involved the commercialization of analytical procedures (e.g. fees for testing) and the commercialization of experimental products (e.g. vaccines).
>
> (Pickstone, 1993, p. 238)

These practices were not primarily oriented towards advancing scientific disciplines but to the creation and sale of techno-products. The human genome project is an illustration of how blurred the boundary line has now become:

> The Human Genome Project, an international quest to spell out the precise sequence of the three billion letters in the human genetic code, is still more than a decade from completion. But in a rapid blurring of big science and big business the effort has already created its first millionaires.
>
> One is J. Craig Venter, who as a Federal employee and the National Institute of Health developed a crucial technique for spelling out – or 'sequencing' – long strands of genetic code. Then, a little more than a year ago, he left to join a venture to commercialize the technology. Now, even before they have a product, Dr. Venter and his backers have raised millions of dollars by selling public shares of stock in their venture, Human Genome Sciences Inc., of Bethesda, Md.
>
> (*The New York Times*, Sunday, 30 January 1994)

This trend towards fusing science and technology and to commodifying the products of both is part and parcel of wider nineteenth century movements to sell science to industrialists and politicians, a movement which saw scientific and technological progress as a motor for economic and social progress. The Royal Institution, for which Davy worked, had as part of its mission the task of 'selling' science to wealthy progressive landowners and industrialists and to encourage them to invest their capital in research science. So while Davy and Faraday did conduct original scientific research there, they also had to perform lots of routine soil analysis for farming landowners. This was a practical way of trying to convince landowners of the significance of chemistry for agriculture:

> The knowledge of the composition of soils, the food of vegetables, of the modes in which their products must be treated, so as to become fit for the nourishment of animals, is essential to the cultivation of land; and [the landowner's] exertions are profitable and useful to society, in proportion as he is more of a chemical philosopher.
>
> (Davy, 1839, Vol. II, p. 316)

> Science has done much for man, but it is capable of doing still more; its sources of improvement are not yet exhausted.
> (Davy, 1839, Vol. II, p. 319, quoted in Berman, 1978, p. 66)

Davy was explicit about who he was trying to convince of the value of scientific knowledge, and it was not the likes of miners: it was those with sufficient power, influence and capital to invest in research science. Thus when working on his safety lamp he was working for the mine owners, not the miners, who had no wealth to invest in science. This affects the character of research to the extent that two groups had rather different primary concerns. The miners wanted a reduction in accident rates; the owners wanted to be able to salvage more coal from 'crept' workings, where concentrations of methane were high and ventilation poor, without significantly increasing accident rates. Davy's view of the wider economic and social role of science is clearly illustrated in the following remarks:

> The arts and sciences ... are in a high degree cultivated, and patronized by the rich and privileged orders. The guardians of civilization and of refinement, the most powerful and respected part of society, are daily growing more attentive to the realities of life; and giving up many of their unnecessary enjoyments in consequence of the desire to be useful, are becoming the friends and protectors of the labouring part of the community. The unequal division of property and of labour, the difference

of rank and condition amongst mankind, are the sources of power in civilized life, its moving causes, and even its very soul; and in considering and hoping that the human species is capable of becoming more enlightened and more happy, we can only expect that the whole of society should be ultimately connected together by means of knowledge and the useful arts; that they should act as the children to one great parent, with one determinate end, so that no power may be rendered useless, no exertions thrown away. In this view we do not look to distant ages . . . [but] look for a time that we may reasonably expect, for a bright day of which we behold the dawn.

(Davy, 1839, Vol. II, p. 323, quoted in Berman, 1978, p. 67)

This vision was by no means unusual. A little earlier we find John Farey making similar connections between economic and social progress and the use of new technology:

The high state of wealth and civilization which the English people have attained within the last half century, has been greatly promoted by the application of the power of the steam-engine to various purposes of the useful arts, in aid of manual labour. In an uncultivated state of society, all that the higher classes consume must be obtained by the degradation and slavery of the mass of the population; for unless the industry of the working class is systematically applied, and aided by the use of machines, there can be but little surplus wealth to maintain an educated class in society, and produce that state of general affluence which is conducive to the progress of civilization, and the development of intellect.

It is only in comparatively modern times, that the natural powers of currents of wind and water have been applied to facilitate laborious operations; but at the commencement of the last century, in addition to the general application of wind and water powers, a new element was subjected to the laws of mechanics in England, and with great success. The productiveness of labour has been so greatly increased by this gigantic auxiliary, and by the improved system of manufactures and commerce to which it has given birth, that those conveniences of life, and attributes of wealth, which were formerly considered to be one of the distinctions of the first classes of the community, are now acknowledged to belong equally to that middle class which may be said to consist of labourers, who apply their minds to useful industry, instead of their hands.

This change has produced a great advancement in the state of society. The desire of supplying the artificial wants thus created, has excited a great energy of mind, and an active exercise of knowledge amongst the middle class, which has influenced the whole mass of society, so as to have produced a high state of civilization; and in its consequences has induced a refinement of habits, manners, and sentiments which can only result from a general diffusion of wealth and knowledge. The condition of the labouring class has been greatly improved at the same time, and a more rapid improvement will follow, from a perseverance in that system of education which is now in active operation amongst the common people.

(Farey, 1827, Preface)

Here additionally we find added to the total vision the ingredient of economic theory which gives technology a socially progressive role because, and to the extent that, it increases productivity. It is within the framework of this vision that, as was seen in Chapter 2, efficiency becomes a crucial evaluative concept. Techno-science, as defined by Latour and Pickstone, is a product of this socio-economic vision which intimately interconnects science and technology with industrial capitalism.

TOP-DOWN VERSUS BOTTOM-UP DEVELOPMENT

In spite of these nineteenth century visions, it remains the case that prior to the twentieth century most technology was not developed from the top down, was not the result of application of research science. A consequence of the trend towards a top-down approach is that artificial environments must be created to ensure success. This may be the origin of the sense that technology is fundamentally opposed to the natural and the feeling that it is a monstrous system which threatens to dominate and control every aspect of our lives. It has been the preparedness to ride roughshod over the variations of naturally occurring conditions that has made it possible to use standardized procedures and devices by standardizing the environment.

There are definite costs to such an approach. As an example, consider standardized designs for modern high rise apartment buildings, designs that include circulation ducts for central heating and air-conditioning, and put them up anywhere in the world where there are the energy resources to power the heating and/or air-conditioning. Yet a building design appropriate for New York or London may make little sense in the context of Honolulu. It may provide comfortable living, but at a very high cost because of the need constantly to run air-conditioning. Buildings designed to suit Honolulu's climate would be unfit for habitation in New York or London: they would be impossible to keep warm or dry in winter. To this extent such technologies are less embedded in local culture and ways of life, but their implementation requires overriding and/or ignoring distinctive local features if it is to work. It is for this reason that the development, manufacture and marketing of such technologies is attractive to multinational corporations.[4] The instrumental view of technology, with its associated conceptions of science and of technology as, ideally, applied science, is a mere ideology. On its own it would not have the powerful grip and influence that it does. It requires the vision that, having been sold to industrialists and governments in the nineteenth and early twentieth centuries, has become integral to their practice, the practice of techno-science.

Technology developed bottom up tends to be developed in response to locally occurring specific practical problems. It draws on existing local cultural and material resources and adapts existing procedures and practices. To this extent bottom-up developed technology is much more deeply culturally embedded, much less readily transferable to other situations. It is therefore more difficult to market, especially to market trans-nationally. Its production methods, moreover, are likely to be such that these, too, cannot just be transported to another setting, one where labour currently happens to be most cheaply available.

To take but one extended example of this contrast, consider the difference between horticultural techniques advocated for the English gardener by the nineteenth century gardening writer, William Cobbett, and the trends in twentieth century agriculture, of which the so-called Green Revolution is but one example.

Cobbett writes for a very specific audience – the English professional gardener whose function is to ensure year round supplies of a good variety of high quality fruit and vegetables for the table of a large country house. This is not subsistence farming; this is sophisticated horticulture with a presumption of capital resources for construction of the best possible growing environments for the produce required. Neither is it market oriented; the goal is not to generate profits but to provide plentiful supplies reliably and within the available resources. The clear presumption is that once the initial capital investment is made, the only really significant input is labour.

Since the English climate is relatively cool, crops such as oranges, grapes, peaches, cucumbers, melons and tomatoes cannot be reliably grown without protection and input of heat. Cobbett gives instructions for the construction of a walled garden (walls in part for securing crops from theft, but equally to give protection for plants and to provide a variety of growing conditions), with four different wall aspects, for fruit trees espaladed along the walls. Included in the garden will be hot beds and greenhouses. The whole technique of using hot beds for growing in England crops that it would not otherwise be possible to grow, or for extending the growing season of other crops, such as lettuces and peas, is something whose development is highly culturally embedded. The crucial material necessary, apart from ground (each frame he suggests should be 12 feet by 4 feet) together with wood and glass to make the frame, is stable manure (preferably from corn-fed horses bedded on wheat straw) or at least litter from cow stalls or pigsties. In other words, it is a technique developed when horses were a primary means of transport and source of motive power. It would be difficult to implement where this is no longer the case. It uses what would, in the context of the economy of a large country house, be a readily available material and exploits the fact that stable manure, in the process of decomposing into very fertile soil, generates substantial amounts of heat. Cobbett gives detailed instructions for managing the manure so as to generate a good 'fermentation'. As with almost all the techniques he discusses, this is a labour-intensive process.

Apart from detailed instructions for techniques of cultivation for each of 167 kitchen garden plants and fruits, Cobbett discusses the control of 'vermin' and, at some length, the question of seed. Under the discussion of peas, for example, there is advice about varieties and description of their differing characteristics. The advice includes suggestions about which varieties to sow and in what sequence to ensure supply for the longest possible season, as well as methods of cultivation. But Cobbett also notes that because, in a kitchen garden, it is always necessary to have more than one variety in bloom at the same time, it will not be possible to save seed very successfully. So, to produce one's own seed for the following year would require additional ground with well-separated plots for each variety. Here we see limits to the possible self-sufficiency of the kitchen gardener. To have a range of true-bred varieties available to the gardener presupposes in many cases a separate kind of growing, growing for seed production rather than for consumption. Cobbett does not advocate total reliance on seed merchants, but gives separate advice for each crop. While the existence either of seed merchants, or of some external source of seeds of known varieties, is assumed, the overall presumption is that the gardener will be self-sufficient, allowing part of the crop to go to seed, and with a reasonable degree of confidence about what that seed will grow into.

Contrast this nineteenth century approach to making fruit and vegetables available for as much of the year as possible with that whose evidence we see on late twentieth century supermarket shelves. Instead of relying on local growing and storing, exploiting varietal variation and varied growing techniques to extend the season, we find a very limited number of varieties grown all over the world and shipped to multiple, often very distant, destinations. Regional climate variations, together with refrigeration, and the availability of transport – shipping, rail, truck and airfreight – are used to ensure year round availability of both basic and more exotic foods. Many of the limited number of varieties now supplied have been the product of agricultural research, in particular of programmes of hybridization. Once hybrids are used growers must purchase new seed from the seed companies. They cannot hope to save seed from their own crop and grow the same variety in the following year. Many of these varieties have been selected for their transportability and appearance, their mass producibility – which includes the possibility of mechanical picking, disease and pest resistance, ease of processing, etc. – not for their flavour or nutritive value. Commercial growers must grow for the market and that allows bulk buyers (not consumers) to dictate what is grown. Bulk buyers, including food processors, are one group who have the capital to finance research and development of new varieties, varieties answering to their specifications. The scientific approach to food production becomes top down and centralized. It is not a matter of using locally developed procedures for maximizing production by exploiting varieties adapted to local conditions but of maximizing production of a uniform, consistent product, one designed to meet marketing and production needs, priorities set a long way from the site of production. To do this with standard varieties requires standardizing a growing environment – altering the environment, to conform to these standard conditions by the addition of chemicals, pesticides and water as necessary. But it is not *just* a question of altering the growing environment. There must also be alterations in farming practices and hence alterations in the organization of farmers' lives. Thus it was for its social consequences that the Green Revolution attracted most criticism, even when others have held it up as a triumph for science.

Because the Green Revolution has been held up both as an example of scientific achievement and as an example of all that is wrong with science, it will be useful for us to examine the sources of these differing valuations in more detail, but first we should take a wider look at the relations between technology, culture and politics.

5

TECHNOLOGY, CULTURE
AND POLITICS

The conflicting visions we spoke of earlier profoundly influence
how we view the relationship of technology to politics and other
culturally embedded practices. Both visions, we argued in Chapter
1, involve seriously distorted views of the nature and place of technology in the contemporary world. If we do not work from a more
realistic view of our technology, we will misunderstand how it
interacts with politics, culture and other social forces. We will, that is,
not only misunderstand technology, but culture, politics and society
generally. So our concern is not just abstractly philosophical; it has
concrete social and evaluative implications, as became evident in the
conclusions drawn in Chapter 2. There we argued that technologies
regularly embody values, norms and power relations. Their interconnections with culture and politics will be the subject of the present
chapter. Examples such as Davy's lamp, the introduction of a
hydraulic palm seed oil press in Nigeria, and even pasteurization
show that we cannot ignore the cultural embeddedness of technology.
Yet because the myth of value-free technology dies hard and because
the myth has little understood, though far-reaching, consequences,
the ways in which technology, culture and politics interact warrant
further exploration.

CULTURE AND HUMAN LIFE

Humans are social animals. That is, we thrive only if we participate
in a broad range of social and cultural activities. One who doesn't
is, as Aristotle (*Politics* Book I) says, either a 'brute' or a god, but
not a man. Life in a community, in short, is our natural milieu.
Those who see community life as a burden, an imposition that,
however necessary, limits freedom, deeply misunderstand our relation

116

to our community, and the culture it embodies. Mary Midgley makes the point forcefully: 'Culture is not opposed to freedom. It makes it possible'(Midgley, 1978, p. 287). For we cannot live *well* without culture – any more than an otter can thrive without swimming. Culture isn't decoration: our nature as humans demands that we create a culture if we don't have one and that we sustain it if we do. As anthropologists document, cultures are endlessly varied – though they all respond to common human needs: regulation of sexual impulse, control of violence, rites and rituals of passage, etc. To thrive, however, everyone needs to live in a *particular* flourishing culture. No one, of course, must accept every element of their culture. Far from it. Almost everyone sometimes challenges, reinterprets, flouts, twists, ignores, distorts or opposes *some* cultural products: that, too, is part of our nature.

Depending on one's purposes – even agenda – 'culture' and 'cultural' can denote sharply different domains. Writing in the 1860s, for instance, Matthew Arnold identified culture with a society's greatest intellectual and artistic achievements because, he believed, these elevate society beyond the brutal, crass and mundane. Clearly, this isn't a value-neutral description. Not only does it require criteria for distinguishing 'higher' from 'lower' – criteria which Arnold was happy to provide – but it almost inevitably relegates technology to the 'lower' forms of achievement in favour of science, which in turn takes second place to the 'arts'. Furthermore, its narrowness obscures the way in which high culture is shaped by, and in turn shapes, technology. Histories of culture, construed in this way, pay attention to the Bible and its translation into vernacular languages while ignoring Gutenberg's printing press which made it possible for everyone to read it.

According to another characterization, 'culture' refers to all those practices, art forms and representations considered in isolation from economic, social, political and technological backgrounds in which they flourish. In studying nineteenth century art, for instance, one might focus exclusively on the emotionalism, colour and spontaneous brush work of a French Romantic like Delacroix in rejection of the rationality, line and deliberated execution of a neo-classicist like David. While this focus and this understanding of culture has merit, it also turns attention away from both technology and politics. It takes nothing away from Mozart's indisputable genius to recognize how he composed for the instruments of his day in the context of princely courts.

We find Clifford Geertz more helpful. For him, 'culture' denotes 'an historically transmitted pattern of meanings embodied in symbols; a system of inherited conceptions expressed in symbolic forms by means of which [human beings] communicate, perpetuate, and develop their knowledge about and attitudes towards life' (Geertz, 1973, p. 89). This partially captures the sense in which technology can embody values and meaning. But it, too, unduly limits what we wish to capture by 'culture'. For, by focusing on conceptions, it stresses the mentalistic while underplaying the materiality of culture and the extent to which culture is embedded in and sustained by everyday practice. Culture does refer to ways in which we express ourselves in religion, narrative myths, language, sports and even body language, but it also includes characteristic ways in which people dress, farm, organize their society, make and use tools. Within this broader characterization we can distinguish, even if not wholly separate, various cultural forms, e.g. religious, political and aesthetic. So in 'culture' we shall include all those social and symbolic practices – artistic, religious, sporting, linguistic, political, labouring, child-rearing – in which people participate and which they have some ability to describe, however rudimentarily. (See Nerlich, 1989, p. 2.) Bees live complex social lives and make exceedingly beautiful hives. What they cannot do is describe or reflect on either. People can. They may misdescribe, misunderstand and misinterpret, though not everyone entirely and always. If cultures were wholly transparent, we would have no need for social scientists; if they were wholly opaque, we couldn't assess whether social scientists added to our understanding. Cultures are, as it were, translucent: we initially recognize ourselves in them 'through a glass darkly' hoping to see them and ourselves with greater clarity and less distortion.

We don't, of course, live in a 'culture' *per se*: we live in communities of various sizes and degrees of complexity, from small, nomadic villages to enormous mega-states. These communities embody, shape and reflect culture in its myriad forms. The cultural life of a people consists primarily of a set of practices, authority relations, institutions, habits, traditions, values and attitudes. We follow Alasdair MacIntyre in defining a 'practice' as a complex, demanding activity with (a) standards of excellence and (b) goods both internal and external to them (MacIntyre, 1984, pp. 175–8). Engineering, for instance, requires education, training and skill. A particular engineer can be successful both in terms of external goods (e.g. earning a living and acquiring prestige) and in terms of internal goods (e.g. designing

118

and building bridges that are economical, functional and elegant). Attaining internal goods requires that one submit to those standards of excellence that lie at the core of the practice, as these are articulated within a tradition. This necessarily places the practitioner within a social context, namely that of the historical tradition that has given rise to its standards, approaches, and ways of thinking and feeling.

Living practices change. Sometimes change is forced by external pressures, but often change is generated internally, as standards, approaches, ways of thinking and feeling are found wanting. Technology plays no small part in both external and internal changes. Arguably, for instance, the move away from realism to abstraction in art was hastened by the invention of the camera, and the invention of tubes of paint – another nineteenth century invention – created conditions for greater spontaneity and demanded less in terms of craft training. Technologies can also transform a practice from within. As instruments become more finely calibrated, for example, engineers raise their standards of tolerance which, in turn, enables them to design and build increasingly fine and economical devices.

Change is not always progress. Practices can atrophy or decay, and this, too, for external or internal reasons. Technology again plays a part. Navigational skills, for instance, become less important – or at least significantly different – as better devices for fixing location are invented. Today satellites enable unskilled navigators to know their position on the high seas within a matter of metres. Sometimes external goods overwhelm the internal goods of a practice leading to its decay. The need to 'publish or perish', some argue, has led to the corruption of scholarly practice. Practices, in short, never run on 'automatic pilot', at least not for very long. They need constant attention and renewal to thrive.

To flourish most practices need institutional support. A group of friends can get together with a minimum of fuss to play string quartets; a symphony orchestra cannot. It requires an organization of considerable complexity, whose exact nature depends on the wider economic, legal and political context in which it is to exist. In the United States such an orchestra must at least be legally incorporated, which means conforming to requirements specifying governance, relations of authority, limits of liability, and charitable status. The governing body will in all likelihood hire fund-raisers, publicists, financial advisers, attorneys, booking agents, librarians, programme annotators and sound engineers. As institutions inevitably take on a life of their own, practitioners and institutional officials often find themselves at odds. The governing body, for example, may shape programmes to reflect its own musical tastes, not that of the orchestra. Because time is expensive, orchestras often don't rehearse as extensively as conductors wish, precipitating a decline in standards. Here, too, technology plays a role. Many orchestras depend on recording contracts to make ends meet. Sophisticated recording techniques enable sound engineers to splice together discrete elements to make a symphony and even augment music once recorded, so the orchestra doesn't have the pressure – or sense of pride – of producing a single, sustained work. In a socialist country, such as the former USSR, orchestras were not subject to the same kind of economic pressures, but were, by being an integral part of the state system, subject to political control and were at the mercy of state bureaucrats.

Such interactions conspire to place practitioners and institutions at odds. Sometimes the tension can be creative; too often it stultifies, undermines or destroys. But it would be unrealistic to think either that most practices could endure without institutionalization or that practices and institutions could exist in perfect harmony. To this we must add a further complication. Those involved in the institutionalized life of a practice are often themselves practitioners! Sound engineers, attorneys, librarians, financial experts, for instance, have their own standards of excellence, their own internal goods. In living up to their standards and in realizing the goods of their practices, they may find themselves at loggerheads with those they were originally called on to serve. Similar remarks could be made about relations between other practices and the institutions on which they depend.

These observations suggest that technology plays an important role in nearly all aspects of culture, including politics. But how? Examples could be drawn from any area of social life. Recognizing that no facet of culture can be sharply separated from any other, here we will focus on only two domains, one concerning domestic political life, the other technological transfer from First to Third World nations. This not only gives us more than enough to examine, but it addresses concerns fundamental to liberal democracies.

TECHNOLOGY AND POLITICAL LIFE

Langdon Winner writes:

In the late twentieth century technology and society, technology and culture, technology and politics are by no means separate. They are closely woven together in a multiplicity of settings in which many forms of human living are dependent upon and shaped by technological devices and systems of various kinds. Our useful artifacts reflect who we are, what we aspire to be. At the same time, we ourselves mirror the technologies which surround us; to an increasing extent social activities and human consciousness are technically mediated.

(Winner, 1993, p. 284)

His insight helps clarify the ways in which technology and politics are 'woven together'.

First, politics clearly influences which technologies get developed (see Goldhaber, 1986). Military technologies provide the most obvious examples: nuclear bombs and submarines, radar-evading aircraft, 'smart' bombs, and 'Star Wars' laser weapons. Not only were none of these technologies inevitable, but without concerted political effort none would have been developed. Further, because of decisions to develop these particular technologies, other possible weapons systems were effectively consigned to the dustbin. For no nation has the intellect, imagination, will or money simultaneously to think through and develop more than a few possibilities. Political judgement clearly influences strategic thinking, and 'need' for new weapons grows out of chosen strategies. Although the Soviet Union and the United States knew which weapons systems the other was developing, for instance, each (for its own reasons) nevertheless concentrated on those most in accord with its own military traditions, risk assessments, organizational proclivities, and sense of the politically and morally possible.

For example, during the Cold War nuclear strategists developed a virtual theology of distinctions: for example, *Mutual Assured Destruction* and *No First Strike*. One fascinating and disturbing dispute concerned *Counter-Strike* vs. *Counter-Value*. Under counter-strike strategic weapons were targeted; under counter-value ordinary *people* were targeted as well, on the grounds that this terrorist threat would act as a more effective deterrent. Which weapons get developed depends in large part on which strategy wins political approval. But to win political approval, strategies must be convincingly sold to the electorate. And this accounts for much of the double-speak and propaganda associated with nuclear strategies and weapons. 'Counter-value', for instance, hardly conveys the horror of targeting major urban areas for obliteration; and charming names such as 'Minute-man' and 'Patriot' conjure up the tribal memories of Paul Revere, Patrick Henry, and other early American heroes. Technology plays an important role in selling these strategies to the public. Television is particularly influential in shaping how we view both the effective-ness and acceptability of whatever any interest group – governmental or otherwise – peddles. This is such a well-known story that there is no need to rehearse it here.

If the choice of military hardware is the most obvious illustration of the way in which politics influences technology, it isn't the only example. Wherever one looks, '[t]he state can be found promoting the introduction of technology, using it to sustain national prestige, deploying it to maintain internal and external security, and subsidiz-ing its research and development' (Street, 1992, p. 46). In the United States, for example, the supercollider and the genome project could not survive let alone thrive without massive governmental support. The development of Concorde, the British–French joint venture, illustrates how non-economic considerations – e.g. national pride, a desire to cement international relations, political vanity, a perceived need to revive public enthusiasm, and a desire to keep a nation's best brains at home – conspire to lead governments to opt for technologies which made little sense from the beginning. Large projects have the advantage of appealing both to the public's imagin-ation and to politicians' desire to provide tangible economic benefits to their constituents, whether or not it serves the broader public interest.

Of course, not all governmental influence on the direction, fund-ing and regulation of technology leads to 'waste, fraud and abuse'; far from it. But what cannot be denied is that the state is deeply implicated in technology development at every stage. The influence is often indirect. By creating favourable tax breaks or tariff walls, for instance, government makes it possible for firms developing particular new technologies to grow and prosper; by not extending similar breaks to other technologies, it discourages their growth and devel-opment.

Legal decisions, too, shape how technology is used and under-stood. In the United States, for instance, governmental bodies may not eavesdrop on conversation using ordinary telephones without court authorization; but what about conversation conducted over cordless phones? A recent case in the United States addressed just this question. A lower court held that such a conversation – because broadcast by radio waves – was 'analogous to carrying on an oral communication in a loud voice or with a megaphone'. It followed earlier decisions that had ruled that cordless phone users could have no reasonable expectation of privacy in their calls because of the ease by which the calls could be monitored. At the time of those decisions, some cordless phones had a range of over 700 feet and were subject to interception by standard radio scanners, radio receivers, and other cordless phones (many of which were pre-set to the same frequency). An appellate court, however, focused on the important role that telecommunications play in today's society. It noted that 'wireless' technology is a fast growing area in telecommunications. According to the court, 'the decision as to whether cordless telephone conversations are protected by the Fourth Amendment [against 'unreasonable searches and seizures'] may ultimately determine whether any telephone conversation is protected by the Fourth Amendment'. Further and significantly, this court noted that more recent cordless phones employ an evolved technology; many are limited in range to about 60 feet, 'barely beyond the average house or yard', and are no longer pre-set to the same frequency. Since cordless phones now transmit on frequencies not used by commercial radio, conventional radios can no longer intercept cordless communications. Although the conversations can be monitored by radio scanners, the court further noted that only a small percentage of the populace own such scanners. In addition, new cordless phones also incorporate the ability to scramble their signals. Respecting the new technology, the appellate discerned that, 'Surely the reasonableness of an expectation of privacy becomes greater when the conversation can only be intercepted using specialized equipment not possessed by the average citizen. . . . [I]n spite of the fact that a defendant uses a cordless phone', continued the court, 'the circumstances may show that he also has a reasonable expectation of privacy'.[1]

Here we see courts struggling to reconceptualize wireless telecommunications from one category to another. This process continues, and will involve Congress, business interests and law enforcement organizations, as well as technological experts. Once the eventual result becomes embodied in laws, regulations and – most importantly – business practices and conversational traditions, the outcome will appear as natural as it seems artificial and contrived now.

John Street shows how the state is involved with technology as regulator, as customer, and as underwriter.[2] In whatever guise, the state encourages, discourages, directs and shapes. As we have just seen, as regulator the state can determine whether ordinary and cordless telephones will be treated alike. But the effects can be even more extensive. Lewis and Booth (1989) show how differently the United Kingdom and United States have regulated public airwaves. Until the Thatcher revolution, the United Kingdom looked on broadcasting as a public service, so authorities carefully controlled who could broadcast and what they could broadcast. In the United States the development of radio and television was seen as a commercial enterprise, with listeners regarded as potential customers; airwaves, consequently, are far less regulated. Street argues that this difference reflects different assumptions about the role and responsibilities of government, different interests surrounding the development of radio in each state (especially differing military considerations), by different patent laws, and differing ways of distributing access to airwaves (Street, 1992, pp. 49–50).

The state is also a leading customer of technology. One thinks immediately of the vast sums spent on military and police technology, but the state is a leading customer of technology across the board. Ross Perot, for example, became a billionaire by selling software to the US government for use in processing medicare forms. Even foreign aid involves the state as customer. In 1986, for instance, India received £65 million in aid in the form of twenty-one Westland W-30 helicopters intended for offshore oil exploration – paid for by the British government and ultimately, of course, the British taxpayer. The state underwrites enormous chunks of technological innovation and development, and not just for military purposes. Sometimes this is done passively through tax breaks. But the state also funds technological innovation and development more directly through alliances with universities, research institutes and commercial interests. And when the state is involved, political choices based on political interests and values play a central role in determining what does and does not get funded.

There is an evident danger in speaking of the *state*, *government* and *politics* in the abstract. All are made up of numerous individuals, alliances and pressure groups vying against each other and forming temporary alliances to shape institutions and policies. All involve individuals intent on ensuring that *their* vision and values should be furthered by technology. So any serious investigation of how government and politics shapes and is shaped by technology must attend to *particular* people, alliances and groups to discern their particular motives and intentions. For instance, the long-lasting birth control implant, *Norplant* – hailed as a solution to teenage pregnancy – has been condemned by some African-Americans as a not-so-subtle technique of keeping minorities from outnumbering whites, especially in large cities. Whether true or not, critics rightly draw attention to *other* implications of this technological fix than those welcomed by its advocates.[3]

If political choices shape technology, it is equally true that technologies shape political choices. New weapon systems can obviously create new political opportunities: states possessing nuclear weapons, for example, have political options other nations envy. Civilian technologies also transform the political landscape. So-called 'public access' cable television, for instance, enables certain groups – previously on the fringes of political life – to launch public appeals beyond the imagination of orators on Hyde Park Corner, creating novel political opportunities and problems. On the one hand, it allows dissidents to bypass the gate-keepers of political orthodoxy; on the other hand, it also allows hate groups to spread their message of racial hatred. Can we devise a principled way of permitting the one but not the other, without seriously compromising a commitment to freedom of expression? No one can now answer this question with any degree of confidence.

It is commonplace that political and cultural values are expressed in language, and the ideas so expressed are subject to intense public scrutiny and debate. Political language reveals a great deal about us: our commitments, our hopes, our fears, and where we believe we fit in the order of things. We have argued that the same is true of artefacts. Our technologies, however, speak silently, covertly, and are seldom seen as central to political or cultural discourse. Langdon Winner suggests two reasons why this is so. First, most people do accept the instrumentalist account of technological devices: a tool is just a tool. If our argument so far has been sound, this may partially explain why technology hasn't seemed an appropriate object of political and cultural attention; it is, however, no justification. Second, and more sinister, is Winner's suggestion that the ideologies embedded in things tends to be hidden because 'they have been implanted there by those who do not wish those ideas to be known or widely discussed. The apparent solidity of useful things sometimes provides a mask for persons and groups who wish to exercise power while avoiding responsibility' (Winner, 1993, p. 289). Winner's charge is sometimes well taken; for example, 'spiking' cigarettes with highly addictive nicotine. In such cases those developing and peddling technologically enhanced objects go to great lengths to keep their interests hidden from public view. But if, as maintained earlier, it is natural – even inevitable – for individuals and groups to embody their interests and values in what they make, then ordinarily no conspiracy need be posited. For we all, quite unconsciously, embody our ideologies, interests and values in the technologies we make and employ. So Winner's indictment is too sweeping. Still, Winner reminds us that those with power often use it irresponsibly. And he is right to insist that unconscious interests, values and commitments should be brought to light and subjected to critical scrutiny. How values, ideas and interests embodied in technologies remain hidden from view becomes a bit less mysterious if we reflect that many technologies take their place comfortably *as part of the ordinary everydayness of our surroundings*. It is this more than anything that obscures the political and cultural message of so much technology.

Yet how can concealed values become part of public discussion, debate and deliberation? *If* technology shapes forms of life, *if* it reflects not only who we are, but what we aspire to be, and *if* it mediates our relationship to the world, then which technologies get developed for what purposes must be a central concern for any democracy. For no democracy can thrive if the deepest and most far-reaching questions facing it remain hidden. Winner does not exaggerate when he says that modern civilization has systematically ignored how fundamental questions facing the body politic appear in the guise of 'neutral' technologies (Winner, 1993, p. 289). And we follow him in urging that we cultivate ways of democratizing technological policy making and innovation. Winner's 'three maxims' summarize his approach: (1) *No innovation without representation*; (2) *No engineering without political deliberation*; (3) *No means without ends*.

1 **No innovation without representation**. Here Winner echoes American patriots, who objected to British taxation without representation. The suggestion is partly that technological innovation involves a kind of hidden tax. As we shall see when we look at the automobile, this is literally true: the private automobile is heavily subsidized through government (and hence taxpayer) subsidy. The point goes deeper, however. Those most affected by a technology often have the least to say about its development and use, as Davy's lamp illustrates. Were the sentiments of miners consulted, the lamp would surely have been redesigned, if not

abandoned until better ventilation systems had been installed. In this respect, however, times have not changed much. Today, it is true, technological innovations must meet governmental safety standards in most industrialized nations. But this has not eliminated, and cannot eliminate, all risks. The effects of widespread and long term use of a new material or product are in many cases impossible to predict with any kind of precision. Some effects which could be foreseen are not because the research focus is on effects relevant to the purchasers' concerns, and not those relevant to the concerns of the people who will have to work or live with the material or product. Safety regulations, of necessity, are framed in general language to cover the introduction of both known types of devices and materials and unanticipated technological developments. They cannot, therefore, direct attention at all the possible problems that might arise in connection with a specific innovation. Part of the problem is that the *buyer* of innovative technology is not always – not even usually – the *user* of it, as Davy's lamp again illustrates. Because interests of buyers and users often diverge if not conflict, what seems a boon to one may be a bane to the other. Just as we no longer tolerate taxation without political representation, so a robust democracy should not allow technological innovation without representation, both at political and shop floor levels.

2 **No engineering without political deliberation**. Most applied science and engineering occurs without any political deliberation. Oddly, military engineering probably receives the most political deliberation, though it is usually kept in the hands of a select group and not widely discussed. Still, there are occasionally public, political debates about whether to build a certain bomber, missile system or space platform. Generally, however, civil engineering goes on outside the spotlight of public inspection and therefore political discussion. Civil technological innovation goes on in the 'private' sphere, and proponents of the distinction between public and private take the distinction literally. What a private corporation wishes to do is *private*, where that means 'nobody else's business'. The absoluteness of the distinction, however, cannot be maintained. Liberal democratic societies find attractive the slogan that what consenting adults do in the privacy of their own homes is no one's business but their own. Even this slogan has limits. We don't admit that it extends to child abuse, for example. When applied to engineering, the distinction between public and private

becomes even more problematic because the *effects* of private engineering decisions spread far beyond corporate front doors.

3 **No means without ends**. To consider ends in isolation from the means needed to attain them amounts to sheer sentimentality or wishful thinking. To divorce means in isolation from intended or probable ends constitutes a form of wilful blindness. Scientists and engineers face the latter temptation frequently. They can become so caught up in the intellectual challenges of their projects that they ignore, deny or suppress knowledge of how the science or technology will most likely be used. Nothing better illustrates this temptation than Robert Oppenheimer's remark that building the atomic bomb posed 'a sweet technical problem'. He was, of course, absolutely correct and it would be absurd to fault anyone for becoming deeply engaged by working on cutting-edge technology. Yet we also need to keep in view – as Oppenheimer did – the ends for which the technology is being developed. Later, when we consider the case of Joseph Rotblat, we shall see what complications that introduces. Here we need only stress that techno-science carries with it moral and political responsibilities as well as engrossing challenges.

For these maxims to become more than slogans entails far more democratization than those with power are likely to relinquish graciously. For it would require far more open access to business and industry than prevails almost anywhere, at least on a large scale.[4] Yet unless our understanding of what constitutes a *public matter* is extended to include what profoundly affects the public, it is unlikely that fundamental change can occur: we will be left with picking up the pieces and trying to regulate the worst effects brought about by 'externalities'. The fact that this kind of democratization would require changes in the political status of business and industry serves as a reminder of the tight connections between economics and politics, connections which have been strengthened by technology development policies which have focused on seeking to use research science as the base for technological innovation. The costs of this kind of research have become prohibitive, so excluding all but governments and large trans-national companies from playing the role of funding agencies. The extent to which government-funded research is or is not dominated by the economic imperatives of big business and the extent to which it is or is not able to be responsive to public concerns thus has a crucial bearing on the extent to which it would be possible for these maxims to become more than slogans. The other important question is whether it is inevitable that technological innovation should be so expensive that it is effectively put beyond the control of all except those with vast financial resources. That is, is the top-down approach the only one which is realistically available now and for the foreseeable future? This is a question to which we will return in the more concrete context of asking to what extent it is possible, by technical innovation, to alleviate the problem of hunger.

Politics can be distinguished from economics but it cannot be separated from it. Labour and industry have much at stake in all the examples we've considered, and they exert considerable influence to ensure that political decisions reflect their economic interests. Labour and management find themselves on the same side when their interests coincide; for example, when fighting tariffs that keep their products out of foreign markets. Frequently, of course, economic interests do not coincide, and we find them at loggerheads over any technological innovations that will likely lead to large scale unemployment. Technological innovation within industry in developed countries has, as we have already seen, been driven in the direction of job reduction by demands for increased efficiency and productivity. Fewer people are used to produce more goods or deliver more services. The idea that this is desirable, that it constitutes a form of social progress, is linked to the low status of work in the conception of what constitutes true human fulfilment. However, the application of this ideology of progressive social development is flawed because it ignores the reality of the deprivations suffered under existing social and economic conditions by those who are without work. It is not therefore surprising that labour movements have resisted technological innovations which threaten jobs. But the structure of the scenario has inevitably cast labour (especially organized labour) in the role of an anti-progressive force, and management as the progressive, pro-technology force. The issue which is submerged by this type-casting is whether there might not be economically viable ways of organizing the production of goods or the provision of services, using technologies which have been designed not to replace a workforce, but to enhance its capacities and improve its working conditions. Again this is a question about whether there really is only one ineluctable scenario for technological development (as both pessimists and optimists often claim). If there is not, then it is clear that some of the choices to be made about directions of technological development are in fact political, not technical choices, which is an issue that arises quite crucially in the context of agricultural development and to which we will thus return.

Lest we be tempted to oversimplify, however, we will first look at a very different kind of example: the automobile. This is to serve as a reminder that technology, culture, politics and economics can become intertwined in many different ways. The exact way in which these interconnections are formed has always been to do with the particular technology and the particular economic, cultural and political climate into which it is introduced.

THE AUTOMOBILE

Perhaps nothing better illustrates the integration of technology, culture, politics and economics than the automobile. As we noted earlier, automobiles reinforce and glorify values of individualism: mobility, privacy and control. They make it possible for us to go where we wish when we wish and, if we wish, by ourselves. Behind the wheel, we are in control of our route, destination and speed. Automobiles allow us to live far from our work, so that those with automobiles can escape (and ignore) the noise, squalor and inconveniences of city life. Because the vast majority of all motor vehicles licensed in the United States and the United Kingdom are automobiles and because they eclipse all other forms of transportation, we may speak of a *car-* or *auto-centred* transport system.[5] All told, there are nearly a half *billion* automobiles worldwide (Freund and Martin, 1994). Because automobiles are so much a part of our landscape, they seem natural, ordinary. We have difficulty believing that less than a century ago, cars were a rare, luxury item. Yet they now dominate the transportation systems of every developed nation.

Statistics reveal the dominance, and some consequences, of a car-centred system of transport:[6]

- There are 1.7 automobiles for every man, woman and child in the United States; Western Europe isn't far behind with a ratio of 2.5:1 (*Motor Vehicle Manufacturers Association*, 1992, pp. 8–41).
- Nearly 60 per cent of all US households had *two* or more vehicles in 1990, compared to about 10 per cent in 1960.
- In the United States, 11 million cars are junked annually.
- About 10 per cent of arable land in the United States is taken up

by the automobile infrastructure; in Los Angeles, two-thirds of the land space belongs to the automobile.

● Each mile of roadway requires about 25 acres of land; railways, by comparison, use about 85 per cent less land yet trains can carry 67 per cent more passengers than automobiles.

● Automobiles consume over 10 per cent of all energy used in the United States. More generally, in 1985 the transport sector consumed 6 per cent of all oil used in the United States; 44 per cent of oil used in Western Europe; 5 per cent of oil used in Japan; and 49 per cent of oil used in Third World countries (Renner, 1988, p. 16).

● Automobiles account for one-fifth of the dollar value of all retail sales in the United States; in 1989, roughly 14 per cent of the workforce was involved with some aspect of motor vehicle transportation; and in 1990, nearly 18 per cent of total television advertising in the United States was devoted to selling automobiles (Freund and Martin, 1994, p. 135).

● Road vehicles accounted for 37 per cent of the total metric tons of all air pollutants from controllable emissions. According to World Bank figures, 76 per cent of the 4.4 million tons of pollutant emissions produced by humans in Mexico City were attributable to motor vehicles in 1989 (Faiz *et al.*, 1990).

● Roadside dust in Nigeria has a higher lead content than leaded paint (Freund and Martin, 1994, p. 31). (While new cars in the United States no longer use leaded gas, a billion gallons of leaded gas are still sold, largely for older cars (Hilts, 1991, p. 7). Both the United States and the United Kingdom continue to export leaded gasoline to developing nations while curtailing sales in their own countries.)

● Vehicular deaths are the leading killer of Americans aged 5 to 43 years. Motor vehicle accidents were the fifth leading cause of death among Americans in 1989, ahead of diabetes, suicide, AIDS or homicide (Freund and Martin, 1994, p. 6). In the United States, the odds of dying in a motor vehicle accident are three times greater than dying by homicide (*The Philadelphia Inquirer*, 24 July 1994, E3).

Statistics alone cannot reveal the automobile's political and cultural significance. Auto-centred transport is not apolitical: it was made possible by political and economic decisions and even now has widespread political dimensions. Much of this is hidden, partly on

131

purpose, but more because the system combines public and private consumption masking total costs. For example, without government subsidies in terms of land purchase, road construction and maintenance, and policing, automobile transportation would be far more costly than it is. Freund and Martin cite several studies showing that:

> The total public expenditure for these services in the United States was estimated at $300 billion in 1990, about 7 percent of the GNP. Only 62 percent of these costs were recovered from driver (user) fees such as gasoline taxes, leaving a subsidy of $114 billion in 1990.
>
> (Freund and Martin, 1994, p. 131)

Indirect subsidies in terms of governments' picking up the tab for social costs resulting from car-centred transport add to this subsidy: health costs associated with pollution and accidents; environmental costs; disposal costs; and congestion – which alone was estimated to cost $150 billion in the United States in 1990. As Freund and Martin (1994, p. 132) observe, 'Contrary to the popular myth that auto-centred transport is the outcome of technical imperatives, consumer choice, and free enterprise, in fact it would not have become entrenched without the benefit of massive government subsidy.' They cite a study by Marcia D. Lowe (Lowe, 1990, p. 4) that 40 per cent of the expenses of the Pasadena (California) police department are auto related; were they permitted to impose a tax to offset these costs, it would add 39 cents to every gallon of gasoline sold within the city.

Government subsidies are not accidental. They are the result of political decisions. In the United States, the Interstate Highway Act of 1956 initiated massive 'freeway' construction, not because of a groundswell of popular demand, but because of a carefully orchestrated campaign by car makers, road builders, trucking companies, and the oil industry. They skilfully exploited Cold War fears by appealing to national defence needs in arguing for the necessity of adding 41,000 miles of highway. Perhaps Dwight Eisenhower had this in mind when he warned of a 'military–industrial complex' in his final address to the nation as President. Peter Freund and George Martin similarly identify three interest groups that dominate transport policies, which they call 'the auto–industrial complex': the private-sector lobby; central city business interests, 'which seek to facilitate access to businesses and to increase property values in downtown areas' (Freund and Martin, 1994, p. 134); and public-sector highway and transport departments, including professionals and bureaucrats whose jobs depend on a car-centred transport system.

It was not always thus. In the United States, at least, mass transit dominated urban transport well into the 1930s. Thirty years later, however, urban electric railways were replaced by buses and cars. Freund and Martin tell us how:

> General Motors played a leading role in this change, through the National City Bus Lines and other of its subsidiaries. The 1,100–mile Pacific Electric Red Car System in Los Angeles and Orange Counties was purchased and torn up by GM, Firestone Tire and Rubber Company, and Standard Oil Company of California; the system was gone by 1962. Similarly dismantled was the Key System Lines connecting San Francisco and East Bay cities.
>
> (Freund and Martin, 1994, p. 135)[7]

Governments either allow such things to happen or actively encourage it. At least in the United States, we know that PACs (Political Action Committees) and special interest groups buy access to politicians at every level of government. Between 1981 and 1988, for instance, PACs opposed to clean air legislation gave political candidates $23 million; GM alone spent $1.8 million to oppose clean air legislation. Langdon Winner draws our attention to the overpasses on the parkways on Long Island, New York. Designed by the late Robert Moses, master builder in New York of 'public' works from the 1920s to the 1970s, they were deliberately built with a low clearance. This effectively prevented public buses – whose passengers are predominantly poor and African–American – from using the parkways to get to Jones Beach, an acclaimed Moses-designed 'public' beach (Hall, 1988, quoted in Freund and Martin, 1994, p. 117). Incidents like these – and they are not unusual, only striking – suggest that we should take with a large grain of salt claims that technological innovation and development drives itself.

What is often overlooked politically is that benefits and burdens of automobiles are not equally shared: benefits tend to be privatized, burdens socialized. Even in the United States, not everyone owns, or can own, a car: the poor, the elderly, the disabled, the uninsurable, and children are all effectively bared from the existential pleasures and economic necessity of owning an automobile. Costs, however, are distributed more widely, being borne by those who drive only a few thousand miles yearly out of necessity, don't drive at all out of choice, or cannot drive.

Voices calling attention to the 'malefits'[8] of an auto-centred transport system have trouble being heard. This is so for several reasons. Given that the livelihoods of so many people in advanced industrial societies depend on automobiles, the message isn't welcome; heeding it might mean loss of job, home and respect. (It is instructive to see how difficult it is, for similar reasons, to close military bases, cease manufacture of nuclear weapons, cut back on the number of people in uniform even when it is conceded that the predominant argument for a robust military – a belligerent Soviet Union – has ceased to exist.) Further, the automobile has become a necessity for many people. As mass transit systems have shrunk in service and scale, many people have no choice but to purchase a car. Although what is rational individually may be collectively irrational, no individual can or should be expected to harm him- or herself when there is no reason to expect his or her sacrifice, by itself, matters much. These people can hear, but, unless practical alternatives become available, they have little reason to listen. And the auto-industrial complex has no reason to hurt itself by suggesting alternative modes of transportation. Here politicians too often abdicate leadership, and simply repeat the refrain of those who, if they are crossed, can ensure their electoral defeat. The auto-industrial complex, moreover, does what it can – through advertising, lobbying and manipulation – to obscure the costly and destructive consequences of an auto-centred system. Finally, both the ordinariness of the car and its potent cultural significance mask and transform it into something much more than 'a hunk of junk'.

The bare statistics cited at the beginning of this section give only a sketchy picture of the enormous impact of automobiles on society. It is only a slight exaggeration to refer to the result as a *car-* or *auto-centred culture*, not merely an auto-centred transport system. Like capitalism, the motor car has insinuated itself into the fabric of society, so that we have difficulty even imagining a world where automobiles aren't king. On one level, for instance, a car-centred culture appears democratic and helps level social differences. True, some cars cost five or six times more than others, and that sets the owner of a luxury car apart from the masses. Still, low-priced autos can take one as far and (nearly) as fast as a luxury car. As Freund and Martin note, however, 'Autos are costly to buy and operate, they impose their social and environmental costs unequally, and they dominate the social organization of space to the disadvantage of many people' (Freund and Martin, 1994, p. 56).

The latter needs elaboration. Sixty years ago, a 9 year old child would be expected to go to familiar places, or even downtown, by foot, bike or bus. Comparing 1971 to 1990, one set of researchers in the United Kingdom found that space usable by children had actually *decreased*. Parents gave increased traffic as their principal reason for curtailing their children's mobility: 'personal freedom and choice arising from widening car ownership has been gained at the cost of freedom and choice for children' (Hillman *et al.*, 1990, p. 106). Thus, at least in this respect, children mature more slowly than just prior to World War II.

Highways are not alone in eating up space; so do malls, which are a direct consequence of a car-centred culture. Because people live in suburbia or exurbia, because cities have become clogged with traffic – both factors leading to the decline of cities – malls now ring large urban areas. Both they and their parking lots gobble up space. Not only do malls usually blight the landscape, but they create their own significant environmental problems, from runoff problems (leading to flooding) to the destruction of natural habitat. And, of course, they themselves create a need for more cars and more highways. For how can one reach a suburban mall unless by car?

Automobiles have been particularly hard on women. We mentioned above that an auto-centred culture curtails the freedom of children to explore beyond their immediate neighbourhood. Consequently, this not only slows the maturation of children, but turns mothers into chauffeuse to and from school, to and from shops, to and from malls. This, too, adds to the hidden cost of cars. But doesn't the car at least liberate women from the confines of the home? An editorial in the *Economist* proclaimed that the automobile is the 'greatest mobile force for freedom in the rich democracies', a liberator of women.[9] Unfortunately, the *Economist* overlooks ways in which the automobile negatively affects women's lives. Judy Wajcman notes that 'with the advent of the car, home-delivery services and corner stores gradually disappeared to be replaced by car-oriented supermarket complexes resulting in a significant increase in the proportion of time women spend on consumption activities' (Wajcman, 1993, p. 129).

Where public transportation does exist, it favours men over women, and is especially hard on mothers. Transit systems are designed to move large numbers of people from home to work and back again. Mothers, however, often work part-time, so needing to travel at times when public transportation operates sporadically. Further, their job opportunities are frequently limited by the availability of public transport, since fewer women than men own cars, especially poor, single mothers and older women. The dominance of the automobile and the correlative decline in the quantity and quality of public transport, moreover, often places more women at risk. They are especially vulnerable to sexual harassment and violence while using or waiting for public transport. As noted at a forum on Women and Transport in 1988:

> Urban motorways and rural trunk roads cut through women's lives, driving a noisy, polluting, dangerous wedge between their homes and workplaces, schools and health centres, causing them to walk roundabout routes, through hostile subways or over windy bridges, diverting and lengthening bus journeys, and creating unsafe, no-go areas of blank walls and derelict spaces.
>
> (Kramarae, 1988, p. 121)

So women, even more than men, *need* a car if only for protection, since large American and many European cities are unsafe for pedestrians.

The disappearance of the neighbourhood shop, home delivery services, and the decline of public transportation adversely affect the elderly. Often unable to drive, negotiate busy streets on foot, or use inadequate public transportation, elderly men and women find themselves confined to their homes or apartments, wholly dependent on the goodwill of relatives, neighbours, or social services to meet the most basic needs, including the need for fellowship. They are subject to most of the disadvantages younger women face, and more. A similar story could be told about the disabled.

Not only does an auto-centred culture compress space, it also compresses time. For as we live further and further from our work, we spend more of our time commuting. We also spend significant chunks of time in cars ferrying non-drivers – children especially – from place to place. And we spend increasing amounts of time stalled in traffic: in 1990, for instance, the *average* California driver wasted 84 hours per year locked in traffic jams and spent more than $1,000 per year in wasted time and fuel.[10] London rush-hour traffic averages about 7 miles per hour – about as fast as a horse-drawn carriage of the previous century. Still, even if automobiles don't save time getting us to town or across town, they do, generally, get us across country with astonishing speed. We relish this 'time saved'. Even this is misleading, however. For time spent driving long distances is time spent *not* doing something else. Even travel by train or bus, for instance, frees drivers to read, doze or engage in more relaxed conversation. So we must treat conclusions about time saved with caution.

Given that we have become a car-centred culture, driving long distances has become a virtual necessity: friends and family no longer live nearby, and are only conveniently accessible by car. So it isn't surprising that there is a genuine 'need' for large, fast, comfortable cars on wide, expensively maintained motorways. In the United States motorways are euphemistically called 'freeways'. And so they are, at least in the sense that no one has to pay directly to use them and they give car drivers freedom to go where and when they wish. Costs are well hidden in petrol taxes, county and state taxes, and governmental subsidies. At some level, of course, everyone knows this. Yet, at another level, few wish to confront the true economic costs. Imagine our dismay if our cars, like taxis, were equipped with meters showing the true costs of operating an automobile! Highway costs are only part of the *public* story, as we've seen. *Private* costs also add to the expense: insurance and depreciation, for instance. No meter could easily calculate *indirect*, though undeniable real, costs. Were Western nations less dependent on foreign oil, for instance, it is at least arguable that the recent war against Iraq would have been avoided, saving both money and lives. Exxon was (rightly) chastised for its negligence in the Alaskan oil spill, but we cannot expect a vast sea transport system of oil *without* significant spills.

The alliance of those whose livelihood depends on a robust auto-mobile-centred culture helps obscure these costs. They also feed on the cultural symbolism of the automobile: freedom, individualism, mobility, speed, power and privacy. It is commonplace, moreover, to remark that automobiles are seen as having sex appeal and as both revealing and reinforcing social status. That this potent combination of symbols is similarly aligned in all economically advanced nations illustrates just how un-neutral, value-laden automotive technology is. And the automobile itself helps us run from the enormous problems our cities face: when the city becomes unpleasant, we move. While this is, again, rational for any individual, it is a disaster for cities and those who must remain behind.

Our reliance on automobiles also obscures the way in which they impose a social order on us. As John Adams observes:

> Developments in transport and communications have already necessitated many social controls. Speed limits, blood alcohol limits, driving tests and licences, parking restrictions, laws to regulate noise and fumes, laws permitting the compulsory purchase of land for transport developments, compulsory vaccination, and the vast apparatus of customs and immigration are only a few of the most obvious social controls made necessary by increasing mobility.
>
> (Adams, 1981, p. 233)

While celebrating the benefits cars bring, we therefore must not overlook their malefits. More important for our present purpose, however, is simply to see the inextricable web of automobiles, politics and culture. We spoke earlier of techno-science; the automobile provides us with a specimen example of techno-culture.

TECHNOLOGICAL TRANSFER

As used here, 'technological transfer' refers to the export of technologies from countries rich in techno-science to countries, generally poor, lacking sophisticated techno-science. Roughly, we have in mind technologies exported to so-called *developing* or *Third World* countries from *developed* or *First World* countries. (The italicized words are themselves revealing of a certain bias. Better, perhaps, is the *north–south* transfer, though if this simply stands for a coded reference, it does not improve matters much.) This is clearly arbitrary, of course, because technology has been transferred from people to people since before recorded history. Yet the contemporary history of colonialism and Western domination of poor countries in Asia, Africa and Latin America justifies this restriction. While we believe that the central points are fully generalizable to other contexts of technological transfer, they remain to be tested by a thorough historical study. We also avoid, though not entirely, the contentious economic issues surrounding 'dependency theory'. In its incarnation as 'technological dependency' it means that poor economies have to import machines and, consequently, have to stimulate exports of primary goods artificially to generate necessary foreign exchange. Critics of technology transfer conclude that dependent nations are thus held hostage to the economic interests of First World nations and multinational corporations. Proponents point to the successful transformation of the 'newly industrialized countries' of Asia and Latin America as refutation. As we say, we will not enter into this controversy directly. To do so would take us far beyond the aims of our own study.

We saw in Chapter 4, and again here, that there are no universal technologies. Instead, as the Sri Lankan engineer/political economist, Susantha Goonatilake, notes, 'particular technologies carry within them the scars of conflicts, compromises and particular social solutions reached by the particular society [in which they were developed]' (Goonatilake, 1984, p. 121). Not many recognize this truth, including many who are most harmed by the introduction of Western technology into the developing world. Goonatilake demonstrates that countries as disparate as the Soviet Union in the early decades of the twentieth century and India since decolonization have viewed Western technologies with both admiration and envy. Goonatilake believes this admiration and envy goes deep, a claim needing further evidence. Without question, however, those in power and their associates have this attitude. And because there are such great power imbalances in many of these countries, it is the voice of the powerful that counts most.

'In the process of adoption', Goonatilake notes, 'the particular technology that grew up within Europe has been perceived as universal and ahistorical by latecomers to the development process' (Goonatilake, 1984, p. 121). If we are right that techno-science is far from a universal, ahistorical system, one consequence of the absorption of technologies into a developing world will be cultural dependence and a form of cultural colonialism. By swallowing undigested a technology from another culture, a developing nation often also swallows social and power relations that are inextricably bound up with it. Goonatilake offers us a striking metaphor to demonstrate his thesis:

> technology, because it carries the scars of the history of its society of origin and is in fact history in an encapsulated form, acts as a social gene, i.e., as a carrier of social relations from one society to another.
>
> (Goonatilake, 1984, p. 122)

Goonatilake concentrates exclusively on class relations. This is too limiting. The 'social gene' carries much more, from intimate personal values to broad commitments regarding the nature and place of enquiry, science, medicine, reason, tradition and even religion. To continue with the metaphor, sometimes the host rejects the transferred gene; sometimes the gene mutates, and deforms the host; on other occasions, the gene interacts with the host in highly innovative, beneficial ways. The implications of introducing this kind of social gene into a traditional culture are almost always surprising.

We saw this with the well-intentioned introduction of a hydraulic palm-oil press into a Nigerian community. In that instance, the values carried by the gene were rejected, at what cost to traditional community values we do not know. In the case of the introduction of railways in colonial India by the British, the intention was less benign. They were introduced to transport troops quickly to quell rebellions and to carry raw materials to ports for transportation home. But railways caught the imagination of ordinary Indians, and quickly became integrated into the warp and woof of that enormous nation.

Sometimes the host absorbs the gene, but with less happy consequences. In either case, however, Goonatilake rightly concludes that 'a technology which has ingrained within it the historical experience of a particular society tends to rebuild aspects of the society which gave birth to it when transferred to another' (Goonatilake, 1984, p. 133). Results vary from the beneficial to the comic and catastrophic. At least in the short term, the widespread introduction of automobiles and buses into Sri Lanka, for example, has had deleterious consequences. Roads have to be built, often by hand. In Sri Lanka, for instance, barefoot men wielding sledgehammers and chisels break up large boulders into stones and then women smash the stones into variously sized pebbles using hand tools. No protective goggles or shoes are worn by either, which results in serious injuries. Stones are then hand carried to the construction site and laboriously laid in place to form the foundation of the road bed. Once the roads are built, cars and buses must be bought. Since the country is poor, 'reconditioned' cars and buses must be imported, at a considerable cost in foreign exchange, usually from Japan. Used, diesel-burning buses are spectacular polluters. In a hot, humid climate where villages are strung out along roads and where houses and shops have open windows, residents inhale the pollutants day in and day out. (Archaeologists find that remote ancient sites have suffered more damage in the last twenty years than the previous 500.) Automobiles and buses share narrow roads with pedestrians and ox-carts, with predictable results; ill-trained drivers of over-crowded buses only add to the high rate of fatal accidents.

Do the benefits outweigh the malefits? As the per capita income is only about a dollar a day, a private automobile is out of reach for most citizens and, because of expense, privately owned buses are often unroadworthy. Still, buses – both public and private – do enable large numbers of people to travel further afield than ever before. And, with time, roads, vehicles and safety may improve. Here we stress only that the wide-scale introduction of automobiles and buses wasn't from the bottom up, but from the top down and primarily benefits those already relatively well-off and Westernized.

The synergistic relation among technologies in Sri Lanka is further illustrated by hydroelectric dams. Because it is near the equator, Sri Lankans enjoy twelve hours of daylight throughout the year and, until recently, there hasn't been a great demand for electricity, especially in villages. The Jayawardena government, however, launched an ambitious development programme to harness the Mahawelli River. Several nations – including Britain and Germany – eagerly agreed to build dams. They insisted, however, that the dams be larger than the Sri Lankan engineers wished. The reason is that First World governments wanted to subsidize their own engineering and construction firms to build the dams, and the bigger the better. One consequence was that many villages had to be evacuated and relocated because they would be inundated. Not surprisingly, uprooting and moving villages has been socially costly. Another consequence is that the large dams fail to produce electricity when their massive reservoirs fall below a certain level, as happened during a prolonged drought in 1987. (People travelled miles to look down on their former villages, especially their stupas or dagobas, as they emerged after several years of submersion.)

What to do with the electricity? Japan gave Sri Lanka a major television station. It did not, however, give Sri Lankans television *sets*, which they purchased from Japan. Initially, only the wealthy purchased TV sets. At least one TV set can now be found in many poor villages, which pay for expensive petrol to run generators if their village hasn't yet been electrified. The government exercises heavy control over what may be shown, especially news programmes. Television becomes one more way of manipulating public knowledge and perception in a country which is more democratic than many poor nations. Further, because Sri Lanka cannot fill the television day with its own quality programming, many programmes have to be imported. Two programmes watched by nearly everyone who had television in 1987 were *Dynasty* and *MacIver*. (It was rumoured that *Dallas* was withdrawn when governmental officials realized that its chief villain was called by the same initials as their President, J. R. Jayawardena!) Now something can be said for escapism, but it isn't clear that it outweighs the effects of introducing into village culture the strange worlds and values of US fantasy television.

But if the people want the technology, should we withhold it from them? Put this way, the answer is clearly no. Even less than in the rich nations, however, do 'people' in poor nations clamour for the technology they receive. Multinational companies often find willing partners, usually elites, in poorer nations for selling their products. By serving as agents for the multinationals, these elites stand to gain in terms of power, prestige and wealth. Sometimes a government encourages the introduction of a technology because it genuinely believes it will help the less well-off. Even in these cases, however, intended recipients are not generally consulted. If they were, for instance, they would presumably insist that instructions for using the technology be printed in a language they understand and that they be instructed in how to use the technology safely. We suggest that Winner's maxims be transferred before transferring any technology.

Goonatilake develops the metaphor of a social gene in discussing technological transfer. We could equally well speak of social transplants. For when transferred from one society to another, a technology behaves as do organ transplants. There is the immediate 'post-transfer' phase when attention is lavished on it in an attempt to make sure that it 'takes'. After an initial period of optimism (as in the Green Revolution), a period of rejection may begin as the host battles the intrusive foreigner or the transplant itself begins to disrupt the functioning of society. By applying pressure – too often oppressive political, economic or military pressure – the transplant is tolerated if not fully accepted by the whole. At other times, the transplant revivifies the whole, and the 'organism', society, responds with new vigour. Metaphors can be overextended, whether Goonatilake's or our own. At their best, however, they suggest arguments and ways of looking at the world, arguments and ways we have tried to develop here.

6

PLANT BREEDING AND THE POLITICS OF HUNGER

Much has been written about the Green Revolution in agriculture. It has been both heralded as a triumph for modern science and held up as an example of all that is wrong with Western techno-science. Thus if we can begin to understand some dimensions of this controversy we will be starting to move beyond the intractable opposition between optimistic and pessimistic views of technology.

MODERN VARIETIES AND THE 'GREEN REVOLUTION'

The label 'Green Revolution' has been attached to the complex of agricultural innovations that in many tropical and subtropical areas led to the doubling or even tripling of grain production per acre per season in a 20–30 year period beginning in the mid-1950s. This has, for the time being, enabled total world food production to outpace total world population growth. Such phenomenal increases in grain yields would not have been possible without the development and use of modern varieties of wheat and rice developed at the international agricultural research centres in Mexico and the Philippines, funded by the Ford and Rockerfeller foundations. These modern varieties are sometimes also called high yielding varieties. In fact they are early maturing, semi-dwarf (short-strawed) types which are fertilizer responsive and were the product of pursuit of two plant breeding strategies: exploiting hybrid vigour and dwarfing.

A form of plant breeding has been practised ever since humans began to cultivate crops. Within each agricultural community systematic strategies for seed cultivation were developed so that only seed from the 'best' plants was saved for sowing in subsequent years. Techniques such as cross fertilization and grafting were developed in attempts to develop desired traits while eliminating undesired ones. The so-called 'land-races', which provide the genetic base for modern plant breeding, are the product of millennia of development based on such techniques. These techniques were universal until the beginning of this century and are still important for many crops, especially in Africa. As we have already seen, the self-consciously theory-directed scientific approach to plant breeding goes back only to the revival of Mendelian genetic theory, early in the twentieth century, and to the wider social and economic climate of nineteenth and twentieth century United States, Europe and Japan. This provided the impetus for developing agricultural research science with a view to the improvement of agriculture. The Chinese and Japanese, as well as Americans and Europeans, had by the mid-nineteenth century already begun to improve crop yields by using nitrogen-based chemical fertilizers, but the yields of traditional varieties of grain could only be improved to a limited extent this way. This was because they tended to grow tall and leafy, and were then likely to fall over (lodge) making harvesting difficult, especially where mechanical harvesters were in use.

With the development of Mendelian genetics breeders and geneticists experimented on corn and wheat to test their ability to predict and control plant characteristics by inbreeding, to produce genetically uniform strains, and then cross breeding the inbred strains. By 1915 the work with corn suggested that it would indeed be possible to manipulate corn plants on a large scale to generate specialized strains with specific desired characteristics, such as drought or insect resistance. While methods of inbreeding and cross breeding are not in themselves complicated, the jump in scale required to move from laboratory experiments – demonstrating the possibility of manipulating plant characteristics – to actual production of strains with specific desired characteristics meant that it was not something that could be transferred directly from laboratory to farm. The laboratory had instead to be extended with the creation of massive breeding programmes at government-funded experimental stations and at research and development facilities. The latter were set up by seed supply companies and later at the international agricultural research centres set up by the Ford and Rockefeller foundations. The modern varieties of wheat and rice, developed under programmes at the international agricultural research centres, involved cross breeding strains derived from different parts of the world. These modern varieties use fertilizer by converting the extra nutrients into increased seed yield rather than increased leaves and stalks.

That the introduction of modern seed varieties has been instrumental in increasing food production so allowing countries such as India and China to achieve self-sufficiency in grain, even in the face of rising populations, is beyond dispute. But even where food supplies have been growing faster than the population, and even where most of the extra food has been in the form of cheap food grown by smallholders and/or farm labourers, it has not had the effect of significantly alleviating the hunger of the poor. Criticisms of the Green Revolution focus on this failure together with the social, economic and environmental impacts of the changes in agricultural practice which have been implemented to achieve increased yields. The exact nature of the changes that have occurred depends on the context into which the new seed varieties were introduced and the manner of their introduction. Thus to try to understand further the bases of the differing evaluations let us take a specific example.

In the Punjab region of India, with a population of 16.8 million people, 12.1 million of whom live in rural areas, increased grain yields have been dramatic.[1]

	Acreage wheat	Average yield	Acreage rice	Average yield	% gross cropped area in grain
1965–6	1.55m hectares	1.24 t/ha	0.29m hectares	1.0 t/ha	38
1980–1	2.81m hectares	2.73 t/ha	1.18m hectares	2.74 t/ha	59

Here grain input was increasing almost twice as fast as the population, with less year to year variation in yields, more employment per hectare and somewhat lower food prices.

Even in this apparently successful agricultural reform, however, the proportion of people able to afford minimum safe diets has fallen only slowly and then only very recently. This underlines the need to make the distinction insisted upon by Sen (Sen, 1989) between increasing food supply and increasing food entitlements. People can go hungry in the presence of adequate food supply if they lack any food entitlements, e.g. if they are required to pay for food and lack the money to purchase it. Moreover, the Punjab has become one of

145

India's most dangerous and unstable regions, having one of the highest police to civilian ratios in India. There have been a variety of analyses of the causes of this crisis in the Punjab, some putting it down to a religious feud between Sikhs and Hindus, others seeing it as largely a political conflict between the central India Congress Party and the locally based Akali Dal. Yet others see it as a conflict over agricultural policies between the central government and Punjabi farmers, who organized through the Akali Dal. Vandana Shiva (1991) argues for the latter and in the process presents a damning ecological critique of the Green Revolution in the Punjab, where farmers find themselves cultivating increasingly less fertile, saline, waterlogged and chemically polluted land. Still others emphasize the effects of the new form of agriculture on artisans and labourers who suffered as the land they leased or share cropped was repossessed by farmers and worked by wage labourers and as the common land, used for subsistence, was enclosed and brought under cultivation by farmers. And although the new farming methods did increase the demand for labour, this was supplied by importing some 200,000–300,000 seasonal labourers from Bihar to break strikes by Punjabi workers, thus keeping agricultural wages down. These multiple analyses show that the social and environmental story of the 'successful' Green Revolution in the Punjab is much more complex than mere figures on grain production can reveal, although even these figures reveal the scale of changes in land use.

Techno-pessimists blame the introduction of modern seed varieties for rural unemployment, poverty and hunger, urging a return to traditional indigenous agricultural practices. On the other hand:

> Techno-optimists would, in effect, (i) maximize public and private food crop research, (ii) leave it to others to improve social and demographic conditions, and (iii) expect the extra food output and the new technologies to improve poor people's lives at any constellation of social forces, and with minimal effect, good or bad, on that constellation.
>
> (Lipton, 1989, p. 9)

To go between these positions and beyond the opposition between them will require making the case that modern seed varieties are not solely responsible for the evils of the Green Revolution and therefore that plant science may still have a positive role to play in solving the problem of hunger. Simultaneously it will require not merely acknowledging the inevitable connections between plant

146

breeding research agendas and wider political, economic and social ideologies, but insisting on them; that is, recognizing that it is unrealistic to think that plant breeding programmes which ignore them could solve the problem of hunger or that plant breeding alone, even when trying to take such factors into account, could provide any such solution. In other words it means insisting that this is a problem for which there is no purely technical fix, whilst not forgetting that it has a technical dimension.

ARE MODERN VARIETIES THEMSELVES TO BLAME?

Critics have argued that the high response varieties of grain must bear the brunt of the blame because to achieve high yields they require high inputs of fertilizer and water, because they require frequent repurchase of seed, and because they are tied to the large scale, mechanized, high input farming characteristic of the North American plains. In other words, a condition of their successful use is the transformation of land and of farming to make them uniform with the conditions presupposed by the seed developers. Indeed many adverse environmental and social effects noted in the Punjab are the result of mechanization by some large farmers, high inputs of fertilizers and pesticides, changes in the scale of farming and in patterns of land use. But just how tight is the technical connection between modern seed varieties and the kind of changes in agricultural practices which in many places accompanied their introduction?

During the period of the Green Revolution changes in Indian agriculture[2] were geared towards providing cheap food surpluses for the growing urban industrial centres (though it remains the case that 705 of India's 850 million people derive their livelihood from agriculture). After independence India adopted a pattern of strong central government focusing on industrial rather than agricultural development. It was only in response to near famine conditions in the early 1960s that urgent attention was paid to implementing centrally planned reforms in agricultural practice. However, even in the period 1952–65 the Indian government, with financial and personnel support from USAID and the Ford and Rockerfeller foundations, set up an indigenous agriculture research system modelled on US institutions. Thus the Indian Agricultural Research Institute was set up in New Delhi and universities modelled on US land-grant universities were set up around the country. The aim was to train agricultural scientists to do the research necessary to adapt the new, high yielding, modern varieties of wheat and rice to Indian conditions and to train scientific experts who could provide a farm extension service. Because of the low prestige of agriculture-related professions there was difficulty attracting good students into the university programmes until the government implemented a policy of awarding top administrative positions to scientists rather than to civil servants. These scientists were largely US trained. In the period 1962–7 there was a general reform of agricultural bureaucracy to help agricultural reform. As a part of this reform an agricultural research service was established on the model of those of the United States and the United Kingdom, which gave power and credibility to agricultural scientists as well as assuring them of potential careers. During this period high yielding varieties of Mexican wheat were tested under Indian conditions. In the period 1965–75 the planned changes in agricultural practices were implemented by means of an aggressive policy of providing incentives for adoption of the new techniques. In 1965, accompanied by a massive radio, press and cinema publicity campaign 1,000 trial plots around the country were sown using 250 tons of seed imported from Mexico. A minimum of 2 hectares of each selected field was devoted to the new seed and was entrusted to the supervision of agricultural scientists. Provision was made to compensate farmers if no bumper crop resulted. The yield was 5,000 tons of seed which was immediately bought up by farmers demanding the new 'miracle' seeds. To meet this demand a further 18,000 tons of seed were imported from Mexico. The wheat varieties were subsequently modified by Indian research scientists to fit both the Indian consumers' preference for amber and white wheats over the Mexican red, and the varied soil and climatic conditions in India which differed from those in Mexico.

There are several things to note about the manner of introduction of modern varieties of wheat, and rice, into India. First it was clearly recognized that the seeds would not succeed without further research to adapt them to Indian conditions. The establishment of a research base in India was therefore important to the success of the project. Second, this was part of a centrally planned agricultural reform where the expertise, which includes assumptions about the way to improve agriculture, was provided by the United States. This meant that the seeds came as part of a preconceived package of reform measures designed to make Indian food production more closely resemble that found in the United States. So the seeds were only introduced into regions such as the Punjab, where reforms in agricultural practice such as increased mechanization, use of chemical fertilizers and installation of irrigation systems, were already under way. Many environmental and social consequences to which critics point are a product of these developments, not the use of modern seed varieties as such.

It could be argued, however, that the capital investment required for these other 'modernizations' would not have been made if there had not been the promise of high yields from use of the modern varieties of wheat and rice, because otherwise the benefits would not have been high enough to justify the economic cost. This is probably true, but it merely points to the significance of the surrounding political and economic climate, not to inevitable features of the use of the new seeds. The point is that in India the new seeds were introduced as an integral part of a package of techniques, including the purchase of seed, chemical fertilizers and irrigation, which was such that to adopt them would require capital investment before obtaining any increased yield at harvest. So other government policies, such as those regarding the extension of credit, granting of subsidies, fixing of wage rates, taxation and so on, played a crucial role in determining who would be in the best position to take advantage of the reforms, whether it would be smaller or larger landholders, those mechanizing or those employing farm labourers. Thus the use of modern seed varieties was not on its own responsible for the specific form that changes have taken in Punjab. In fact:

> Although tractors, mechanical threshers and other machinery are usually explicitly incorporated in the Green Revolution package, figures show that while poorer farmers have eagerly adopted improved varieties and fertilizers, which raise yields and income, they have lagged significantly behind larger farmers in investment in all forms of mechanization or labour saving products like pesticides. In countries like Java, Thailand and India few tractors are to be found at all.
>
> (Bray, 1986, p. 60)

Comparison between yields on larger and smaller farms, furthermore, has shown that small landholders have generally been able to achieve higher yields than large landholders because they are able to put in more labour per hectare.

In this connection it is important to note the different requirements of wheat and rice. While wheat production can be readily mechanized it is much more difficult to do so with rice. The main reason the new seed varieties boosted rice production dramatically was that they were quick maturing and so made it possible to get two crops a year where previously there had only been one. This requires more labour and more input in terms of fertilizer and water, but not necessarily mechanized tilling, planting, weed control or threshing. The most important mechanization would be as pumps, for irrigation, and the most significant capital outlay would be entailed in provision of an adequate system of irrigation. Wet rice cultivation is difficult to mechanize where the mud in the paddy fields is deep and when, as is usually the case, fields are small because of the way irrigation is organized. The constraint imposed by the demands of rice cultivation is illustrated by the pattern of agricultural development in nineteenth century Japan:

> The *shōnōsei* tradition of family farming made many Western innovations in agriculture unsuitable for adoption in Japan. In the late nineteenth century, the period of the Meiji Restoration, Western agronomy and agricultural technology were greatly admired in Japan: officials and students were sent abroad to study, and foreigners were hired as advisers by the newly established Ministry of Agriculture. Many Western breeding techniques and some new crop varieties proved successful and were widely adopted, but Western machinery and farming methods often proved quite unsuitable. . . . It was not simply that peasant farmers were incapable of adapting to the new Western technology, rather Western technology and centralization of management, though appropriate to capitalist farming, were fundamentally unsuited to wet-rice production. Many capitalist entrepreneurs set up as farmers in Japan in the late nineteenth century, and those who ran livestock farms or grew industrial crops often prospered . . . but capitalist entrepreneurs who set up in rice farming invariably failed.
>
> (Bray, 1986, p. 213)

Since the 1950s, however, the Japanese have developed small to medium scale machinery suitable for rice cultivation. They found that, even on co-operative farms where land consolidation had taken place, use of large scale Western-type machinery entailed a considerable reduction in rice yields, although it improved the productivity of labour. In her detailed discussion of rice cultivation Bray shows just how important are factors other than seed for obtaining high yields. The question of mechanization is itself complex and the problems posed to it vary with terrain and soil conditions. What becomes clear is that the attempt to transfer the large scale machinery, used for rice cultivation in the United States, may have damaging environmental effects, reduce overall yields, displace labour and create imbalances between large and small, wealthy and poor, farmers.

In Japan, where great care and effort has gone into designing appropriate, small and medium scale machinery, yields have not suffered. This careful research into mechanization was carried on against a background of government-supported improvements in irrigation systems and of price supports for rice farmers. The particular mix of social, research and economic policies made it possible to reduce the labour requirements of rice cultivation without exacerbating income differentials between rich and poor farmers and without depriving poorer farmers of opportunities for farm work. For this reason many economists look to the Japanese experience for a possible model for developing countries where land is scarce and labour plentiful. But there are problems. The complex machinery has now become too expensive, representing too large an investment for individual small farmers. Moreover, Japan is a developed industrialized country with an indigenous research and development base able to afford to invest in its agricultural infrastructure. Other developing countries lack these resources.

Those countries in which the introduction of modern varieties did result in increased grain yields were those which either already had, or were able to develop, their own agricultural research expertise, including a detailed knowledge of their soil and climate conditions and existing agricultural infrastructure. Where this knowledge base is lacking (many African countries) the introduction of modern varieties was not on any account a success. Without the requisite knowledge base it is not possible to undertake breeding research to adapt imported varieties to local conditions or to know exactly what additional infrastructure might have to be put in place to ensure increased yields. To think otherwise is to forget that, as with other technologies (see Chapter 4), there are conditions which have to be in place before the introduction of modern seed varieties can result in consistently improved yields. So though the modern varieties will give improved yields without a shift to large scale, capital intensive and highly mechanized farming, they nonetheless do carry with them many other features of technologies which have been top-down developed. They do require purchase and use of chemical fertilizers and adequate, reliable supplies of water, i.e. they do require the right, relatively controlled sort of growing environment, and to secure this some modifications in farming practice and its infrastructural supports have to be made. Because these varieties can extract more nutrients from the soil, their continued use can lead more rapidly to decreased soil fertility than continued use of traditional varieties would. Besides, because the seeds are the product of breeding trials which require meticulous controls and the recording of large amounts of data on trial hybrids, it can never be economically feasible to hope to provide varieties specially adapted to very specific local conditions. Instead, the strategy has to be to breed for characteristics that will allow for good performance over a range of conditions. Although the earliest high yielding varieties were drought intolerant and without fertilizer performed worse than traditional varieties, more recently developed varieties are more drought resistant and perform as well as or better than traditional varieties, even without the use of chemical fertilizers. But the net result is a trend towards uniformity in varieties and therefore towards modifying growing conditions to suit those varieties available. This runs directly counter to the result of using traditional selection strategies that tend to multiply varieties. For when farmers select their own seeds they are selecting those best suited to their own particular growing conditions.

Because modern forms of plant breeding cannot be conducted at farm level, but have to be carried out at specially designed research institutes (whether publicly or privately funded), farmers wishing to start using modern seed varieties have to purchase seeds which embody the research priorities of those who hold power in research institutes. These may or may not coincide with the farmer's own priorities. For example, when hybrid corn was introduced in the United States in the 1930s, the new, higher yielding hybrids had also been bred with a view to facilitating mechanized harvesting. Thus ears were borne on shorter, stiffer stems which, whilst better for mechanical harvesters, made hand harvesting very difficult. Clearly this would be welcomed by those farmers wishing to move to mechanized harvesting, but not by those who wished to rely on traditional sources of farm labour. This is just one of many examples where the development of new varieties has been aimed not merely at increasing yields but at facilitating mechanized harvesting, improving ability to withstand long distance transport or improving shelf-life. These are not characteristics to which either farmers or consumers would give top priority.

The modern varieties of wheat and rice were bred with the primary aim of increasing yields, not grain quality or nutritional value, and without regard to the means (in terms of inputs) that would have to be used, or the consequences of having to employ these means in very diverse contexts. Thus apart from actual grain yield per plant attention has also been focused on those characteristics, such as disease resistance, which most directly affect yield. As Lipton (1989) points out, however, the primary concern of the smaller, poorer farmer is not increased yield *per se*, but food security. Such farmers value yield stability more than breeders do, often preferring a safe 2 tons per acre to an unstable average of 3 tons, which may be achieved by a bumper harvest one year followed by a bad harvest the next. Unstable yields require that seed be stored from one year to the next, but storage presents its own problems. Construction of good storage facilities would require capital investment. Poor storage facilities result in losses through deterioration in quality and destruction by pests. Similarly poorer farmers, with small amounts of land and available labour, frequently intercrop rather than planting uniform stands of a single crop. This can spread risk if one crop does better in wet years and the other in dry years. It can also reduce the need for chemical fertilizers, as when beans (nitrogen fixing) are intercropped with maize. Poorer farmers are thus more interested in achieving stability, sustainability and in cross-crop effects (Lipton, 1989, p. 29).

Furthermore, the tendency of plant breeders to give priority to herbicide tolerance works against the interest of agricultural labourers whose employment in weeding would thereby be eliminated. To this extent Lappé and Collins are correct when they point out that:

> Clearly, the technology that has been introduced in the Green Revolution is not socially neutral. . . . The existing Green Revolution technology, therefore, is a choice *not* to start by developing seeds better able to withstand drought or pests. It was a choice *not* to concentrate first on improving traditional methods of increasing yields, such as mixed cropping. It was a choice *not* to develop technology that was productive, labour-intensive, and independent of foreign input supply. It was a

choice *not* to concentrate on reinforcing the balanced, traditional diets of grains plus legumes.

(Lappé and Collins, 1978, pp. 153–4)

Similarly Lipton comments that while:

Plant breeding must be left to plant breeders; priority setting must not be.

Priorities *are* set by *someone*, irrespective of the state of knowledge at the time.

(Lipton, 1989, pp. 31–2)

REVISING THE GOALS OF PLANT BREEDING RESEARCH

To continue plant breeding with its present research goals and the presumptions implicit in those will not solve the problem of securing food entitlements for the poor, even if the needs of sub-Saharan Africa, where sorghum, millet, legumes and roots, rather than wheat or rice, form the staple food crops, receive more attention than they have in the past. This is because these breeding priorities will, by focusing on increasing yields despite inputs, and on improving potential for mechanization and chemical weed control, tend to help big farmers more than small ones,[3] and tend to reduce employment opportunities, whereas:

Economic benefits to the poor arise mainly via food price restraints and higher levels of hired employment, rather than via 'small farm' income; and the benefits are embodied mainly in extra entitlements to food, rather than in extra availability of food.

(Lipton, 1989, p. 337)

Thus, Lipton argues,

the appropriate question is not, as it might have seemed twenty years ago, how research and interventions involving M[odern] V[arietie]s can best increase total food supply per person. This is no longer credible as the key to the poverty impact of such intervention. Instead, the appropriate question is: what pattern of MV research and interventions will best help poorer families (and the society that surrounds them) to improve their per-person entitlements to food?

(Lipton, 1989, pp. 346–7)

Could scientific plant breeding research agendas be set to be more likely to have a positive impact on the problem of hunger? First, as our examples have made clear, the environment to which seeds have to be adapted is not merely the physical environment, it includes also the economic, political and cultural environment into which they are to be introduced. Thus one would have to recognize not only that poverty relieving crop and variety mixes required for humid and semi-arid areas will be different, but also that the same will be true for areas between which there are social and economic differenes. For example, areas where most people are smallholders, are near landless rural employees of large landholders, or live in towns and cities are also such that the characteristics of poverty reducing crops will be different in each case. The issue of how exactly the research agenda for scientific plant breeding might be altered, if plant breeding is to contribute positively to resolving the problem of hunger, is too complex to pursue in depth here, but Lipton does develop suggestions that include emphasizing sustainability, stability and employment implications, rather than simply focusing on increasing yields while minimizing labour inputs.

BIOTECHNOLOGY TO THE RESCUE?

As Lipton himself notes, however, there are features of the whole strategy of using scientific plant breeding as the main basis for agricultural improvement which inherently limits the possibility of making a successful impact on the problem of hunger. The first problem is that to fashion breeding programmes in a way that takes more account of the social setting into which new seeds are to be introduced requires a detailed knowledge of existing farming systems and of the various resource bases present: geographical, climate, physical infrastructure, population density and distribution, level of skills, patterns of work and domestic relations, etc. Much of this knowledge is lacking for precisely those areas, such as sub-Saharan Africa, where the problems of hunger are most acute.

The second problem has to do with the selection of research goals and attempts to increase the number of characteristics that a programme aims to breed into plants. If there are n goals in a breeding programme, each with probability of 1 in m of being attained, the probability of developing a successful modern variety that attains all n goals will be only 1 in $n \times m$. So if each goal has a 1 in 10 chance of being attained, each new goal reduces the chances of achieving all goals by a factor of 10 and, because it will require more and longer trials, research costs will be raised by at least that factor. This is why the prospects of recombinant DNA techniques associated with the new biotechnology have been so eagerly anticipated by some.

Gene transfer via rDNA is now technically possible for maize and rice, although commercial application is generally agreed to be at least ten years away. However, of the corporate money invested in biotechnology research devoted to agriculture by far the largest proportion has gone into developing herbicide-resistant crops. Calgene, which has equity investments from Plant Research Venture Fund, FMC Corporation and Continental Grain, has done contract research for herbicide resistance in rape, soybean, sunflower, corn, tobacco and cotton (Kloppenburg, 1988, pp. 212–13) and has cloned a gene for resistance to the widely used herbicide Roundup. This emphasis within commercial research is not perhaps surprising given that many major seed companies are now owned by trans-national chemical and pharmaceutical corporations such as Ciba-Geigy, Sandoz, Upjohn and Monsanto. Kloppenburg (1988, p. 248) lists thirty-two major research projects on breeding for herbicide resistance. These are devoted to a very limited number of crops, not all of which are food crops, several being for the timber and paper industries. As Kloppenburg asks:

Does the Sudan really want access to a Funk Seed Company sorghum line that, through recombinant DNA transfer, has had a bacterial gene added that provides resistance to a proprietary herbicide produced by Funk's corporate parent, the transnational agrichemical plant giant Ciba-Geigy Corporation?

(Kloppenburg, 1988, p. 287)

Lipton points out that poor rural people could well lose out with the introduction of herbicide-resistant crops. If they cannot afford the new seed or the herbicide and have fields close to those where the herbicide is used, their crops will be damaged by drifting spray. If herbicide use greatly cuts production costs for those farmers able to use it, farm prices may well fall, so increasing the economic vulnerability of those unable to afford the seed/herbicide package. In addition, herbicides are directly designed to reduce farm labour. In areas of high unemployment their deployment would merely decrease further the number of jobs and therefore the number of those with food entitlements.

The effort expended on this type of research seems to have more to do with securing markets for chemical inputs to agriculture than with solving the problem of hunger. Indeed, the problem with bio-technology research to date is that most funds spent on it have come from the private sector, and much of this has come from the pharmaceutical industry for medical applications, by chemical companies for the development of fermentation techniques to improve the industrial processing of farm products. The firmly commercial priorities within biotechnology research are not only not designed to benefit the poor but are likely to lead in directions which make their position more precarious. For emphasis is placed on cash crops and animal production, so diverting more grain to animal feed, and on displacing agricultural labour.

One of the inherent problems with biotechnology research is its high fixed cost. So private-sector investors in such research have sought to increase their potential return on investment by securing legislation in the United States which allows patenting of plant varieties, techniques and even information gained from DNA sequencing. In addition they have encouraged political trends that have effectively weakened public-sector competition. Government funding for research has been reduced and much university-based research has been privatized and commercialized, with insistence that it has to pay its way. So for example Agrigenetics Corporation's contract with Cornell University researchers for investigating cytoplasmic male sterility on corn contains provision such as the exclusive right of Agrigenetics to file for patents on the results of funded research, restrictions on the dissemination of information provided to the researchers by Agrigenetics, six week publication delays to permit review of papers and speeches by Agrigenetics, six month publication delays to permit filing of patents by Agrigenetics, and university forfeiture of royalties to any product or process that Agrigenetics is not permitted to maintain as a trade secret (Kloppenburg, 1988, p. 233). For reasons such as these Lipton draws the conclusion that the hope for conducting research into developing modern varieties under the modified goals which he suggests would be required before their introduction could benefit poor people lies with the international agricultural research centres. These centres allow open access to germ plasm, research methods and results and are not directly constrained by commercial imperatives. However, this hope can be realized only if these centres can secure continued funding. Moreover, they are at a competitive disadvantage, since private-sector researchers have access to their results but not vice versa. It can be argued that these centres have themselves massively contributed to the transfer of knowledge, embodied in the germ plasm of land-races, from poorer, less developed countries, to wealthier developed ones. These wealthier countries have, via their patent laws, in turn used this knowledge as a mechanism for the commercial exploitation of some of the very countries from which the knowledge was derived. It is possible to draw up very rough balance sheets of the return on investment that the developed world makes on its continued funding of the international agricultural research centres. From the centre in Mexico from which wheat germ plasm is obtained the per annum return is reckoned to be on the order of a hundredfold, whereas for the rice research institute in the Philippines, from which semi-dwarf varieties have been obtained, the return is about twentyfold. In other words the benefits derived by the developed world from the transfer of genetic material have been and continue to be enormous. When they can in turn obtain exclusive patent rights over genes and DNA fragments, however, the opportunities for reciprocal benefit to less developed countries from retransfer of that genetic material are minimized.

ON THE ECONOMIC 'IRRATIONALITY' OF REVISED RESEARCH GOALS

More fundamentally Lipton's suggestion that scientific plant breeding should be directed towards solving the global problem of hunger, which requires increasing the food entitlements of the poor people in each country (including those in developed countries), runs counter to the ideology that has shaped our technological culture. Plant breeding has never been a pure science, one aimed at intellectual understanding, devoid of concerns for utility or applicability. A 'pure' science seeking understanding of the biological mechanisms of heredity in plants and of the environmental and genetic factors affecting plant growth would have no intrinsic connection to the purposes of agriculture. Its field would cover chickweed and stinging nettles as well as wheat and rice. It would not merely have no particular breeding priorities to suggest, but would not have breeding as a goal except in so far as attempts to determine plant characteristics might be thought to shed light on genetic mechanisms. The broad framework of Darwinian evolutionary theory only provides a basis for evaluating a plant's characteristics with respect to whether they contribute positively or negatively to the likely survival of the species to which it belongs. Modern, scientific plant breeding thus has the character of a techno-science, in which its research objectives are responsive to agendas set by those prepared to fund that research.

Now the idea that, when setting a techno-science agenda, one should ask 'What kinds of seed development would benefit poor people?' would be judged 'irrational' by the standards which have guided private-sector, and even much public-sector, research and development in the major industrialized countries. The conception of technology which has governed much of this development was clearly articulated by Michael Polyani:

> Technology devises the means for the achievement of certain ends and such a process is rational only if it is economic. The ingenuity of a technical process is an intellectual joy, but does not by itself make it valid as a technology. No amount of ingenuity will technically justify a process for extracting tap-water from champagne. Correspondingly, any invention can be rendered worthless and indeed farcical by a radical change in the values of the means used up and the ends produced by it. If the price of all fuels went up a hundred-fold, all steam engines, gas turbines, motor cars and aeroplanes would have to be thrown on the junk heap.
>
> (Polyani, 1955, p. 37)

In other words, one of the factors shaping the development of Western techno-science has been the assumption that improved technologies are those that can be economically justified, which increase profits (for someone) or which reduce expenses (to someone). Since research and development has to be funded, it is only rationally justifiable to fund research that at least holds out the prospect of producing an economic return on investment. Research focused on the needs of the poor, by definition, is not going to hold out any such prospects. Poor farmers cannot pay high prices for new seeds, just as poor people and poor countries cannot afford to pay high prices for newly developed medicines. The idea that technological progress is strictly co-ordinate with that leading to economic progress, viewed in terms of rendering production processes increasingly profitable, is founded on the kind of optimistic trickle-down economic vision of social progress expressed by Farey in the quotation on pp. 110–11. Unless that vision can be displaced suggestions such as

Lipton's will not appeal to those called upon to fund the international agricultural research centres. As Kloppenburg remarks:

> There is no question that bio-technology holds unprecedented promise for plant improvement. But we cannot rely on private industry to explore the full range of technological possibilities. . . . Is industry likely to use the perenniality of *teosinte* to breed a perennial corn and thereby eliminate half the American seed market? Will companies produce genetically diverse multi-lines or composites that cannot be effectively protected under patent law or breeder's rights legislation?
>
> (Kloppenburg, 1988, p. 286)

Is there an alternative vision available? Herman Daly, an economist who has worked for the World Bank for the past six years, made some suggestions for revising the way economic accounting is done which, if adopted, would go some way to effecting such a displacement. His recommendations revolve around the notion of natural capital – i.e. counting natural resources as part of a nation's capital. His first suggestion is to stop counting the consumption of natural capital as income. Economists have not counted soils, forests, clean water, clean air, mines, etc., as capital. If they were to do so then income from exports of timber from old forests would not be counted as foreign exchange income but as capital transfers. Such a recategorization would have the effect of changing international lending and development policy dramatically. Thus the World Bank when considering whether to fund a dam or road would introduce the loss of natural capital into its accounting projections. One might add that germ plasm should be counted as part of natural capital and its transference subject to the kinds of regulation and compensation that might be expected to accompany such transactions. His second suggestion, one that he would see as needing to be applied first in developed countries, is to tax labour and income less and 'throughput' more. Here 'throughput' means the flow of energy and materials from the earth, through the economy and back to the earth as waste. Thus Germany, for example, is already beginning to address the waste issue with laws that seek to make manufacturers responsible for the ultimate fate of their products. The third suggestion follows up on this: it is to maximize the productivity of natural capital and invest in increasing it. This would require economists to shift from thinking that the most limiting factor in an economy is either labour or human capital to recognizing that it now is very often natural capital, for example, as when fish catches are limited not by the numbers of fishing boats, but by the remaining fish stocks, or agricultural production is limited not by available labour but by available water. This recognition would undercut the presumption that economic efficiency dictates development of technologies that use labour more efficiently by reducing jobs and make it possible to link economic efficiency with efficient use of resources. To effect such a change would require economic incentives to be restructured in countries such as the United States where in many instances the efficient use of materials is actually discouraged by the tax structure (Meadows, 1994, p. 11, Young, 1994, p. 34).

LOCAL KNOWLEDGE AND THE LIMITS OF TOP-DOWN DEVELOPMENT

Some such reorientation of economic accounting would be necessary to secure funding for the kind of research advocated by Lipton. Even supposing that such support were secured, however, it might still be questioned whether science-research-based strategies are those which will have either the most direct or the most positive impact on the problem of hunger. Lipton himself recognizes that such research is powerless without a basis of detailed knowledge of the whole range of agricultural and social conditions within which it is to be applied, and that this is lacking in many countries where the problem of hunger is most severe. That knowledge can only be gained locally and its acquisition again requires organization and funding. Even national governments concerned to improve their own agricultural base have often not given priority to acquiring this knowledge. One reason for this is that, as we have already noted, there is a tendency – encouraged by instrumental views of technology – to ignore the dependency of technologies on conditions pertaining in the environment in which they are deployed. When foreign experts are relied on they frequently have little detailed knowledge of local conditions and tend to assume that techniques which work in one part of the world will work just as successfully in another. There is, in addition, perhaps a deeper problem. Namely, the authority status accorded to scientific expertise and the low status accorded to the knowledge embodied in practical skills. This in turn creates a presumption that top-down development is the only sensible direction in which to go.

Most of the debates between technological optimists and pessimists

161

have been based on taking it for granted that the central assumption underpinning the development of Western science has been that pure science yields a form of theoretical understanding which will always enable practical goals to be achieved more effectively than craft skills. Techno-optimists take this claim to have been demonstrated by the technological achievements of the twentieth century of which the increased yields achieved with the Green Revolution are but one example. Techno-pessimists, however, dispute the assumption and along with it the whole idea of using scientific analyses to improve craft skills. Instead they argue that positive valuation of science is the product of a particular culture, and therefore not universal. Indeed it is because adoption of this assumption leads to the devaluing of traditional craft skills and the forms of culture and society in which they are embedded, that critics of technology wish to reject it. On their view conservation of traditional forms of life is crucial to the possibility of people being able to lead fulfilled human lives.

The thrust of our arguments has been neither to treat this assumption as demonstrated nor to treat it as discredited, but to suggest that it is not a correct formulation of the assumptions which have underpinned the growth and development of Western science and technology. As we have seen, the idea of 'pure' science is in tension with the ideology distinctive of modern science, the ideology that links its status and its function to the development of improved technologies and techniques. The assumption underlying the project of modern science, so characterized, is that it is possible to develop methods of problem solving that combine intellectual with practical skills. Further, that such methods will be superior to those relying solely on practical craft skills, in the sense that they will make it possible to do things that were not previously humanly possible. And, finally, that it will make it possible to improve the conditions under which we live. Modern techno-sciences are a product of this assumption and their existence lends credibility to it. They are also, however, the result of certain conceptions of what constitutes an improvement in society, of what constitutes an improved technology and therefore of a certain way of posing the practical problems. For this reason they have no automatic claim to be superior to, or even to be immediately relevant to, the practical problems faced by communities that do not share those conceptions.

Modern scientific plant breeding, although it has in developed countries for the most part displaced breeding by selection, built upon the practical skills of farmers in those countries, including the skills employed to improve varieties through seed selection. Today the knowledge embodied in such skills would be classified as craft knowledge because it was not the product of any theoretical understanding of the factors that determine reproduction and development in plants, but of centuries of empirical trials and errors.[4] Given the status currently accorded to scientific experts and scientific expertise in developed countries, and frequently by those in power in less developed countries, this classification is also a valuation. Craft knowledge is treated as inferior to scientific knowledge, craft skills as less valuable than those associated with 'scientifically' developed seeds and methods of cultivation. But, as we have also seen, assignments of value are the product of value judgements, of evaluations, and there is always room to question their dependence on the cultural location from which the corresponding evaluation was made.

Clearly in a culture in which understanding is prized and in which intellectual skills are associated with a social status superior to that associated with craft skills, a scientific understanding of plant growth and reproduction is likely to be valued over the skills of farmers who select seed without possessing that knowledge. It is this traditional linking of practical skills involving manual labour with low social status which results in their tendency to be undervalued. And this undervaluation is often reinforced when the introduction of new technology under expert advice displaces traditional skills and renders them inapplicable.

For example, the process of growing corn in the United States in the late nineteenth century required farmers to be knowledgeable about the many factors, such as soil composition, insect pests, length of growing season, rainfall and so on, that could affect the yield of their corn. Conditions varied from farm to farm and from region to region so that by 1900 selective breeding had produced many varieties of corn exhibiting distinctive physical characteristics and suited to diverse growing conditions. Farmers learned how to 'read' corn, i.e. how to see these physical characteristics as indicators of yield, quality and of insect and drought resistance. An experienced farmer could identify Reids Yellow Dent or Western Ploughman at a glance and know which, if either, would be well suited to his or her fields, whereas a non-farmer would be hard pressed to make such identifications (Fitzgerald, 1993, p. 229). In the period 1910–30 farmers were encouraged by agricultural experimental stations and the USDA to take a more active part in the development of improved varieties of corn by selection, and to adopt a more scientific

approach. This was the development on which the previously discussed programme at Reading College was modelled. Thus during
the 1920s farmers themselves were the linchpin of efforts to improve
corn yields. Farmers practising these more systematic methods of
selection, especially with an eye to disease resistance, saw their yields
improve 5–10 bushels per acre above those of farmers who did not.

Their knowledge of the corn plant and its range of variations,
and of their own fields and ecological peculiarities, were powerful
tools in shaping their own economic stability. While some farmers
no doubt put less stock than others in the potential return from
these crop-improvement efforts, all shared a form of knowledge
and a sense of perspective that many experts/breeders, especially a
generation later, did not possess. Like their counterparts in the trades,
farmers acted out of pride and economic self-interest; an indifferent
farmer, like an indifferent carpenter, could not expect to survive
(Fitzgerald, 1993, p. 334).

The introduction of hybrid corn in the 1930s, however, cut
farmers out of the seed development process and transformed their
relation to the large seed companies. Hybrid varieties are produced
by first inbreeding to achieve genetically uniform strains and then
cross breeding these inbred strains. While the methods of doing this
are not in themselves too complicated, the corn resulting from a
single trial at cross breeding might have no agriculturally desirable
characteristics at all. For it is just as likely to inherit the less
desirable characteristics of both parents as to inherit the desirable
ones. Only multiple attempts with hundreds of thousands of ears
per year, accompanied by scrupulous control and record keeping,
could hope to turn up those crosses that might prove useful. In
addition the seed industry adopted a more complex process of double
crossing. Thus the development of hybrid varieties could not be
carried out on the farm. Besides, with hybrids corn farmers could
not save the seed from one year's crop to sow for the next year
without significant decreases in yield. This meant that having once
converted to hybrid seed they had to abandon the idea of developing
a strain suitable for their own farm conditions. The skills associated
with this kind of development project now proved to be of no use
even in judging which seed to purchase. Visual characteristics were
no longer a reliable guide to growing characteristics:

> Like machinists on the shop floor presented with numerically
> controlled machine tools, farmers were presented with hybrid

corn in the mid-1930's. And as other workers had found before and would find afterward, the deskilling properties of the technology seemingly lay, not with the human agent proffering it, but rather within the inert technology itself.

(Fitzgerald, 1993, p. 338)

To select seed most likely to do well on his or her land the farmer now had to turn to the agricultural experts for advice, or rely on that afforded by seed company representatives, thereby effectively delegating their cognitive authority and an element of autonomy to geneticists and seed merchants.

Such examples show the rationale behind political resistance to modern techno-science as it has been developed and then transferred to less developed countries. It is readily viewed as an instrument of colonialism or cultural imperialism, given its tendency to devalue and ignore traditional knowledge. Nevertheless, any kind of problem solving requires change, requires something to be done differently. It is unrealistic to attempt a return to or a preservation of all elements of a traditional culture in the changed circumstances of increased populations, existing trends to urbanization and industrialization. This goes for cultures which are already highly technological as well as for those to which techno-science is being transferred. In seeking to resolve the problem of hunger through agricultural development, we have seen that the top-down approach, relying on scientific plant breeding, has several, in principle, limitations. It is inherently limited to the development of a few seed varieties that fulfil research goals, even were those goals directed towards the poor, over the widest variety of contexts. The financial burden of its research, not to say its demand for trained scientists, makes it impractical to demand scientific plant breeding research into crops and crop mixes to suit every marginal environmental niche.

This limitation has started to receive recognition within the agricultural research community, partly because of failures of conventional agricultural development policies in Africa, where the international agricultural research centres have spent more per head per hectare and tonne of food, than elsewhere and with less permanent effect. That failure is now acknowledged to be in part a result of the top-down, technological package approach adopted by Green Revolution agriculturists. So there are now some who are pressing for recognition of the value of local craft knowledge and for finding ways of integrating it into programmes for local crop development, while not denying the very real benefits to be gained from appropriate use of modern varieties:

> the great challenge for local crop development is to find means through which local knowledge of crop genetic resources can be validated and linked to world science, while at the same time ensuring that control of the knowledge remains within the community.
>
> (de Boef, et al., 1993, p. 13)

> It is only by elevating producer knowledge into the current framework of development that sustainable food-production systems can be maintained . . . people still need a better understanding of the systems within which they exist. Focusing on high technological research only seems to compound the problem of improving basic lifestyles. It is only when attitudes to the use of modern science for research are changed from being laboratory to people-oriented that we will be able to develop a holistic approach to true agricultural and local knowledge advancement.
>
> (Opole, 1993, p. 164)

Monica Opole gives one example of the kind of work necessary to bring about such a reorientation. She describes the work of the KENGO Indigenous Vegetable Project in Kenya. This project aimed to improve traditional production systems by working with women who grow indigenous vegetable crops to extend their knowledge base. One aim of the project was to develop new forms of relation between scientists and farmers by developing new ways of linking local knowledge to scientific expertise. It arose out of experience of the failures of conventional development methods which have urged the displacement of indigenous vegetables by modern exotic vegetables such as tomatoes, onions and *Brassica* species. The last need to be grown with pesticides which apart from the economic cost of purchase pose a health risk because farmers lack an understanding of the nature of pesticides and of the need for a time lapse between pesticide use and harvesting.

One reason why agricultural extensionists have urged displacement of indigenous vegetable crops by these exotics is that it was believed that they were poisonous and nutritionally inferior to the exotic cultivars. Here the expert 'knowledge' came into direct conflict with people's experience. But here the expert 'knowledge' was not based in substantial analysis, but reflected cultural bias that can all too easily cover and serve to mask the existence of gaps in research. An important part of the project was thus to use participatory research to select twelve varieties of indigenous vegetables for co-cultural agronomic trials and nutritional analysis. The species were selected by local people on the basis of taste preferences, acceptability, present levels of nutritional and medicinal use and commercial viability. Samples were collected from farms and tested both for nutrients and toxins, specifically nitrates and tannin. These analyses were able conclusively to demonstrate that the varieties selected were by no means nutritionally inferior to introduced exotic vegetables. Levels of nitrates and tannin were found not to be high enough to be a cause of concern. The effects of using chemical fertilizers as opposed to manure were also studied. The indigenous crops tended to do better when cultivated with organic fertilizers than with inorganics, and problems showed up with long term use of inorganic fertilizers, such as increased frequency of attack by aphids and root worms.

The point of such studies is that they educate both local producers and locally based agronomists in a way which better prepares the ground for co-operative development of improved methods of food production. One factor contributing to the lack of recognition of local knowledge is that it takes the form of craft knowledge and is implicit in existing practices. The role of craft knowledge both in the formation of modern science and in its continued application itself tends to be ignored in standard images of science and its application (see Chapter 4).

To take a slightly different kind of example, but one very relevant to the problem of providing adequate and affordable food, let us briefly consider fermentation processes. In developed countries their traditional fermented food products (bread, beer, cheese, soy sauce, yoghurt) have been systematically studied and modified in various ways to facilitate mass production. None of this would have been possible without drawing on the craft knowledge of traditional 'brew masters'. The traditional processes had to be studied before they could be modified to produce acceptable products on a larger scale and more safely.

Yet even in such countries development does not always take the route of industrialization and total displacement of traditional techniques. Developments in European cheese production over the last fifteen years illustrate this point. On the farm, small scale cheese production has increased. This has resulted in production of a greater variety of cheeses, since the specific conditions of each production site and method impart distinctive characteristics. Success in modern, small scale cheese making .involves learning traditional craft skills while exploiting what modern biochemistry, temperature control and sterilization technology have to offer. The economic incentive for such production depends on the prevailing conditions of the overall agricultural policy. When all milk could be sold directly from the farm to large dairies at heavily subsidized prices, there was little incentive. But this changed with the imposition of strict quotas on the amount of milk that farmers could sell. The economic viability of small scale production further depends on the availability of marketing mechanisms and consumer demand. In this case consumer demand still outstrips supply even at the relatively high prices that such cheeses command. It is, in fact, very difficult fully to replicate traditional, small scale fermentation conditions on an industrial scale and in such processes the actual conditions can make very definite differences to factors such as taste and texture, which affect consumer acceptability.

When food experts from developed countries come to give advice to less developed countries they tend to dismiss their fermented food products as unhygienic, unpalatable and of dubious nutritional value – a judgement that the Chinese would endorse in regard to cheese. But they do so without undertaking the kind of study that would be necessary either to justify this opinion or to refute it and begin collaborative research to investigate the potential for improvement in quality (judged by consumer preferences), supply and in hygiene. It has to be acknowledged that it is not an easy task to seek to understand the biochemistry of these processes, as often there are several bio-organisms involved:

> One of the worst problems in mixed culture fermentation is the control of the optimum balance among the microorganisms involved. This can, however, be overcome if the behaviour of the microorganisms is understood and this information is applied to their control.

> (Hesseltine, 1992, p. 55)

Nevertheless, the Japanese have shown what can be done in this direction with the production of soy sauce. Their state of the art machinery, using computerized control to ensure optimum conditions for microbial growth and activity, was a product of combining study of all aspects of traditional brewing practice with biochemical theory. In this respect, as in their approach to rice growing, the Japanese have shown that it is possible to combine elements of top-down with bottom-up development.

PERCEPTIONS AND POLITICS

Confronted by a problem as complex as that of world hunger, a brief chapter cannot pretend to come up with solutions. But this was never our aim. Our aim was to try to show ways of mapping the geography of the issues in which science and technology are involved and to show that perceptions of science and technology themselves crucially affect the way in which such problems are approached. It seems clear that to move beyond the conflict between techno-optimist and techno-pessimist approaches it will be necessary to adjust our vision of science by recognizing the extent of the commercial content of existing techno-science and by recognizing the value of the contribution that practical skill and expertise has made to it. But, as we have also indicated, these are not minor adjustments for the contrary assumptions are deeply woven into the economic, social and political culture and institutions of developed countries. It is for this reason that the problem of hunger is not just a technical problem; it is also a political one, though, as we have argued, technological development could, under the right political and economic conditions, have a role to play in its solution. The task of securing those conditions will be all the more urgent as the global demand for grain again begins to outstrip supply. It is estimated by both Chinese and Western analysts that if Chinese economic expansion were to continue at its present rate, with Chinese annual per capita consumption of grain rising to 400 kilograms (the current level in Taiwan and half the US level), then by 2030 China alone would be looking to import over 350 million tons of grain a year. But since 1980 annual world grain exports have only averaged about 200 million tons, of which almost half comes from the United States (Brown, 1994, p. 17). Moreover, China is by no means the only country expected, given current trends, to be requiring huge imports of grain. Such a shortfall in the world supply of grain, under free-market conditions, would drive up prices and exacerbate the problem of securing food entitlements in developed and developing countries alike.

Technology finds itself deeply implicated in politics and culture whether considered within the society that creates it or the society to which it is transferred. As we continually stress, this in itself is neither good nor bad; it could not be otherwise. Were we speaking about art, religion, language or law this would be accepted as commonplace. Attitudes towards science and technology are different, however. Here the grip of universality and value neutrality holds us firm. By argument and example, we have tried to show that science and technology, especially as we move to techno-science, interact in subtle, powerful ways with the most familiar forms of social life. If we have stressed negative implications by our examples, it is only because organized groups cheer the positive. We need reminding that, even when technologies are beneficial on balance – perhaps especially when this is true – technology cannot be separated from either culture or self-understanding. Only then can we become fully responsible for the technology we develop, use and transfer to others.

7

WHO'S RESPONSIBLE FOR THIS MESS?

The degree to which scientists and technologists are answerable for their creations is controversial. Champions of the neutrality thesis, as we have seen, reject ascriptions of responsibility because, they believe, no one is accountable for a technology, except the individuals who put morally neutral tools to illicit use. Curiously, pessimists who see technology as hopelessly out of control also implicitly relieve the makers and developers of technology of responsibility. For if technologists themselves are little more than victims of uncontrollable forces, then it would be absurd, not to say cruel, to blame them for being victimized. Thus whereas techno-optimists more frequently blame accidents on the errors of human operators, techno-pessimists tend to blame technology itself for accidents and other undesired consequences of its use, not its users or developers. One of the consequences of rejecting these two extreme positions is that it becomes possible, and indeed natural, to ask 'To what extent are scientists, engineers and technical experts to be held responsible for their products?' and similarly 'To what extent are we as users and consumers to be held responsible for the uses we make of technological devices, and for the effects of their use?' and 'When unwelcome side effects occur, how is blame to be apportioned?'

In the course of indicating the network of concepts and considerations opened up by these questions, we will encounter examples of the kinds of dilemmas which can confront the conscientious research scientist, the conscientious engineer working on development and production in high-tech projects and conscientious users and consumers of technology. Here we assume that conscientious people are those who seek to do their jobs well and to act in a morally and professionally responsible fashion. Thus it is clear that this discussion will also be about what it is to be conscientious.

CONSCIENCE AND CONSCIENTIOUS ACTION

We begin with two quotations from C. P. Snow – scientist, scientific administrator in the British government during World War II, novelist, and author of the influential *Two Cultures* (Snow, 1964):

> I respect, and to a large extent share, the moral attitudes of those scientists who devoted themselves to making the bomb. But the trouble is, when you get onto any kind of moral escalator, it is impossible to know whether you're ever going to be able to get off.

> (Snow, 1961, p. 258)

> There is of course one way to contract out [of moral responsibility]. . . . It consists of the invention of categories – or, if you like, of the division of moral labor. That is, the scientists who want to contract out say, *we* produce the tools. *We* stop there. It is for *you* – the rest of the world, the politicians – to say how the tools are used. . . . This is the doctrine of the ethical neutrality of science. I can't accept it for an instant . . . we nearly all feel intuitively that the invention of comfortable categories is a moral trap. It is one of the easier methods of letting the conscience rust.

> (Snow, 1961, p. 256)

The experience of Joseph Rotblat, a brilliant young Polish scientist who worked on the atomic bomb, illustrates just how difficult it is to 'get off the moral escalator'. His revealing story is worth recounting in detail. By the end of 1938 Rotblat was convinced that it was theoretically possible to manufacture an atomic bomb of unprecedented power. What was his reaction?

> my first reflex was to put the whole thing out of my mind, like a person trying to ignore the first symptom of a fatal disease in the hope that it will go away. But the fear gnaws all the same, and my fear was that someone would put the idea into practice. The thought that I myself would do it did not cross my mind, because it was completely alien to me. I was brought up on humanitarian principles.

> (Rotblat, 1986, p. 16)

Why, then, did he agree to work on the bomb? His opening remark gives his general answer: 'Our hopes and fears, our resolutions and actions, are influenced by an infinite number of small events

172

interacting with each other all the time' (Rotblat, 1986, p. 15). His particular answer was:

> I convinced myself that the only way to stop the Germans from using it against us would be if we too had the bomb and threatened to retaliate. My scenario never envisaged that we should use it, not even against the Germans. We needed the bomb for the sole purpose of making sure that it would not be used by them: the same argument that is now being used by proponents of the deterrence doctrine.
>
> (Rotblat, 1986, p. 17)

Interestingly, Ludwig Wertenstein, pupil of Madame Curie and director of Warsaw's Radiological Laboratory where the young Rotblat worked, declined to give any moral advice to Rotblat:

> On the moral issue . . . he was unwilling to advise me. He himself would never engage in this type of work, but he would not try to influence me. It had to be left to my own conscience.
>
> (Rotblat, 1986, p. 17)

Two days after Rotblat returned to Liverpool, the war broke out and Poland was overrun.

Rotblat confronted a moral issue early in his research in Liverpool:

> Chadwick . . . gave me two young assistants. One of them presented a problem: he was a Quaker and as such had refused to do war work. He was therefore sent to Liverpool University for academic duties – but was diverted to work with me on the atom bomb! I was not allowed to reveal to him the nature of our research, and I had qualms of conscience about using him in such an unethical way.
>
> (Rotblat, 1986, p. 18)

But he did use him in just that way, as he himself was later to be used. For in March 1944 – over a year before the two atomic bombs devastated Hiroshima and Nagasaki – Rotblat was present at a dinner party in Los Alamos, at which General Leslie Groves, Military Commander of the Manhattan Project and Robert Oppenheimer's military counterpart – said, 'of course, the real purpose in making the bomb was to subdue the Soviets' (Rotblat, 1986, p. 18). This stunned Rotblat:

> I felt deeply the sense of betrayal of an ally. Remember, this

was said at a time when thousands of Russians were dying every day on the Eastern Front tying down the Germans and giving the Allies time to prepare for the landing on the continent of Europe. Until then I had thought that our work was to prevent a Nazi victory, and now I was told that the weapon we were preparing for use was intended for use against the people who were making extreme sacrifices for that very aim.

(Rotblat, 1986, p. 19)

So Rotblat asked permission to leave the Project and return to England. Permission was granted, but he returned to England only after a close call with US security forces. They were suspicious of Rotblat's motives and intentions. This illustrates just how difficult getting off the escalator can be, especially in wartime.

Why did so few scientists follow Rotblat's lead? He offers three reasons. The most frequently given reason, he says, 'was pure and simple scientific curiosity'. And we should not discount this powerful motivation. After all, anyone who invests time, education and effort in a project is unlikely to abandon it easily; indeed, immersion in an exciting research project frequently prevents one from recognizing a moral problem at all. Second, 'Others were prepared to put the matter off even longer, persuaded by the argument that many American lives would be saved if the bomb brought a rapid end to the war with Japan.' Despite this understandable and persuasive reason, we must note both that the Manhattan Project was initiated because of fear that *Germany*, not Japan, would develop and use the bomb and that there was evidence available at the time that Japan was willing to surrender if only the Emperor would be spared (Rotblat, 1986, p. 19). Finally, still others 'were not willing to take an individual stand because they feared it would adversely affect their future career'. While this may strike some as a petty, even dishonourable, reason, we must recognize that careers can be, and ideally should be, much more than simply jobs: a career can become integral to a sense of accomplishment, and therefore to self-identity and a sense of self-worth. Scientists with a social conscience, Rotblat concludes, were a minority in the scientific community: 'The majority were not bothered by moral scruples; they were quite content to leave it to others to decide how their work would be used' (Rotblat, 1986, pp. 19–20).

Here we have clear confirmation of Snow's remarks. Rotblat's ride on the moral escalator changed him profoundly:

Work on the atom bomb convinced me that even pure research soon finds applications of one kind or another. If so, I wanted to decide myself how my work should be applied. I chose an aspect of nuclear physics which would definitely be beneficial to humanity: the applications to medicine. Thus I completely changed the direction of my research and spent the rest of my academic career working in a medical college and hospital.

(Rotblat, 1986, p. 22)

Rotblat does not speak from the vantage point of the classroom, but from that of a scientist who, as Oppenheimer put it, has 'known sin'. And as anyone who has known sin also knows, one can sin again:

Not being an absolute pacifist, I cannot guarantee that I would not behave in the same way, should a similar situation arise. Our concepts of morality seem to get thrown overboard once military action starts. It is, therefore, most important not to allow such a situation to develop.

(Rotblat, 1986, p. 21)

Rotblat's reflections deserve attention because they illustrate how anyone who deliberates conscientiously about a moral matter thinks, whether or not one agrees with that person's particular judgements. His reflections show how easy it is to board Snow's moral escalator, yet how difficult it is not only to decide when to get off, but also to have the courage to do so.

What then is 'conscience', this thing which apparently can rust, which people don't wish to advise one about, and which has trouble knowing when to get off escalators? It is easily misunderstood. 'Conscience', the satirist H. L. Mencken once remarked, 'is the inner voice which warns us that someone may be looking' (Mencken, 1920). More seriously, people often think that conscience consists in nothing more than an unpleasant *feeling*, a pang of guilt accompanying something we do which we believe is wrong. And there are moral nihilists[1] who would see all moral judgements as merely expressic is of personal taste based on feelings and for whom having a conscience could be nothing more than having such feelings. This would be one basis on which it might be held that matters of conscience are wholly personal and individual; that it is inappropriate for others to offer advice on how one should feel.

While conscience is undeniably affective, there is more to it than

175

that. For if conscience were simply a matter of guilty feelings, then one would be well advised to rid oneself of it as quickly and painlessly as possible. For unless guilt is somehow grounded in something other than feeling, it can be easily manipulated, always a nuisance, and too often emotionally crippling. If, however, conscience can be either mistaken or corrupt, then it seems that there must be a strong cognitive, or rational, element to conscience. In which case we will have to part company with the moral nihilists, who deny the possibility of genuine moral reasoning, and assume that rational deliberation is a part of moral judgement.

John E. Smith characterizes conscience as 'a capacity for self-critical appraisal' (Smith, 1980). This is fine as far as it goes, but it needs further elaboration. For 'appraisal' involves evaluative judgement – the application of standards, principles and precepts to a case at hand. Otherwise, so-called appraisal would be nothing more than an expression of subjective preference. After all we expect house appraisers, or valuers, working for mortgage companies to know what to look for, what standards to apply, and how to apply them. Appraisers do not always agree, of course, but if competent, they can cite reasons for their assessments, appreciate the reasoning of their colleagues, and alter their evaluations in the light of those analyses. So, too, with self-critical moral appraisal.

Smith notes that conscience has a double significance, a significance giving content to what has just been said:

> [Conscience] implies, first, a synthetic or synoptic grasp both of particular decisions and actions and of a pattern of conduct running throughout life as a whole, set in relation to an *acknowledged* norm sitting in judgment on their quality, validity, and excellence. . . . Second, [it] implies that the person makes the judgment *with* himself . . . that it is properly *self-referential*.
>
> (Smith, 1980, p. 556)

In seeking to act in accordance with the dictates of conscience a person acknowledges certain norms as binding, while at the same time also recognizing that they are self-imposed. But because conscience involves judgement, it can be fallible:

> It is not enough to proclaim that a given action is prohibited because it is 'against conscience' as if this declaration were, all by itself, the sufficient reason. More is required; one must exhibit the norm or standard and indicate what there is about

the proposed action that contradicts or fails to accord with the standard.

(Smith, 1980, p. 556)

In other words, conscientious action is intimately bound up with making moral judgements and with being able to justify both the moral standards appealed to and the specific course of action taken. Rotblat clearly felt that one should not seek to develop a weapon of mass destruction with a view to possibly using it against those who are one's current military allies and offers this as his reason for having refused to contribute further to the Manhattan Project. To acquire a 'critical conscience' is thus to acquire a set of moral beliefs together with a disposition to seek to act in accordance with them. Under moral beliefs we include here beliefs about how one should act, about how one should live, about what sort of person one should seek to be, etc. Once developed, conscience is the disposition or habit of being willing to apply one's moral understanding to one's own conduct; its exercise on any particular occasion is an act of conscience. (Notice, incidentally, that verdicts of one's conscience are restricted to one's own actions: Rotblat's actions could not offend anyone's conscience but his own.)

In suggesting that a conscience is something acquired or which has to be developed, we are disputing Bishop Butler's claim that conscience is 'a faculty in kind and nature supreme over all others, and which bears its own authority of being so' (Butler, 1736) as if it were an in-born, dictatorial, unerring voice. Of course, if it is possible for people to acquire a conscience, it has to be supposed that they have some innate capacity which makes this possible, just as if it is possible for people to learn several languages, they must have some innate language learning capacities. But many of us never learn to speak more than one language, and thus do not convert our full language learning capacities into language speaking abilities. Similarly the innate capacities which make critical self-appraisal possible may fail to develop, whether through lack of an appropriate moral education or through the presence of social forces hostile to, or likely to inhibit, the development of the capacities for critical reflection. To suggest that to have a conscience is to have developed a disposition or a habit is to see the conscientious person as one who not only has a capacity for critical self-appraisal, but as one who characteristically exercises this capacity. A *disposition* is an ability coupled with a settled habit to use the ability in appropriate circumstances. Scientists and engineers, for example, in learning to use quantitative methods (in acquiring a set of abilities) usually also acquire the disposition to apply them to problems at hand. We can, however, imagine engineers who know how to use quantitative methods, but, through laziness or impulse, habitually rely on guess-work instead: they would have the requisite ability, but not the essential disposition. So although conscience may occasionally seem like an ethereal, slightly dyspeptic, organ or like a disembodied, censorious voice, it is better understood as referring to a settled disposition to apply moral principles and precepts to one's own conduct. To act in accordance with this disposition can often require great effort and even courage, as Rotblat's case illustrates. Moreover, because acting in accordance with conscience involves making moral judgements, no such action is immune from criticism, even sub-sequent self-criticism. Even when one understands and seeks to apply appropriate principles, one can easily err in applying them to such complex situations as that which confronted Rotblat. Novel and complex technologies raise novel and tangled moral problems not amenable to old and simple solutions, or at least not clearly so. Of course, we can learn from our moral mistakes as from other kinds of mistakes.

Not only can conscience err, but it can become corrupt. This is possible in many ways. Two are mentioned by Snow and Rotblat: inventing categories that block us from seeing what we are doing and by putting unpleasant matters out of mind, by changing the subject, as it were. Sometimes corruption of conscience becomes inveterate and deep rooted; those corrupted in this way cannot recognize their deeds or situations for what they are even when this is pointed out to them. In addition, for many reasons, not all rooted in preoccupation with the self, people either do not develop their ability to think and act conscientiously or let it atrophy, or 'rust', as Snow puts it. War is especially likely to bring about its eclipse. As Rotblat says, 'our concepts of morality seem to get thrown overboard once military action starts'. For once at war, the inclination to see the enemy as a fellow human being caught up in a tragedy like oneself vanishes, as does the will to resist unjust authority or, indeed, to think about anything but about how to survive the day. Similar pressures arise in economically competitive environments. The immediate thought is to ensure the survival of the company and with its one's job and livelihood; other considerations may get pushed aside. Thus even in peacetime such a crisis mentality can develop which effectively muffles the dyspeptic inner voice, as we shall see in the case of decisions relating to the design and production of DC-10 aircraft.

LEGAL AND MORAL RESPONSIBILITY

A conscientious person, whether research scientist, engineer or user of technology, is one who takes responsibility for (a certain range of) their actions. But what sort of responsibility can people in these various categories be expected to take upon themselves? Was Rotblat being unduly judgemental when he described the majority of the scientists working on the Manhattan Project as not being bothered by moral scruples? All technologies, even well-intentioned ones, cause harm. When this happens who (if anyone) or what (if anything) is responsible? In order to approach these questions it will be necessary to distinguish between various senses of 'responsibility'.

We begin with distinctions drawn by H. L. A. Hart between (a) role responsibility, (b) causal responsibility, (c) liability responsibility, and (d) capacity responsibility (Hart, 1968, p. 212ff.). The names themselves tell us much. Role responsibility refers to the responsibilities we have because of our roles, positions or jobs. As a mother, a woman will have certain responsibilities; as treasurer of her church, she has other responsibilities; and as a member of a design team, still others. When we ask 'Who is responsible for this mess?', we are asking about causal responsibility. To hold someone liability-responsible for the mess is tantamount to declaring that the person should pay damages, be punished, fined, or otherwise make amends. In certain instances, we may declare that someone 'isn't (capacity) responsible' because that person lacks the mental capacity to bear responsibility, perhaps because he or she is a child, mentally deranged, or retarded. These different senses of 'responsibility' are not unrelated and can occur side by side in a single narrative, as the following makes clear: 'Although Jones was *mentally fit* and *in charge* of operations that day and even though he wasn't the *cause* of the accident directly, Jones is still *to blame* for what happened because he egregiously ignored his *duties* by not paying attention; his negligence may make him *liable* for damages or even punishment.' Each emphasized word or phrase employs a distinguishable sense of responsibility. In particular it illustrates how the apportionment of blame is linked to a standard of expected behaviour (Jones ought to have been paying attention) and how, if that expected standard is part of a legal code or contract (such as a job description), failure to live up to it may carry legal penalties.

Hart was primarily interested in questions surrounding legal responsibility. Sometimes legal and moral standards coincide and it is natural that they should do so since basic provisions of criminal and tort law, for example, find their roots in common moral precepts. Furthermore, because jurists have to confront hard cases in which decisions must be rendered, the law influences common morality by providing it with distinctions and principles it might otherwise have overlooked and embed them in social practices that, in turn, shape morality. But it is important to remember that legal and moral responsibilities may not coincide and may even come into conflict. A doctor legally required to perform an abortion may regard this procedure as morally prohibited. Conversely a doctor legally prohibited from performing an abortion may regard him- or herself as morally required to do so.

Apportioning moral responsibility goes hand in hand with determining who is at fault, or who is to blame, whereas typically the necessity of fixing legal responsibility arises because either an aggrieved plaintiff or prosecutor insists that someone has violated the law and thus must pay damages or deserves punishment. Legal responsibility is at once narrower and broader in scope than moral responsibility. It is narrower because it introduces *statutory limitations* on when and against whom complaints can be made; it is broader because it can hold individuals or firms *strictly liable* for harm, though those held liable had nothing to do with causing the harm or could not reasonably have been expected to know that their conduct was harmful.

The special concerns of the law and difficulties in applying it partially explain why our legal system does not always square with our intuitions about fault. As we have seen, the law for the most part concentrates on settling disputes between the state and its citizens or among citizens. Shocking as it may seem, reaching a decision is often nearly as important as making the right decision. Not only must a court settle a dispute to avoid continuing and perhaps worsening conflict, but everyone needs to know what the law demands. Without a stable set of enforceable and enforced rules, planning becomes virtually impossible. In criminal law, this demand typically eventuates in laws that are clear and simple. Much civil law, however, is abstruse, technical and detailed. In both, however, the law strives for clarity and certainty.

Standards of legal responsibility are further complicated by the obligation of judges and juries to hand down sentences, impose fines, and assess damages. To do so in good conscience, they must be certain of who did what and when. In any interesting case this is usually exceedingly difficult to ascertain. Especially in criminal cases, therefore, legal systems in liberal societies choose to err on the defendant's side, as the requirement to prove a defendant guilty 'beyond a reasonable doubt' indicates. Prosecutors often choose to prosecute on a lesser charge to ensure a conviction or not press charges at all if they think they cannot meet this requirement.

Although establishing intent is often crucial in determining criminal liability (e.g. in order to distinguish between murder and manslaughter) the law does not, as it were, concern itself with the state of the defendant's soul (the exception would be in those countries in which there is no separation of religion from the state). Thus legislatures and judges formulate laws which do not concern themselves with motives or with reasons why they might be obeyed or disobeyed: provided that one obeys the criminal law, fulfils one's contracts, and disposes of one's property in prescribed ways, the law usually does not care *why*.[2] Criminal laws in particular are formulated and enforced with minimum assumptions about the intelligence and goodwill of its citizens. This has important implications. First, criminal laws must be simple and easily grasped so that every citizen can understand them. This means that the law cannot always capture nuance appropriate to the moral life. Second, lawmakers frequently draft laws 'defensively', as it were, with the 'bad person' in mind. When framing a law, the legislator must ask, 'How would someone who is either selfish or nasty try to get around this law?' Third, therefore, legal systems in a liberal society rarely demand more than the minimum. Admittedly, if no one exceeded this minimum, life would be miserable for everyone.

For these reasons no self-respecting scientist or engineer would judge his or her conduct above reproach simply because it escaped legal criticism: not only are the standards frequently different, but they are usually less demanding than morality requires. A self-respecting scientist or engineer, in short, does not ask, 'What can I get away with without violating the law or leaving myself open to a law suit?', but 'What precautions must I take to avoid moral culpability for my conduct?' The former looks to a judge sitting on a bench; the latter, to one's conscience as judge.

Appeal to an enlightened conscience demands that we formulate, defend and apply standards setting out the extent of culpability for harm. If we fail to meet those standards, we are at fault and therefore blameworthy.

MORAL AND PROFESSIONAL RESPONSIBILITY

Self-respecting scientists and engineers are, in the first instance, concerned to act as responsible members of their respective professions (a form of role responsibility). Professions are social institutions in which role models are held up, training is given, qualifications demonstrating competence are required, and the conduct of members may be subject to peer review. Lawyers and doctors found guilty of malpractice may be barred from future participation in those professions. Members of professions are thus expected to learn about the standards and codes of conduct pertaining to their chosen profession and to acquire the disposition to apply those standards to their own conduct. For this reason it makes sense to talk of conscientious scientists or engineers – those who are in the habit of critically appraising their own performance by reference to standards which are at once both professional and personal.

But as Rotblat's case illustrates, professional responsibility does not exhaust moral responsibility and people whose professional conduct is beyond reproach may still find themselves with an uneasy conscience over things they have done in the course of their professional life. What then are the relations between professional and moral responsibility? One answer would be that professional people are, in the conduct of their professional duties, morally required to live up to the standards prevailing in their profession. But this leaves the central question of professional ethics wholly open. What are the ethical responsibilities which should be recognized as part of standard practice in the various professions? The idea behind seeking to formulate ethical codes for the various professions is that professionals, as experts in their various fields, wield considerable power over the lives of their clients and others. At the very least this power should not be abused and the pursuit of professional goals should not take precedence over the moral responsibility to avoid causing harm to others. It is on this basis that German scientists who performed medical experiments on unwilling subjects in concentration camps during World War II are criticized, even though the medical knowledge so gained may, from a purely scientific point of view, have been quite valuable. The standards in force governing professional conduct are thus generally aimed at safeguarding the public interest by holding professionals, whether individually or corporately, responsible for the harm they cause, whether directly or indirectly (e.g. by publishing results based on flawed experimental methods, which are then used by others as a basis for practical recommendations).

Thus we need to explore further the concept of moral responsibility specifically viewed as the responsibility not to cause harm. Here we wish to emphasize that technology can cause harm without anyone being at fault. For we know that in human affairs exercising the greatest care and acting conscientiously and with exemplary diligence can still lead to disaster. Nothing we say below is intended to deny this melancholy fact. We are concerned only with avoidable harm; that is, harm which ordinary, reasonable men and women can avoid if they pay sufficient attention to what we know about technoscience, our own practices, and human nature.

In what follows, we will build on three principles of moral responsibility:

1 We are responsible for harm if it is a consequence of something we do or if it follows in the course of nature from our interventions in what is going on.
2 We are responsible when, because of omissions or failures to act, we *allow* harm to occur.
3 We are responsible for harm if we do something foreseeing how others will react to what we do, though we neither cause nor allow the harm that occurs.

Each principle raises conceptual problems, which cannot be adequately discussed here.[3] There are, for example, troubling philosophical questions about omissions. How, for instance, is a *failure* to do something related to *doing* something? Similarly there will be debate over what exactly constitutes harm. However, these problems are not such as to prevent the possibility of agreed evaluations in some central kinds of concrete cases.

Suppose Smith is a trained technician working in a power plant, and his supervisor instructs him to check a pressure valve every 15 minutes and to close the valve immediately if the needle goes into the red zone; for whatever reason – perhaps because Smith is distracted, forgetful or lazy – he fails to do so. An explosion occurs causing the loss of more then fifty lives, very considerable damage not only to the power plant, but also to surrounding property. It can be agreed that the explosion caused harm, even if the exact catalogue has to be negotiated. Similarly it can be agreed that it was the fact that the valve was not closed, but remained open, that was causally responsible for the explosion, and hence it is Smith who is to blame, not for what he did, but for what he didn't do, what he *failed* to do.

Smith's failure to close the valve when the needle moved into the red zone clearly had devastating consequences, but not in the sense that his omission enters a causal story of the sort 'x caused y which, in turn, caused z'. This appears problematic only if we suppose that we are only responsible for those actions which fit into such a story. There is, however, no good moral reason to accept this supposition. As principle 2 above reflects, in and out of techno-science we hold ourselves and others morally responsible for what we *allow* to happen. We speak of Smith's *failure* because we regard it as his responsibility, his duty, to have kept an eye on the pressure valve. His failure allowed a chain of events to ensue that caused harm.

Conceivably, of course, we might *excuse* Smith. Perhaps he wasn't given clear instructions or was kept on duty too long or the meter was dimly lit or he was attending to an emergency, etc. We might blame the designers of the equipment for not using a valve mechanism which would automatically shut if the pressure exceeded safe levels. These might succeed in diminishing his degree of responsibility, or even extinguish it altogether. Pointing out that he is generally inattentive or lazy, however, will *not* relieve him of responsibility!

Principle 3 takes us further. On some occasions, we can clearly foresee that someone will react in a harmful way to something we do, and we can justly be held responsible for creating or exacerbating a situation that leads to harm, though we neither cause nor allowed it. Suppose a gunman grabs a teller during a bank holdup saying, 'If anyone moves, I'll kill the teller'. Believing that the threat is credible, a customer nevertheless makes a dash for the door, and the teller is killed. Again, the customer may have various excuses – some better, some worse. We can say, however, that the customer created a situation that (further) endangered the life of the teller, and that the customer bears responsibility for doing so.

The gunman, obviously, is culpable for killing the teller; he cannot excuse himself because of the customer's action. He is *fully* responsible for what he does. But so, too, is the customer for creating a situation that (further) endangers the teller. The question is not 'Who is the morally worse person?' or 'Who is most to blame for what happens?' Sometimes these questions can be answered easily, sometimes not. Moral responsibility isn't like a pie, which can only be divided between various people so that the total equals 100 per cent. In a conspiracy, for example, *each* member of the conspiracy can be fully responsible for the harm caused though each member made discrete contributions to the outcome; for example, one bought the fuse, another made the bomb, a third hid the device, and a fourth set it off.

Although these examples are non-technological, the implications are not. Techno-scientists frequently create situations where there is every reason to believe that people will misunderstand or misuse technology. Highly toxic pesticides, for instance, are often introduced into Third World countries without adequate instruction or safeguards. While the resulting harm isn't intended by anyone, those who foresee the likely harmful consequences are not without blame.

Three principal types of fault figure in judgements of responsibility: *intentional wrongdoing, recklessness* and *negligence*. One is at fault morally when one does wrong intentionally; that is, when one sets out to do that which one knows or believes is morally impermissible. A legal case involving engineers provides an unequivocal example. A subcommittee of the American Society of Mechanical Engineers (ASME) was formed to be responsible for interpreting a section of ASME code governing low water cut-offs. A court found that two of these engineers conspired to misinterpret the code so that a new product would be declared unsafe. What motivated the conspiracy? One engineer on the subcommittee was employed by a rival company. He and another member deliberately and knowingly caused harm, and did so contrary to their sworn legal and professional responsibilities.[4] Deliberately to misinterpret a section of ASME code is a clear failure to live up to professional standards.

Morally speaking, this is an easy case: there is no justification or excuse for what the engineers did. It also illustrates the previous point that *both* engineers can be *fully* responsible for the harm they caused. Many cases are not so clear. For a slightly more complicated case, consider the decision to launch the 'ill-fated' *Challenger*. Quotation marks are placed around the term 'ill-fated' because it is now evident that human misjudgement, not fate, led to the disaster. This case is more complicated for several reasons. First, the *Challenger* disaster is not an instance of intentional wrongdoing: no one set out to cause death and destruction. Second, many of those involved felt themselves to be bound by conflicting obligations, and were not motivated – directly, at least – by crass self-interest. In at least one instance, the conflicting obligation was structural. An engineer opposed to launch because of cold weather was also a manager, and at a crucial, last minute meeting was told to 'wear his managerial hat'. In his managerial role he overruled himself as an engineer, approving the launch. He clearly felt a conflict between two sets of role responsibilities.

The *Challenger* disaster involved both recklessness and negligence. These terms are often confused, but the distinction is clear enough. Recklessness is the wrongful disregard of known risks, as when one knowingly speeds in a crowded pedestrian precinct. Recklessness shares with intentional wrongdoing a knowledge of likely outcomes. The moral difference between them lies largely in this: in intentional wrongdoing, one *tries* to cause harm; in reckless behaviour, the harm isn't intended, but one doesn't *care* (or *care enough*) whether the harm occurs. Negligence, like recklessness, involves the unintended infliction of harm, but is the fault – not of wilfully disregarding risks – but of failing to live up to a morally (or legally) acceptable standard of conduct. Smith, for instance, might have *recklessly* failed to check the valves because – although he knew the risks – he just didn't care; or he might negligently have failed to do so; that is, without living up to standards of conduct *which he should have known* even if he didn't.

There is little point in trying to decide, in the abstract, which is worse: intentional wrongdoing, recklessness or negligence. Intentional wrongdoing seems worst, because one deliberately sets out to cause harm. It is worse in one sense, because people are more likely to hit a (bad) target if they aim at it. In another sense, however, recklessness is worse, or at least as bad. For people who just don't care or who recklessly disregard evidence are likely to cause at least as much harm as intentional wrongdoers. Executives of cigarette companies, for instance, who claim that their business is simply to sell cigarettes, by not examining the evidence regarding diseases caused by smoking, could hardly do more harm than if they set out to do so. Negligence *seems* the least blameworthy because a negligent person isn't trying to do anything harmful nor exhibiting carelessness. Yet if it is one's *responsibility* to exercise 'due care', then one is exhibiting a defect of character in failing to take this responsibility seriously.

As with intentional wrongdoing, excuses are available for the reckless and the negligent person. The reckless person can say –

sometimes successfully – that he or she didn't think the endeavour was *that* risky. After all, this person may say, we launched in temperatures almost this cold before. Or, the person may say, 'although I had it in the back of my mind that this was risky, I was preoccupied with other thoughts, and wasn't paying very much attention to the risks'. A negligent person may say – sometimes successfully – that he or she was overtired or preoccupied or otherwise incapacitated, physically or mentally, so that his or her failure to exercise 'due care' should be excused. As J. L. Austin once said, however, even successful excuses seldom get us out of the fire – only into the frying pan.

Lack of knowledge in techno-science often leads to harm, as the discussion of the Green Revolution in Chapter 6 shows. Only *culpable* ignorance, however, counts as negligence. This can occur when the ignorance is *affected*. If, for instance, one deliberately shields oneself from knowledge about probable risks or contrary evidence, then one's ignorance is affected, and constitutes no excuse. So, too, is ignorance that results from a failure to look for possible adverse consequences. Not only is this bad techno-science, but the resulting ignorance is affected and thus negligent: standards of responsibility require more than just looking at the up-side of technology.

Some culpable ignorance, however, isn't affected, but results from overlooking, misinterpreting or underemphasizing something. A trained accountant who overlooks or misinterprets certain figures, for example, may do so negligently if he or she doesn't meet the standards of the profession. Similarly, a scientist or engineer may not pay sufficient attention to what he or she is doing and so the resulting damage sustains a charge of professional negligence.

The discussion thus far suggests what Curd and May call the *malpractice model* of professional responsibility (Curd and May, 1984, p. 9). It limits culpability to *generally accepted and followed* standards in one's profession. The following case illustrates this model of responsibility.

A Turkish DC-10 crashed in 1974 near Paris shortly after takeoff killing all 346 people aboard. Because a baggage handler at Orly International Airport failed to lock the rear cargo door securely, when the differential between the air pressure inside and outside the cargo bay reached a critical value, the door blew out causing rapid decompression which, in turn, caused the cabin floor to collapse. The collapsing floor severed the flight control cables which ran through the floor, cables which enabled the pilots to control the plane. The President of McDonnell Douglas initially tried to pin blame on the baggage handler, though both McDonnell Douglas and the Federal Aviation Administration (FAA) were well aware that the latching system on the DC-10 was unreliable, for a similar accident occurred over Windsor, Ontario, two years earlier. In that incident, fortunately, only some cables were severed and the pilot, in a feat of extraordinary skill, landed the plane safely. Investigation of this accident revealed that the fault lay in the design of the locking mechanism: the external handle could be in the 'door locked' position without fully engaging the locking pins. To compound the problem, no warning lights were installed to alert flight crews that the pins were not fully engaged.

As early as 1969 engineers at Convair, who designed the latching mechanism for McDonnell Douglas, expressed doubts about its safety. In 1970 a member of the McDonnell Douglas design team wrote an internal memo after an explosive decompression in a ground test. None of his information was forwarded to the FAA nor caused McDonnell Douglas to call for changes in its prototypes. It should also be noted that Lockheed and Boeing used significantly different latching mechanisms for their wide-bodied planes which worked well. However, McDonnell Douglas were at that time operating under severe financial constraints. They had gained the order to build a wide-bodied jet on condition that it be cheaper to purchase and cheaper to operate than those of its competitors Boeing and Lockheed. These pressures seem to have led management and some engineers to the conclusion that corners had to be cut as well as making them reluctant to make design modifications that would add to the overall weight of the plane. Just after the Windsor accident, moreover, and two years before the Paris disaster, the Director of Product Engineering, F. D. Applegate, had written a memorandum to his superiors at Convair in which he had been severely critical of McDonnell Douglas for pushing Convair to develop this new latching system:

> My . . . criticism of Douglas . . . is that once this inherent weakness was demonstrated by the 1970 test failure, they did not take immediate steps to correct it. It seems to me inevitable that, in the twenty years ahead of us, DC-10 cargo doors will come open and I would expect this to usually result in the loss of the airplane.
>
> (Eddy *et al.*, 1976, p. 185)

The authors of *Destination Disaster*, a documentary account of the Paris crash, conclude that:

> to some of its designers, the faults of the DC-10 had been obvious long before [1972]. And to judge by their written prophecies, neither Windsor nor the later tragedy outside Paris could have come as much of a surprise.
>
> (Eddy *et al.*, 1976, p. 165)

Interestingly, Applegate himself seemed more concerned about Convair's potential legal liability than about anyone's moral responsibility.

Those engineers who designed and tested the DC-10 and the door mechanism were morally and professionally culpable for their recklessness, even though they were acting under considerable pressure. The harm caused by the badly designed latching system was not only clearly foreseen, but the harm was avoidable, for had the mechanism been redesigned to meet industry standards, the likelihood of a catastrophic accident would have been no worse than that prevailing in the industry generally.

Notice that the malpractice model does not permit any balancing of risks against possible benefits. It ignores benefits altogether by restricting itself exclusively to harm caused by failure to live up to principles and practices prevailing in one's profession. This seems too restrictive, since it limits moral culpability for harm caused by not following prevailing professional standards: it says nothing about what standards *should* prevail. While the malpractice model has its place and while it doesn't impose impossible burdens on techno-science, the malpractice model sets standards too low to satisfy moral demands. 'Prevailing standards', after all, not only embody thoughtful moral deliberation, but also reflect past practices, hoary traditions, a desire to avoid trouble, an interest in protecting members against suits, and an eagerness to protect members from economic pressures – not to mention the results of compromises with employers, government and clients. Prevailing standards, furthermore, though partially shaped by law suits, legislative action and administrative agencies, primarily reflect the practices and thinking of techno-scientists *themselves*. It expresses no great cynicism about human nature to suggest that no group of professionals (or any other group) is the *sole* best judge of what standards and procedures best safeguard the public interest.

Recognizing the limitations of the malpractice model, Curd and May therefore advance a *reasonable care* model of professional responsibility. The significant departure from the malpractice model lies in this: a member of a profession has a duty to conform to the prevailing standards of that profession 'unless those standards are lower than those that a nonprofessional would adopt in a given situation', in which case the professional has a duty to conform to this higher standard.

Curd and May illustrate this model with another DC-10 disaster, this one near Chicago in 1979 when an American Airlines DC-10 crashed shortly after takeoff killing all 274 on board. Just before liftoff, the left engine ripped loose from its mounting, causing the plane to yaw to the left rolling its wings into a vertical position from which it could not recover. While there were some initial design problems, they need not detain us. The structural cause of the O'Hare crash was a nearly foot-long crack in the rear bulkhead of the pylon attaching the engine to the wing. Subsequent inspection revealed similar cracks with sixty-eight other DC-10s.

The problem arose because maintenance crews at American Airlines (and Continental) followed improper practices. Instead of removing pylons and engines separately, as specified by McDonnell Douglas, maintenance crews – to save time and thus money – removed them as a unit. In remounting the heavy assemblies, misalignments occurred cracking flanges of the rear bulkhead.

Given prevailing standards in the aircraft industry, engineers involved in designing the rear engine assembly of the DC-10 have a moral case that they did not violate the malpractice model of responsibility: the FAA, after all, approved the design. But we have seen that this does not suffice to defeat a charge of negligence, and therefore moral culpability, if the standards themselves are inadequate. Like most government agencies, the FAA sets only *minimal* standards of safety. Further, the FAA exists not only to ensure safety, but to promote air travel.[5] As Curd and May argue, 'reasonable risk is not the same as minimally acceptable risk, especially in industries where there is a great potential for harm' (Curd and May, 1984, p. 18). Because of the air disaster in Paris five years earlier, Curd and May argue that McDonnell Douglas – and, by implication, their engineers – were morally required to meet higher standards of care: 'when a hazardous design defect has been found in one of the products of a company, that company then has a duty to make sure that product is safe, *not just in respect of the known defect*, before the product is allowed back into the public sector' (Curd and May, 1984, p. 18). There is no injustice in holding design engineers responsible for the

Chicago accident besides management and maintenance crews. For the negligence of the maintenance crews could reasonably have been anticipated by McDonnell Douglas' engineers as a response to their design. Why?

> It has been estimated that it would have taken an extra 200 man-hours per engine to service them as McDonnell Douglas recommended. What is more important, McDonnell Douglas knew that maintenance crews were using the less time-consuming and more hazardous procedure. . . . In December, 1978, and again in February, 1979 (several months prior to the Chicago crash), cracked flanges were discovered in planes belonging to Continental that had been serviced in this way. . . . Once the McDonnell Douglas engineers saw that the risk of cracks in the flange was no longer remote, they should have taken action to reduce the chances of a serious accident.
>
> (Curd and May, 1984, p. 19)

Richard De George disagrees. He argues against both models of professional responsibility, at least in as far as they apply to engineers working in large firms:

> Engineers in large firms have an ethical responsibility to do their jobs as best they can, to report their observations about safety and improvement of safety to management. But they do not have the obligation to insist that their perceptions or their standards be accepted. They are not paid to do that, and they have no ethical or moral obligation to do that.
>
> (De George, 1981)

We cannot expect engineers – and, by extension, techno-scientists generally – to place their jobs in jeopardy, De George contends, by going over the heads of their superiors. Further, engineers are not paid to make *ultimate* safety decisions; that is the province of upper management. The moral responsibilities of engineers (and techno-scientists), at least in large corporations, are limited to their *contractual obligations*.

Is it demanding too much to ask people to risk their jobs to protect public safety? Depending on the likelihood and degree of harm, a conscientious professional may have to be prepared to pay that price. Had some engineer come forward at McDonnell Douglas, hundreds of lives would have been saved. In exacting this cost, we should keep in mind that scientists and engineers enjoy high status and above average incomes; with both come heavy responsibilities. Until techno-scientists of large corporations and governments are better protected from retaliation by their employers, however, we may excuse their reticence to some extent for failing to live up to standards and practices that ought to prevail. As Curd and May conclude 'Professionals should not be expected to be saints, but neither can they avoid moral responsibility by hiding behind professional codes or the corporate veil' (Curd and May, 1984, p. 26).

De George's second argument limps badly. Techno-scientists in large corporations do have contractual obligations to report design weaknesses to their superiors. But *moral* duties are seldom exhausted by contractual obligations, nor are they less stringent. *Legal* obligations usually express a bare minimum with which life in a complex developed society cannot exist. Moral responsibilities carry heavier burdens. The question is not 'What is the minimum I must do to avoid legal liability?' but 'What must I do to meet acceptable moral standards?'

De George's exclusive reliance on contractual obligations between techno-scientists and their employers overlooks completely those most likely to bear the brunt of intentional wrongdoing, recklessness and negligence. For whether we discuss Davy's lamp, automobiles, seeds, pesticides, or aircraft it is almost never the techno-scientist or his or her employer who suffers, but others not party to the contract. As slow moving as it is, Anglo-American law has recognized this for nearly a century: manufacturers cannot stand behind 'privity of contract' to protect themselves from negligence.[6]

We would take issue with Curd and May in one respect and go further in another. We agree that once techno-scientists find a flaw in one aspect of a design, they should re-examine the entire product. The case they discuss, however, turns on even narrower grounds. For once it is discovered, as it was here, that users are *abusing* their products, it is their moral responsibility to redesign to prevent this kind of abuse. This requirement has special importance when considering technological transfer. For often, as we have noted, products and techniques are introduced into cultures where they are not well understood. Given that we *know* this to be the case, techno-scientists and the corporations for whom they work must take precautions to reduce mishandling and abuse. Obviously, not all contingencies can be imagined. Products designed only for use in technologically sophisticated countries, for instance, can end their lives in less technologically sophisticated countries. That we cannot envisage all contingencies, however, does not imply that we cannot envisage any.

We would go further than Curd and May for reasons alluded to above. Even – perhaps especially – the well intentioned can overlook or ride roughshod over the perceptions, attitudes and interests of those whom they believe they are helping through technology. The Green Revolution provides us with an example. Harms caused were not the result of wilful wrongdoing or reckless disregard of risks, but a certain *hubris*. Had techno-scientists worked more closely with those who would actually be directly affected by technological innovations, different technological strategies might have been adopted, strategies more attuned to the cultures where they were introduced. To be surprised time and again that things don't work out as intended when either radical new technologies are introduced into a familiar world or familiar technologies are introduced into unfamiliar worlds is simply affected ignorance. Given that we know that the effects of any such introduction are even more unpredictable if the contexts into which they are being introduced are not carefully researched, it would seem that those involved in technology transfer should be held responsible for conducting this kind of research prior to making the transfer. In other words, to continue to assume that technological products work in the same way and with the same effects independently of the environments in which they are used may also constitute wilful negligence.

We see here how conscience and responsibility come together. For although we have defended general principles of the moral responsibilities of professional people, it would be both foolish and wrongheaded to suggest codified rules. It would be foolish because concrete cases are more complex and nuanced than any code could capture; it would be wrongheaded because it would suggest that our sense of moral responsibility can be fully captured by a code. We see the matter, instead, as a matter of applying these general principles to concrete cases openly, forthrightly and conscientiously. As Joseph Rotblat discovered, there are no easy answers; but there are clear wrong answers, and many pitfalls in attempts to find the right answers.

CONSUMER RESPONSIBILITY

It is perhaps even more obviously foolish to think that the responsibilities of conscientious consumers of techno-products and users of techno-devices might be codified in any way. Everyone living in a developed country falls into this category and with so many kinds of people, situations and products to be covered the task would be mind-numbingly complex. But here again application of the three general principles concerned with preventing harm to others may take us some distance towards seeing what might be the responsibilities of conscientious consumers and users of techno-products.

As we have argued, techno-optimists tend to place too much responsibility on users for the harms resulting from the use of techno-products and techno-pessimists too little. Users of products such as guns and cars are of course responsible for the way they use them. To drive under the influence of alcohol is irresponsible because, as traffic accident statistics make very clear, this markedly increases the likelihood of being involved in an accident and of causing harm to other road users. On the other hand, if fewer guns were freely available there would be fewer opportunities for their misuse. If there were fewer cars on the road there would be fewer traffic accidents, as well as less traffic congestion, air pollution and fuel consumption. But in a car owning culture it is very difficult for people not to own and use a car. Their options have already been limited by the prior direction of technological and cultural development. Whole environments have been built around the assumption that they will be inhabited by car drivers, and are hence extremely hostile to pedestrians and cyclists.

Both decisions about what directions of research and development to pursue and about what to produce and market restrict the options available to potential users and consumers of techno-products but are not directly within their control. In democratic countries, however, factors such as the structure of taxation, safety regulations, emissions standards, even the availability of products such as guns or of beef produced by use of growth promoting hormones, being matters of legislative policy, are a result of public opinion and preferences as expressed through the ballot box. These legislatively imposed structures do in turn affect research, development and marketing decisions. Thus some of the responsibilities of consumers, those relating to possible harms caused within their own countries, are political responsibilities.

However, because many techno-products are developed and produced by trans-national corporations there is a more global dimension to the possible harms caused by specific kinds of consumption, or by the use of specific technologies. The population of the developed world consumes a disproportionately large amount of the world's natural resources. On average residents of industrial countries use nineteen times as much aluminium, eighteen times as much in chemicals, fourteen times as much paper and thirteen times as much iron and steel as their counterparts in non-industrial countries (Young, 1994, p. 30). Their patterns of consumption, including energy used to power technological products from computers to cars and air-conditioners, affect labour, economic and environmental conditions in less developed countries, frequently causing harm to the inhabitants of those countries. The manufacture and consumption of techno-products generates large amounts of toxic waste, some of which is now being dumped in countries sufficiently desperate for hard currency or sufficiently unaware of the hazards, to allow it in.

It is clear that no individual consumer is responsible for such problems and that it would be inappropriate to burden individuals with responsibility for the harmful effects of a complex set of political, industrial and economic institutions, because individuals, one by one, have no power to alter the structure of such institutions. This is what is correct in the techno-pessimist's portrayal of our situation. But that portrayal is inaccurate to the extent that it suggests that individuals are left with no options, or that the actions they take as consumers and users of techno-products make no difference. The system is sustained and perpetuated in large measure by the consumption patterns of those in developed countries. Changes in these patterns can bring about changes in the kinds of products manufactured and the way in which they are manufactured. Thus consumers cannot be entirely let off the moral hook by being relieved of all responsibility for the harms caused by their patterns of consumption.

One of the most obvious harms, and one which has received attention, is the production of waste and the problems caused by trying to dispose of it. Consumers generally have shown themselves more than willing to participate in recycling projects once suitable systems have been set up for collection or drop-off for recyclable materials. A greater problem has been persuading them to buy products made with recycled materials and hence in convincing manufacturers that it is worth their while setting up plants to process recyclable materials. Other, often more serious harms are less visible and hence receive very little attention. The optimistic instrumental view of technology makes it easy to overlook the embeddedness of all techno-products – all the infrastructure of manufacturing processes and transport necessary to sustain their production and supply and the cost of maintaining conditions under which the devices can be successfully used.

For example, take a bag of Columbian coffee beans found on a typical supermarket shelf in the United States. The beans will have been grown on trees which required several doses of insecticides. These may very well have been manufactured in the Rhine river valley, contributing further to the pollution of one of the most polluted rivers in Europe. The farmers who sprayed the coffee trees with pesticide almost inevitably inhaled small amounts of it, even if they were taking precautions. Residues from pesticide spraying wash down the mountainside and collect in streams. The kind of packing frequently used for coffee consists of four layers constructed of polyethylene, nylon, aluminium foil and polyester. The three plastic layers are made from oil which may well have been shipped from the Middle East, in tankers fuelled by more oil and fabricated in factories in Louisiana's 'Cancer Corridor', where toxic industries have been disproportionately concentrated in areas where the residents are black. The aluminium layer is likely to have been made in the Pacific Northwest from bauxite strip mined in Australia and shipped across the Pacific on a barge fuelled by oil from Indonesia. Bauxite mining in Australia has violated the ancestral lands of the Aborigines. Refining of bauxite in electric furnaces requires large amounts of power. In the Pacific Northwest this comes from a hydroelectric dam on the Columbia river, construction of which destroyed the salmon fishing subsistence economy of native Americans.[7] Of course it also might be the case that the aluminium layer was produced from recycled cans.

One of the problems facing consumers and users of techno-products seeking to make responsible choices is lack of information both concerning the products between which they need to choose and concerning the implications of that choice. It is often very difficult to know where the components of a product, such as a car, bicycle or computer, have been made, and even more difficult to ascertain the conditions of their manufacture, the kind of process used, the amount of pollution caused, etc. Nor is it always easy to get information about the side effects of using a product such as a paint, or a weedkiller. Consumers have successfully agitated for more labelling on food products, listing ingredients and nutritional content in order that they may be in a better position to make responsible choice regarding their diet. In some countries household appliances also have to carry information on energy use, water use, etc. The next step in making the exercise of consumer responsibility more possible is information relating to the manufacturing process. Never to try to get this information is again a case of affected ignorance.

Techno-products, not surprisingly, are advertised and marketed via beguiling images of mastery and control, of the freedom, autonomy and liberation from labour conferred by technology. This is where the optimistic view of technology positively encourages reckless use, even as it seeks to shift the moral burden for any resultant harms onto users. As users and consumers we should not be seduced by these images either into forgetting that the product brought to us had to be produced and that materials had to be used in its production, or into expecting too much of it. It is unrealistic to think that techno-logical solutions to practical problems come without side effects, which have the potential for creating new problems. At the same time we should not underestimate our dependence on technology. What we perhaps have to become is more mindful users of it.

As we said at the outset, our attitudes towards technology are intimately bound up with our aspirations as human beings, with the dream of a possible future humanity which guides our lives in subtle and often unnoticed ways. We have been arguing that if our dream is of a society in which all labour is taken over by robots and humans are freed to live healthy, comfortable and leisurely lives, or if it is of an idyllically pastoral pre-industrial society, then it is a dream which needs adjusting because it is seriously unrealistic. The reality is that we are products of a techno-culture and that technology cannot free all humans to lead the lives of wealthy Athenian citizens or of wealthy Indian princes. In fact, as we have seen in many instances, technology often simply allows us to go on doing stupid things in clever ways.[8] The questions that technology cannot solve, although it will always frame and condition the answers, are 'What should we be trying to do? What kind of lives should we, as human beings, be seeking to live? And can this kind of life be pursued without exploit-ing others?' But until we can at least propose answers to those questions we cannot really begin to do sensible things in the clever ways that technology might permit.

NOTES

2 FACTS, VALUES AND EFFICIENCY

1 This accords with the original meaning of 'fact'. The term derives from the Latin *factum*, meaning 'deed', or 'thing done'.

2 The term 'epistemic fallacy' was coined by Roy Bhaskar. He develops his account in Bhaskar (1975, pp. 36ff). Acceptance of Bhaskar's general point does not entail acceptance of his particular version of scientific realism.

3 We are indebted to Nerlich's general account of values and their transformation.

4 Polyani reinforces his distinction between observation and invention by arguing that the distinction is recognized in law, since inventions can be patented, whereas observations cannot. With the move towards the commodification of knowledge, to viewing knowledge as a form of property, that distinction is no longer legally recognized. It is now possible to patent, or to claim property rights over, things which would once have been classified as scientific discoveries.

5 The question of the expression of values in science is more complicated and we will return to this in Chapter 3.

6 The developmental, user, environmental and cultural contexts will be addressed in Chapter 7.

7 Even if, one day, nuclear weapons, like artefacts unearthed by archaeologists, are found only in museums, they will tell our successors that twentieth century humans were prepared to do the unthinkable.

8 In the discussion that follows, we are indebted to Billington (1983, pp. 266–7).

9 We are familiar how 'pro-life' and 'pro-choice' serve as codes for moral and value stances. Descriptions of RU-486 as either 'abortifacient' or 'medicine' similarly express our own and even society's commitments.

3 SCIENCE, SCIENTIFIC METHOD AND THE AUTHORITY OF EXPERTS

1 In this he was not immediately successful. Arguably the reorientation that he envisioned was not fully achieved until well into the nineteenth century. See for example Cunningham and Williams (1993).

2 For a fascinating study of this tradition and its links to the attitudes of modern science see Noble (1992).

3 The history and uses of this metaphor are traced in Mayr (1986).

4 For more on this reorientation see Lachterman (1989).

5 This shift can be clearly seen in the work of Newton. In *Principia* he introduces the law of universal gravitational attraction as a mathematical law, a law of action for which he explicitly says he will offer no causal explanation. Later, however, in the queries appended to his *Opticks*, he discusses what properties may be thought to belong to the essence of matter and seems still to be thinking in terms of trying to provide an Aristotelian-style causal explanation of gravitational attraction, one grounded in the natures of the material bodies which are attracted to one another. Later commentators on *Principia*, including Hume, assumed that the great advance of the new science was that it had focused on laws of action, putting aside the quest for Aristotelian (formal) causes.

6 From the manual of Dr Daniel W. Cathell quoted in Evans (1993). Evans reports (p. 803) that instruments represented mechanization, efficiency and scientific reasoning, the finger symbolized clinical experience, time-honoured methods of physical diagnosis, and the sanctity of the doctor/patient relationship.

7 See for example de Boef *et al.* (1993).

8 See for example Newton-Smith (1984).

9 Note that Bacon here means natural philosophy, or what we now call science.

10 This fascinating story is told in Gordon (1968).

4 FROM APPLIED SCIENCE TO TECHNO-SCIENCE

1 By AD 100 there were ten aqueducts supplying 250 million gallons daily. Much went to public baths but this still left 50 gallons per head for the 2 million inhabitants. This is much the same amount that is used today by a citizen of New York or London. (See Cartwright and Biddiss, 1972, p. 9.)

2 The lamp was introduced in 1816. In Durham and Northumberland in 1798–1816 there were twenty-seven explosions and 447 deaths, in 1817–35 there were forty-two explosions and 538 deaths (Berman, 1978, p. 175).

3 For another discussion of this episode see Albury and Schwartz (1982).

4 Indeed this idea has in many instances become a part of corporate mentality. So, for example, Hewlett Packard not only designs computer technology for use anywhere in the world, but has a single standard

design of building shell to be used for any of its facilities, wherever they may be in the world and whether they are for production or offices. While this may represent a saving in architectural design fees, it does not make for energy-efficient buildings or for spaces especially well suited to the work carried on in them.

5 TECHNOLOGY, CULTURE AND POLITICS

1 *US vs. Smith* Z91–5077 (5th Circuit Court of Appeals) 12 November 1992. Unfortunately for the plaintiff, an accused drug dealer, the court denied his appeal on the particular facts of the case.
2 We are indebted here to Street (1992, Ch. 3).
3 In addition, *The New York Times* (8 July 1994) reports that many women are finding that – only a few years after its introduction and contrary to initial advertisements – having Norplant removed can be both painful and disfiguring. The *Times* reports that a group of women has launched a class action suit against the manufacturer of the drug.
4 Certain 'base communities' in Central and South America have forms of participatory democracy that might form a model for what we have in mind. But doubts must remain whether this model would work either for highly industrialized (or post-industrialized) nations or for large nation states.
5 We borrow this term – and much else in this section – from Freund and Martin (1994). Freund and Martin's study shows in detail not only how the industrialized nations have become auto-centred, but what can be done to ween us from overdependence on automobiles.
6 All statistics listed here can be found in Freund and Martin (1994, Ch. 1). We cite sources Freund and Martin draw on where appropriate.
7 A fuller story can be found in Meral (1990). Snell (1974) documents the elimination of interurban rail systems.
8 We owe this term to the late Carl Barus, professor of electrical engineering at Swarthmore College, who believed that engineers too often deceived themselves about the supposed value neutrality of their work.
9 'The Unfinished Revolution', *The Economist*, 25 January 1986, pp. 12–13.
10 Quoted in Freund and Martin (1994, p. 22) from *Advisory Commission on Cost Control in State Government, 'Getting the Most Out of California's Transportation Tax Dollar'*, (Sacramento: Joint Publications, 1990).

6 PLANT BREEDING AND THE POLITICS OF HUNGER

1 These figures and many points in the following discussion are derived from Lipton (1989).
2 Details extracted from Parayil (1992).
3 This is apart from the very considerable environmental problems posed

by implementation of this kind of agricultural system, problems which are in many cases common to developed and developing countries.

4 This distinction is made in a related context, the production of fermented foods, by Leslie Fook-Min Young. 'It is probably fair to say that in the very early days brew-masters were more artisans than technologists' (1992, p. 184).

7 WHO'S RESPONSIBLE FOR THIS MESS?

1 Ayer (1948) defended such a view. Although his version of moral nihilism has been pretty much discredited, the view is not without proponents.

2 When it comes to sentencing and assessing damages, however, judges and juries can properly take the defendant's motives into account.

3 See Donagan (1977, especially Chapters 2 and 4) for an analysis and defence of these assertions.

4 *American Society of Mechanical Engineers Inc. vs. Hydrolevel Corporation*, US Supreme Court, 18 May 1982. Cited in Curd and May (1984).

5 The role of US regulative agencies in promulgating and enforcing safety regulations deserves a study of its own. Because of underfunding, the conflicting roles many agencies have, and a 'revolving door' practice where regulators often become highly paid 'consultants' (i.e. lobbyists) for the industries they were regulating soon after leaving public office, many critics argue that regulative agencies lack the teeth, will and independence needed to control powerful industries. These criticisms will not be pursued here.

6 The lead case in the United States is *MacPherson vs. Buick Motor Co*, (New York Court of Appeals, 1916). Mrs MacPherson was injured because of a defective wheel. It was claimed that she could not sue Buick because no contract existed between the MacPhersons and Buick, only between them and the car dealer from whom they purchased the car. Buick lost. The opinion was written by the great American appellate judge, Benjamin Cardozo.

7 This example is adapted from *WorldWatch*, September/October 1994, pp. 21–4.

8 In the film *Half-Life*, which is about the effects of nuclear testing on the inhabitants of Muroroa attol, a lady from Muroroa says of the Americans that they do stupid things in clever ways.

REFERENCES

Adams, J., 1981, *Transport Planning: Vision and Practice*, London: Routledge & Kegan Paul.

Albury, David, and Schwartz, Joseph, 1982, *Partial Progress*, London: Pluto Press.

Aristotle *Protreptikos, Politics* and *Physics*, in Jonathan Barnes (ed.) *The Complete Works of Aristotle*, Princeton, NJ: Princeton University Press, 1984.

Ayer, A. J., 1948, *Language, Truth and Logic*, London: Victor Gollancz.

Bachelard, Gaston, 1978, *Le nouvel esprit scientifique* 14th edition, Paris: Presses Universitaires de France. Originally published Paris: Alcan, 1934. English edition *The New Scientific Spirit*, trans. Arthur Goldhammer, Boston: Beacon Press, 1984.

Bacon, Francis, 1620, *Novum Organum*, English edition *The New Organon*, Fulton Anderson (ed.), from the translation of Ellis and Spedding, Indianapolis: Bobbs–Merrill, 1960.

——1627, *New Atlantis*, London. Modern edition *The Advancement of Learning and the New Atlantis*, Oxford: Oxford University Press, 1906.

——1964, 'Thoughts and Conclusions', in Benjamin Farrington (ed.) *The Philosophy of Francis Bacon*, Chicago: University of Chicago Press.

Berlin, Isaiah, 1981, 'The Divorce between the Sciences and the Humanities', in his *Against the Current*, Oxford: Oxford University Press.

Berman, Morris, 1978, *Social Change and Scientific Organization: The Royal Institution 1799–1844*, London: Heinemann Educational Books.

Bernard, Claude, 1984, *Introduction a l'étude de la médicine expérimentale*, written in 1865 but not published until 1947. Edition quoted, Paris: Flammarion.

Bhaskar, Roy, 1975, *A Realist Theory of Science*, Leeds, UK: Leeds Books Ltd and Hassocks, Sussex: Harvester Press and Atlantic Highland, NJ: Humanities Press, 1978.

Billington, David P., 1983, *The Tower and the Bridge: the New Art of Structural Engineering*, Princeton, NJ: Princeton University Press.

Borgmann, Albert, 1984, *Technology and the Character of Modern Life*, Chicago: University of Chicago Press.

Bray, Francesca, 1986, *The Rice Economies: Technology and Development in Asian Societies*, Berkeley, CA: University of California Press.

Brown, Lester R., 1994, 'Feeding China', *World Watch*, September/October 1994, Washington, DC: World Watch Institute, pp. 10–19.

Bush, Corlann Gee, 1983, 'Women and the Assessment of Technology', in Joan Rothschild (ed.) *Machina Ex Dea*, New York: Pergamon Press.

Bush, Vannevar, 1946, *Endless Horizons*, Washington, DC: Public Affairs Press.

Butler, Bishop Joseph, 1736, *The Analogy of Religion*, Modern edition, New York: Unger, 1961.

Cartwright, Frederick F., and Biddiss, Michael D., 1972, *Disease and History*, New York: Dorset Press.

Cobbett, William, 1845, *The English Gardener*, London: A. Cobbett.

Cunningham, Andrew, and Williams, Perry, 1993,' "Decentring the Big Picture": The Origins of Modern Science and the Modern Origins of Science', *British Journal for the History of Science*, pp. 407–32.

Curd, Martin, and May, Larry, 1984, *Professional Responsibility for Harmful Actions*, Dubuque, IA: Kendel/Hunt.

Davis, Gregory H., 1981, *Technology – Humanism or Nihilism: A Critical Analysis of the Philosophical Bias and Practice of Modern Technology*, New York: University Press of America.

Davy, Humphry, 1839, John Davy (ed.) *The Collected Works of Sir Humphry Davy, Bart.*, 9 vols, London: Smith and Elder.

de Boef, Walter, Amanor, Kojo, and Wellard, Kate (eds), 1993, Introduction to *Cultivating Knowledge: Genetic diversity, farmer experimentation and crop research*, London: Intermediate Technology Publications.

De George, Richard, 1981, 'Ethical Responsibility of Engineers in Large Corporations: The Pinto Case', *Business and Profession Ethics Journal 1*, (1) pp. 1–14.

Dickinson, David, 1974, *The Politics of Alternative Technology*, New York: Universe Books.

Donagan, Alan, 1977, *The Theory of Morality*, Chicago: University of Chicago Press.

Eddy, Paul, Potter, Elaine, and Page, Bruce, 1976, *Destination Disaster*, New York: The New York Times Book Company.

Ellul, Jacques, 1964, *The Technological Society*, trans. John Wilkinson, New York: Knopf.

——1983, 'The Technological Order', in Carl Mitcham and Robert Mackey (eds), *Philosophy and Technology: Readings in Philosophical Problems of Technology*, New York: The Free Press. Reprinted from Carl F. Stover (ed.) 1963, *The Technological Order*, Detroit: Wayne State University Press.

Evans, Hughes, 1993, 'The Introduction of Blood Pressure Instruments into Medicine', *Technology and Culture*, pp. 784–807.

Faiz, Asif, *et al.*, 1990, 'Automotive Air Pollution Issues and Options for Developing Countries', Washington, DC: World Bank.

Farey, John, 1827, *A Treatise on the Steam Engine: Historical, Practical and Descriptive*, London: Rees, Orme, Brown Green. (Modern edition, Davis & Charles reprints, 1971.)

Feenburg, Andram, 1991, *Critical Theory of Technology*, New York: Oxford University Press.

Ferguson, Eugene S., 1992, *Engineering and the Mind's Eye*, Cambridge, MA, and London: MIT Press.

Fitzgerald, Deborah, 1993, 'Farmers Deskilled: Hybrid Corn and Farmers' Work', *Technology and Culture*, pp. 324–43.

Freund, Peter E. S., and Martin, George, 1994, *The Ecology of the Automobile*, Montreal and New York: Black Rose Books.

Geertz, Clifford, 1973, *Interpretation of Cultures*, New York: Basic Books.

Gibbons, M., 1984, 'Is Science Industrially Relevant? The interaction between science and technology', in Michael Gibbons and Philip Gummett (eds) *Science, Technology and Society*, Manchester: Manchester University Press.

Glas, Eduard, 1993, 'Mathematical Progress: Between Reason and Society', *Journal for General Philosophy of Science 24*, pp. 235–56.

Goldhaber, Michael, 1986, *Reinventing Technology: Politics for Democratic Values*, London: Routledge & Kegan Paul.

Goonatilake, Susantha, 1984, *Aborted Discovery*, London: Zed Books.

Gordon, J. E., 1968, *The New Science of Strong Materials*, Harmondsworth: Penguin Books.

Gowing, Margaret, and Arnold, Loma, 1979, *The Atomic Bomb*, London: Butterworths.

Grandy, Richard, 1992, 'Theories of Theories: A View from Cognitive Science', in John Earman (ed.) *Inference, Explanation and other Frustrations: Essays in the Philosophy of Science*, Berkeley, CA: University of California Press.

Hacking, Ian, 1983, *Representing and Intervening: Introductory topics in the philosophy of natural science*, Cambridge: Cambridge University Press.

Hart, H. L. A., 1968, *Punishment and Responsibility*, New York: Oxford University Press.

Hesseltine, Clifford W., 1992, 'Mixed-Culture Fermentations', in *Applications of Biotechnology to Traditional Fermented Foods: report of an ad hoc panel of the Board on Science and Technology for International Development*, Washington, DC: National Academy Press.

Hillman, Mayer, Adams, John, and Whitelegg, John, 1990, *One False Move – A Study of Children's Independent Mobility*, London: Policy Studies Institute.

Hilts, Philip, 1991, 'California to Test Children for Lead Poisoning', *New York Times*, 12 October.

Hochschild, Arlie R., 1989, *The Second Shift: Working Parents and the Revolution at Home*, New York: Viking Press.

Howard, Robert, 1985, *Brave New Workplace*, New York: Viking Press.

Hugh of Saint Victor, 1961, trans. Jerome Taylor, *The Didascalion of Hugh of Saint Victor*, (c. 1127), New York: Columbia University Press.

Kelly, A., 1986, 'The New Materials', *Science and Public Affairs No. 1*, London: Royal Society.

Kloppenburg, Jack Ralph Jr, 1988, *First The Seed*, Cambridge: Cambridge University Press.

Kovel, Joel, 1983, *Against the State of Nuclear Terror*, London: Free Association Books.

Kramarae, C. (ed.), 1988, *Technology and Women's Voices: Keeping in Touch*, London: Routledge & Kegan Paul.

Kuhn, Thomas S., 1959, 'Energy Conservation as an Example of Simultaneous Discovery', in Marshal Claggett (ed.) *Critical Problems in the History of Science*, Madison, WI: University of Wisconsin Press. Reprinted in Kuhn, Thomas S., 1977, *The Essential Tension*, Chicago: University of Chicago Press.

Lacey, Hugh, and Schwartz, Barry, forthcoming 1995, 'The Formation and Transformation of Values', in R. Kitchener and W. O'Donohue (eds) *Psychology and Philosophy: Interdisciplinary Problems and Responses*, New York: Allyn & Bacon.

Lachterman, David, 1989, *The Ethics of Geometry*, New York: Routledge.

Lappé, Frances, and Collins, Joseph, 1978, *Food First: Beyond the Myth of Scarcity*, New York: Balantine Books.

Latour, Bruno, 1987, *Science in Action*, Cambridge, MA: Harvard University Press.

——and Woolgar, Steve, 1979, *Laboratory life: the social construction of scientific facts*, Beverly Hills, CA: Sage Publications.

Lewis, P. M. and Booth, J., 1989, *The Invisible Medium*, London: Macmillan.

Lipton, Michael (with Richard Longhurst), 1989, *New Seeds and Poor People*, London: Unwin Hyman.

Lowe, Marcia D., 1990, *Alternatives to the Automobile: Transport for Livable Cities*, Washington, DC: World Watch Institute, Paper No. 98.

Lucas, J. R., 1986, 'Dubious Doubts', in M. C. Doeser and J. N. Kray (eds) *Facts and Values*, Dordrecht: Martinus Nijhoff.

MacIntyre, Alasdair, 1984, *After Virtue*, 2nd edition, Notre Dame, IN: Notre Dame University Press.

Marx, Karl, and Engels, Frederick, 1970, *The German Ideology*, (ed.) C. J. Arthur, London: Lawrence & Wishart.

Mayr, Otto, 1986, *Authority, Liberty and Automatic Machinery in Early Modern Europe*, Baltimore, MD: Johns Hopkins University Press.

Meadows, Donella, 1994, 'Daly Medicine', *The Amicus Journal*, New York: Natural Resources Defense Council, p. 11.

Mencken, H. L., 1920, 'Sententiae', in his *A Book of Burlesques*, New York: Knopf.

Meral, Gerald H., 1990, 'Back on Track: Trains in California's Future', pp. 94–100 in Robert L. Dean, (ed.) *The Alternatives to Gridlock: Perspectives on Meeting California's Transportation Needs*, Sacramento, CA: California Institute of Public Affairs.

Mesthene, Emmanuel, G., 1967, *Technology and Social Change*, Indianapolis: Bobbs-Merrill. Selection reprinted in Carl Mitcham and Robert Mackey (eds), 1983, *Philosophy and Technology: Readings in Philosophical Problems of Technology*, New York: The Free Press.

Midgley, Mary, 1978, *Beast and Man*, London: Methuen.

Mitcham, Carl, and Mackey, Robert (eds), 1983, *Philosophy and Technology: Readings in Philosophical Problems of Technology*, New York: The Free Press.

Mowery, David C., and Rosenberg, Nathan, 1989, *Technology and the Pursuit of Economic Growth*, Cambridge: Cambridge University Press.

Musson, A. E., and Robinson, Eric, 1969, *Science Society and Technology in the Industrial Revolution*, London: Curtis Brown, New York: Gordon & Breach.

REFERENCES

Nerlich, Graham, 1989, *Values and Valuing: Speculations on the Ethical Life of Persons*, Oxford: Clarendon Press.

Newton, Isaac, 1686, *Principia*, Modern edition *Sir Isaac Newton's Mathematical Principles of Natural Philosophy and his System of the World*, Andrew Motte's 1729 translation, revised by Florian Cajori, Berkeley, CA: University of California Press, 1934.

——1730, *Opticks*, 4th edition. Modern edition *Opticks or A Treatise of the Reflections, Inflections and Colours of Light*, New York: Dover, 1952.

Newton-Smith, William, 1984, 'The Role of Interests in Science', in A. Phillips Griffiths (ed.) *Philosophy and Practice*, Cambridge: Cambridge University Press.

Noble, David F., 1992, *A World Without Women: the Christian Clerical Culture of Western Science*, New York: Oxford University Press.

Opole, Monica, 1993, 'Revalidating Women's Knowledge on Indigenous Vegetables: Implications for policy', in Walter de Boef, *et al.* (eds) *Cultivating Knowledge: Genetic diversity, farmer experimentation and crop research*, London: Intermediate Technology Publications.

Ovitt, George Jr, 1987, *The Restoration of Perfection: Labor and Technology in Medieval Culture*, New Brunswick, NJ, and London: Rutgers University Press.

Palladino, Paolo, 1993, 'Between Craft and Science: Plant Breeding, Mendelian Genetics and British Universities, 1900–1920', *Technology and Culture*, pp. 300–23.

Parayil, Govindan, 1992, 'The Green Revolution in India: A Case Study of Technological Change', *Technology and Culture*, Vol. 33, No. 4, pp. 737–56.

Pickstone, John V., 1993, 'Ways of Knowing: toward a historical sociology of science, technology and medicine', *British Journal for the History of Science*, pp. 433–58.

Polyani, Michael, 1955, 'Pure and Applied Science and their Appropriate Forms of Organisation', in *Science and Freedom: the proceeding of a conference convened by the Congress for Cultural Freedom and held in Hamburg on July 23rd.-26th. 1953*, London: Secker & Warburg.

Popper, Karl, 1959, *The Logic of Scientific Discovery*, London: Hutchinson.

Renner, Michael, 1988, *Rethinking the Role of the Automobile*, Washington, DC: World Watch Institute, p. 16.

Robins, Kevin, and Webster, Frank, 1988, 'Athens without Slaves . . . or Slaves without Athens', in *Science as Culture*, No. 3, pp. 7–53.

Rotblat, Joseph, 1986, 'Leaving the Bomb Project', in Len Auckland and Stephen McGuire (eds) *Assessing the Nuclear Age: selections from the bulletin of the atomic scientists*, Chicago: University of Chicago Press.

Schrödinger, E., 1952, 'Are there Quantum Jumps?', *British Journal for the Philosophy of Science III*.

Sen, Amartya, 1989, *Poverty and Famine*, Oxford: Clarendon Press.

Shiva, Vandana, 1991, *The Violence of the Green Revolution*, London: Zed Books.

Sinclair, Sir Clive, 1983, Advertisement in *Observer*, 22 May, quoted in Kevin Robins and Frank Webster, 1988, 'Athens without Slaves . . . or Slaves without Athens', in *Science as Culture*, No. 3, pp. 7–53.

Smith, John E., 1980, 'Science and Conscience', *American Scientist*, Vol. 68.

Snell, B., 1974, 'Report on American Ground Transport', *Senate Judicial Committee*, 26 February.

Snow, C. P., 1961, 'The Moral Un-Neutrality of Science', *Science*, 27 January, Vol. 133, No. 3448.

———1964, *Two Cultures and the Scientific Revolution*, 2nd edition, Cambridge: Cambridge University Press

Stamp, Patricia, 1989, *Technology, Gender and Power in Africa*, Ottawa: International Development Research Centre.

Stover, Carl F. (ed.), 1963, *The Technological Order*, Detroit: Wayne State University Press.

Street, John, 1992, *Politics and Technology*, New York: The Guildford Press.

Volti, Rudi, 1992, *Society and Technological Change*, 2nd edition, New York: St Martin's Press.

Wajcman, Judy, 1993, *Feminism Confronts Technology*, Cambridge: Polity Press.

Webster, Andrew, 1991, *Science, Technology and Society*, New Brunswick, NJ: Rutgers University Press and London: Macmillan Education.

Weinberg, Alvin M., 1972, 'Social Institutions and Nuclear Energy', *Science*, Vol. 177, July, p. 34.

Williams, Bernard, 1984, 'Morality, Scepticism and the Nuclear Arms Race', in Nigel Blake and Kay Pole (eds) *Objections to Nuclear Defence*, London: Routledge & Kegan Paul.

Winner, Langdon, 1977, *Autonomous Technology: Technics-out-of-control as a Theme in Political Thought*, Cambridge, MA: MIT Press.

———1980, 'Do Artefacts Have Politics?', *Daedalus*, Z1, Winter, pp. 121–36.

———1993, 'Artifact/Ideas and Political Culture', *Whole Earth Review*, No. 73 (Winter 1991), reprinted in Albert H. Teich, *Technology and the Future*, 6th edition, 1993, New York: St Martin's Press.

Woolgar, Steve, 1989, 'Reconstructing Man and Machine', in Wiebe Bijker, *et al.* (eds) *The Social Construction of Technological Systems*, Cambridge, MA: MIT Press.

Young, John, 1994, 'The New Materialism and Matter of Policy', *World Watch*, September/October 1994, Washington, DC: World Watch Institute, pp. 30–7.

Young, Leslie Fook-Min, 1992, 'Future Directions', *Applications of Biotechnology to Traditional Fermented Foods: report of an ad hoc panel of the Board on Science and Technology for International Development*, Washington, DC: National Academy Press.

INDEX